COMPILED BY
ROBERTS LIARDON

FIRST HAND ACCOUNTS OF THE REVIVAL

FRANK BARTLEMAN'S
AZUSA
STREET

Includes Feature Articles
from *The Apostolic Faith* Newspaper

DESTINY IMAGE® PUBLISHERS, INC.
P.O. Box 310, Shippensburg, PA 17257-0310

"Speaking to the Purposes of God for This Generation and for the Generations to Come"

This book and all other Destiny Image, Revival Press, MercyPlace, Fresh Bread, Destiny Image Fiction, and Treasure House books are available at Christian bookstores and distributors worldwide.

For a U.S. bookstore nearest you, call **1-800-722-6774.**

For more information on foreign distributors, call **717-532-3040.**

Or reach us on the Internet: **www.destinyimage.com**

ISBN: 10: 0-7684-2365-1
ISBN 13: 978-0-7684-2365-5

For Worldwide Distribution, Printed in the U.S.A.
1 2 3 4 5 6 7 8 9 10 11 / 09 08 07 06

DEDICATION

I dedicate this book to my grandparents, Rev. LeBasker and Gladoylene Moore, who led our entire family into experiencing the baptism of the Holy Spirit. In the early 1900s they started over 20 pentecostal churches throughout North and South Carolina. Those were days in which believing in the baptism of the Holy Spirit was not accepted by the Christian community as a whole. It was generally believed that people who spoke in tongues were mentally ill or had a contagious disease that would defile anyone who came in contact with them.

Through it all, my grandparents carried on faithfully and attained, I believe, to the great prize of their High Calling in Christ Jesus. They left this world knowing that all their children, grandchildren as well as their great-grandchildren were born again and had received the precious baptism of the Holy Spirit. I, and the rest of our family, thank you both for your love and faith that was deposited in our hearts and remains to this day!

Roberts Liardon

ACKNOWLEDGEMENTS

To Micki Milam for typing the text and her husband, Don, for helping me in the research for creating the biography of Frank Bartleman.

To Glenn Gohr, and all the good folk at the Flower Pentecostal Heritage Center for the use of photos from their archive. For more information on Pentecostal history I would suggest you visit their Website at: http://www.agheritage.org.

CONTENTS

A BIOGRAPHY OF
FRANK BARTLEMAN
(1871-1935)

Because of his reporting of the revival at 312 Azusa Street, Frank Bartleman became one of the key players in the Azusa Street revival. In his classic book he offers us critical analysis of the revival. Bartleman's extensive reports, along with *The Apostolic Faith* newspapers, are some of the most important sources for understanding the dynamics of what happened at the little mission church on Azusa Street.

Frank Bartleman (Used by permission, Flower Pentecostal Heritage Center.)

Bartleman had long desired to be a part of some momentous revival movement. He was a man on a mission, in search of the holy grail of revival. His search would eventually lead him to Los Angeles just in time to be a part of the Azusa Street revival.

Frank Bartleman was born in Bucks County, outside of Philadelphia, in 1871. He was very close to his Quaker mom, but his German-born father was a stern parent—as most fathers typically were in those times—and it seems clear that they did not have a close relationship. Bartleman once described his relationship with his dad in these words, "I remember as a little child my father asking me in a sarcastic, disparaging manner, what I was living for."[1] He would live his life with a bitterness toward his father that was somewhat muted by his conversion.

Like Charles Parham, Bartleman battled with his health as a young child. No doubt this struggle with his health gave him an appreciation for the healing power of God that would be demonstrated at Azusa.

Russel Conwell, founder Temple University and pastor of Baptist Temple where Bartleman accepted Christ.

Bartleman gave his life to God in 1893 while attending Baptist Temple, the largest Baptist church in the world, in Philadelphia. The pastor, Russel Conwell—who eventually became the founder of Temple University in downtown Philadelphia—had recently written a little booklet, "Acres of Diamonds," a story of a man who left home to search for diamonds, not realizing that there were diamonds in the clay of his own backyard. The message of that book was that most of us overlook opportunities right in our own backyards. This could be the story of Bartleman. He was a man who was in search of the diamond of revival.

Pastor Conwell baptized the 22-year-old Bartleman and offered to pay the young man's way through college. Bartleman refused, explaining that "I made my choice between a popular, paying pulpit and a humble walk of poverty and suffering.... I choose the streets and slums for my pulpit."[2] A future awaited him, but it would be far away from Philadelphia.

IN SEARCH OF REVIVAL

Until Bartleman finally arrived in Los Angeles, he was a spiritual refugee looking for his home. Bartleman left the Baptists, as many were doing at the turn of the century, and joined the ranks of the Holiness Movement because of their passion for sanctification. Bartleman joined the Salvation Army for a while and also went to Moody Bible Institute in Chicago, where he heard the preaching of Dwight L. Moody.

Chicago would not be the resting place for Bartleman, however, and so he moved on. It was as though he was in search of something to satisfy the growing passion in his heart. He left Chicago and headed to the South, where he made the first of his many friends in the African-American community. Still feeling empty and a bit depressed, he returned to Pittsburgh where he met Miss Ladd, his future wife. They were married in 1900, and at this time he became a pastor with the Wesleyan Methodist Church in Northwest Pennsylvania.

Being a pastor turned out to be a negative experience. His expectations concerning the Christian life were much higher than his parishioners. At this time he was becoming more and more disenchanted with denominations, a distaste that he would write about later in life.

From there Bartleman took his wife and daughter and headed to Denver, possibly because of the reports that he had heard about Alma White, head of the Pillar of Fire church. Alma White's ministry in Denver was already growing in its notoriety among the newly emerging Pentecostals. In Denver, Bartleman actively involved himself in evangelistic ministry: printing and distributing gospel tracts, working with troubled people in the slums, and preaching in slums and to the prostitutes on the streets.

GO WEST, YOUNG MAN, GO WEST

Again, the roaming nomad was ready to move on. The next step would lead him ever closer to his coming destiny. He left

Denver and headed off to California with his wife and daughter. In 1904, two years before the start of the Azusa revival, he arrived in Sacramento and was placed in charge of the Peniel Mission. However, the experience at Peniel left a bitter taste, and it eventually failed. Unable to find a place to minister, Bartleman did everything he could to support his family. It was at that time that his second daughter was born. With neither a home nor a job in Sacramento, he packed up his family and left for Los Angeles.

In the beginning, Los Angeles was not a spiritual refuge because Bartleman only encountered more adversity and misfortune. The most tragic event was the death of his precious child Esther who had become the joy of his life. He was broken by her death but quickly recovered and renewed his passion to experience the latter rains of revival.

During 1905, Bartleman worked with some of the churches in the city but found to his disappointment that many of them were lukewarm and not ready for his long desired revival. While in Los Angeles, Bartleman corresponded with Evan Roberts— one of the leaders in the Welsh revival—about his passion for revival to come to California. Bartleman stated that it was these letters that encouraged him to believe that a revival would come.

In June of 1905, Frank Bartleman wrote that Los Angeles was truly a spiritual Jerusalem. He felt that Los Angeles would become the city where God would pour out His Spirit. There was something in the city that inspired him to go on, so he continued to give himself to prayer. He knew that the divisions among God's people were great hindrances to revival and thus he wrote these words in his book on Azusa:

> "Every fresh division or party in the church gives to the world a contradiction as to the oneness of the body of Christ, and the truthfulness of the Gospel. Multitudes are bowing down and burning incense to a doctrine rather than Christ. ...The Spirit is laboring for the unity of believers today, for the 'one body,' that the

prayer of Jesus may be answered, 'that they all may be one, that the world may believe.'"[3]

THE REVIVAL BEGINS

Bartleman finally found himself attending the meetings on Bonnie Brae Street, and when the services moved to 312 Azusa Street, he was there with them enjoying the warmth of Pentecostal fires. Reports of the revival by a Los Angeles newspaper described the revival with harsh and prejudicial language. Bartleman reacted against this reporting, calling it shameful.

214 Bonnie Brae, where it all started, (Used by permission, Flower Pentecostal Heritage Center).

These reporters reacted callously to the mixture of whites and blacks at Azusa Street. In contrast, Bartleman rejoiced at the sight of whites and blacks worshiping God together. His description included the immortal words: "The color line has been washed away in the Blood."

The reports that you will read in this book were first published in 1925 under the title, *How Pentecost Came to Los Angeles—As It Was in the Beginning* and later under the title, *Azusa Street*. Bartleman put the book together from his journal, written during the days of the revival, as well as from news articles. With joy and excitement he wrote about those momentous days as "God walked among them."

Unfortunately, controversy and jealousy eventually ended the blessed work at Azusa Street. Toward the end of his book, Bartleman described with pain how the work of God was destroyed because of a lack of unity.

Bartleman, himself, became embroiled in doctrinal controversy. First, Bartleman sided with William Durham, a pastor from Chicago, who preached the "finished work" view of sanctification. In contrast to Durham's teaching, Charles Parham and William Seymour had both been preaching the second work of

312 Azusa Street, new home for the revival, (Used by permission, Flower Pentecostal Heritage Center).

grace as evidenced in the baptism of the Spirit. Bartleman's position was in direct opposition to the leadership at Azusa. Second, Bartleman would eventually accept the teaching of the "oneness" preachers as proclaimed by Frank Ewart who was rebaptizing his converts in Jesus' name.

Poor health would eventually catch up with Bartleman. Reluctant to join any established denomination, yet committed to mission work right up until the end, Bartleman died as he had lived—an independent. Death came in September 1935 in his beloved Los Angeles.[4]

CHAPTER ONE

BEGINNINGS

I arrived in Los Angeles, California, with my wife and two young daughters, on December 22, 1904. Little Esther, our oldest child, three years old, was seized with convulsions and passed away to be with Jesus on January 7, at 4 A.M. Little "Queen Esther" seemed to have been born "for such a time as this" (Esther 4:14).

Beside that little coffin, with heart bleeding, I pledged my life anew for God's service. In the presence of death, how real eternal issues become. I promised the rest of my life should be spent wholly for Him. He made a fresh covenant with me. I then begged Him to open a door of service quickly, that I might not find time for sorrow.

Just one week after little Esther's departure, I began preaching twice a day at little Peniel Mission in Pasadena. While souls were saved during the month's meetings in Peniel Mission, the greatest victory gained was the spiritual growth of a company of young men attending there. A number were called out by the Lord for future service.

On April 8, 1905, I heard F.B. Meyer, from London, preach. He described the great revival then going on in Wales, which he had just visited. He had met Evan Roberts. My soul was stirred to its depths, having read of this revival shortly before. I then and there promised God He should have full right of way with me; if He could use me.

I distributed tracts in the post office, banks, and public buildings in Los Angeles and also visited many saloons with tracts. Later I visited about 30 saloons in Los Angeles again. The houses of prostitution were wide open at that time, and I gave out many tracts there.

Little Esther's death had broken my heart, and I felt I could only live while in God's service. I longed to know Him in a more real way and to see the work of God go forth in power. A great burden and cry came in my heart for a mighty revival. He was preparing me for a fresh service for Him. This could only be brought about by the realization of a deeper need in my own heart for God, and a real soul travail for the work of God. This He gave me. Many were being similarly prepared at this time in different parts of the world. The Lord was preparing to visit and deliver His people once more. Intercessors were the need. *"He...wondered that there was no intercessor"* (Isa. 59:16 KJV). *"I sought for a man...[to] stand in the gap before Me for the land, that I should not destroy it: but I found none"* (Ezek. 22:30 KJV).

PASADENA FOR GOD!

About the first of May, a powerful revival broke out in the Lake Avenue M.E. Church in Pasadena. Most of the young men who had come forth in the meetings in Peniel Mission attended this church. They had gotten under the burden for a revival there. In fact, we had been praying for a sweeping revival for Pasadena, and God was answering our prayers. I found a wonderful work of the Spirit going on at Lake Avenue. There was no preacher there; yet the altar was full of seeking souls. One night nearly every unsaved soul in the house was saved. It was a clean sweep for God. Conviction was mightily upon the people. In two weeks' time, 200 souls knelt at the altar seeking the Lord. The Peniel boys were involved and wonderfully used of God. We then began to pray for an outpouring of the Spirit for Los Angeles and the whole of Southern California.

I find the following observations in my diary, written at that time: "Some churches are going to be surprised to find God passing them by. He will work in channels where they will yield to Him. They must humble themselves for Him to come. We are crying, 'Pasadena for God!' Some people are too well satisfied with their own goodness. They have little faith or interest for the salvation of others. God will humble them by passing them by. The Spirit is breathing prayer through us for a mighty, general outpouring. Great things are coming. We are asking largely, that our joy may be full. God is moving. We are praying for the churches and their pastors. The Lord will visit those willing to yield to Him."

And the same is true today. Ultimate failure or success for God will be realized just at this point. We must keep humble and little in our own eyes. Let us get built up by a sense of our own importance and we are gone. History repeats itself in this connection. God has always sought a humble people. He can use no other. Martin Luther, the great reformer, wrote: "When our Lord and Master Jesus Christ says repent, He means that the whole life of believers on earth should be a constant and perpetual repentance. Repentance—i.e., true repentance—endures as long as a man is displeased with himself. The desire of self-justification is the cause of all the distresses of the heart." There is always much need of heart preparation, in humility and separation, before God can consistently come. The depth of any revival will be determined exactly by the spirit of repentance that is obtained. In fact, this is *the key* to every true revival born of God.

CONTRACT WITH GOD

On May 12, God dealt with me about giving all my time to Him, turning my back finally and for all time on secular employment. He wanted me now to trust Him fully for myself and my family. I had just received a book, *The Great Revival in Wales,* written by S.B. Shaw. Taking a little walk before breakfast, I was reading this. The Lord had been trying for years to bring me to this decision for His service. We entered into a new contract between us. He was to have the rest of my life fully. And I have never dared to break this contract.

My wife kept my breakfast for me. But I did not return until noon. I had lost my appetite for food. The Spirit, through the book, set me on fire. I visited and prayed with three preachers and a number of workers before I returned home at noon. I had received a new commission and anointing. *My burden was for revival.*

I visited and prayed with people all day long for some time, distributing G. Campbell Morgan's pamphlet on the "Revival in Wales." It moved the people strongly. The spirit of prayer was increasing upon me, and I determined to be "obedient to the heavenly vision." I prayed to the Lord for faith to trust Him fully. "Man shall not live by bread alone."

The Lord blessed me with a further spirit of exhortation to revival among the churches, giving me articles to write for the Holiness press along the same line also. I began to write particularly for the *Way of Faith* and *God's Revivalist.* One night I awoke from my sleep shouting the praises of God. He was getting hold of me more and more. I was now going day and night, exhorting to faith in God for mighty things. The spirit of revival consumed me. The spirit of prophecy came upon me strongly also. I seemed to receive a definite "gift of faith" for revival. We were evidently in the beginning of wonderful days to come, and I prophesied continually of a mighty outpouring.

I had a real ministry to the religious press and began to attend prayer meetings at the various churches to exhort them. G. Campbell Morgan's tract on the "Revival in Wales" spread the fire in the churches wonderfully. I did a great deal of visiting among the saints also and began to sell S.B. Shaw's book, *The Great Revival in Wales,* among the churches. God wonderfully used it to promote faith for a revival spirit. My tract work was continued among the saloons and business houses.

CALIFORNIA FOR CHRIST

In May 1905, I wrote in an article: "My soul is on fire as I read of the glorious work of grace in Wales. The 'seven thousand' in the land, who have kept company with the 'spared ones' (Ezekiel 9), and who have been 'crying and sighing' because of the abomination and desolation in the land, the decay of vital piety in the body of Christ, may well be excused for rejoicing at such a time and prospect as this, when God is once more moving in the earth. But where are the men who will 'stir themselves up to take hold of God?' Let our watchword at this time be 'California for Christ.' God is looking for workers, channels, worms of the dust. Remember, He must have worms. Jesus' life was pressed out in prayer at every pore. This kind comes too high for most people. But may not this be our Lord's 'last call?'"

On June 17, I went to Los Angeles to attend a meeting at the First Baptist Church. They were waiting on God for an outpouring of the Spirit there. Their pastor, Joseph Smale, had just returned from Wales. He had been in touch with the revival and Evan Roberts, and was on fire to have the same visitation and blessing come to his own church in Los Angeles. I found this meeting in accordance with my own vision, burden, and desire, so I spent two hours in the church in prayer before the evening service. Meetings were being held every day and night there, and God was present.

One afternoon I started the meeting in Los Angeles while they were waiting for Smale to appear. I exhorted them not to wait for man but to expect from God. They were depending on some great one, the same spirit of idolatry that has cursed the church and hindered God in all ages. Like the children of Israel, the people must have "some other god before Him." In state church circles in Europe, the pastor is often known as "the little God." I started the service in the evening on the church steps, outside, while we were waiting for the janitor to arrive with the key. We had a season of prayer for the surrounding community. The evening meeting was a steady sweep of victory.

When God's Church becomes what it should be, in love and unity, the doors will never be closed or locked. Like the temple of old, it will be always open. (We saw this later, at Azusa Mission.) God does not have many churches, all of different names. There is no division in a true "Pentecost," neither in true worship. "*God is a Spirit: and they that worship Him must worship Him in spirit and in truth*" (John 4:24 KJV). "*For by one Spirit are we all baptized into one body...and have been all made to drink into one Spirit*" (1 Cor. 12:13 KJV). Ancient Israel, when right with God, was one; how much more should the Church be. We have priests enough to serve continually; and plenty of seeking, needy people to fill the church at all times. How far have we fallen from the early pattern, and even from the type of the Church, Israel! We are so short we scarcely recognize the real thing. Even the Roman Church, though formal, is ahead of us in this. The difficulty and shame is that we are hopelessly divided.

I went to Lamanda Park and, after preaching, spent the night at the parsonage praying and sleeping alternately. I wanted a fuller revelation of Jesus to my own soul. Like the full moon that draws clearer and nearer to our vision as we continue to steadfastly gaze at it, so Jesus appears more real to our souls as we continue to contemplate Him. We need a closer, personal, vital relationship, acquaintance, and communion with God.

*Only the man who lives in fellowship with divine reality can be tasked
with calling the people to God.*

I went to Smale's church again, and again found them list-
lessly waiting for the preacher to appear. Many did not seem to
have any definite idea of why they had come to the meeting. I
began to pray aloud, and the meeting started off with power. It
was in full blast when Brother Smale arrived. God wanted the
people to look to Him, and not to man. Those not having the
glory of God first in view would naturally resent this. But it is
God's plan.

A BURDEN OF PRAYER

I found most Christians did not want to take on a burden of
prayer. It was too hard on the flesh. I was carrying this burden
now in ever increasing volume, night and day. The ministry was
intense. It was "the fellowship of His sufferings," a "travail" of
soul, with "groanings that could not be uttered" (see Rom. 8:26-
27). Most believers find it easier to criticize than to pray.

One day I was much burdened in prayer. I went to Brother
Manley's tent and fell at the altar, there unburdening my soul.
A worker ran in from a side tent and begged me to pray for
him. I attended another meeting that night and there found a
young brother, Edward Boehmer, who had come forth in the
Peniel meetings in the spring, with the same burden of prayer
on him. We were wonderfully united in the Spirit from that
time on. He was destined to become my prayer helper in the
future. We prayed together at the little Peniel Mission until 2
A.M. God wonderfully met and assured us as we wrestled with
Him for the outpouring of His Spirit upon the people. My life
was by this time literally swallowed up in prayer. I was praying
day and night.

I wrote more articles for the religious press, exhorting the
saints to prayer, and went to Smale's again in Los Angeles. Here I

found the people waiting for the preacher again. I was greatly burdened for the situation and tried to show them they must expect from God. Some resented this, being bound by age-old custom, but others responded to it. They were praying for a revival like they had in Wales. This was one of the outstanding features there. In Wales they expected from God. The meetings went on whether the preacher was present or absent. They came to meet God. He met them.

Evan Roberts, evangelist of the Welsh Revival.

I had written a letter to Evan Roberts in Wales asking them to pray for us in California. I now received a reply that they were doing so, which linked us up with the revival there. The letter read as follows: "My dear brother in the faith: Many thanks for your kind letter. I am impressed by your sincerity and honesty of purpose. Congregate the people together who are willing to make a total surrender. Pray and wait. Believe God's promises. Hold daily meetings. May God bless you, is my earnest prayer. Yours in Christ, Evan Roberts." We were much encouraged to know that they were praying for us in Wales.

I wrote some articles for the *Way of Faith*, the *Christian Harvest*, and for *God's Revivalist* at this time. Here is an extract from one written June 1905:

"A wonderful work of the Spirit has broken out here in Los Angeles, California, preceded by a deep preparatory work of prayer and expectation. Conviction is rapidly spreading among the people, and they are rallying from all over the city to the meetings at Pastor Smale's church. Already these meetings are beginning to 'run themselves.' Souls are being saved all over the house, while the meeting sweeps on unguided by human hands. The tide is rising rapidly, and we are anticipating wonderful things. Soul travail is becoming an important feature of the work, and we are being swept away beyond sectarian barriers. The fear of God is coming upon the people, a very spirit of burning. Sunday night the meeting ran on until the small hours of the next morning. Pastor Smale is prophesying of wonderful things to come. He prophesies the speedy return of the apostolic 'gifts' to the church. Los Angeles is a veritable Jerusalem. Just the place for a mighty work of God to begin. I have been expecting just such a display of divine power for some time. Have felt it might break out at any hour. Also that it was liable to come where least expected, that God might get the glory. Pray for a 'Pentecost.'"

LOST IN HIS PRESENCE

One evening, July 3, I felt strongly impressed to go to the little Peniel Hall in Pasadena to pray. There I found Brother Boehmer ahead of me. He had also been led of God to the hall. We prayed for a spirit of revival for Pasadena until the burden became well nigh unbearable. I cried out like a woman in birth pangs. The Spirit was interceding through us. Finally, the burden left us. After a little time of quiet waiting, a great calm settled down upon us. He seemed to stand directly between us, so close we could have reached out our hand and touched Him. But we did not dare to move. I could not even look. In fact, I seemed all spirit. His presence seemed more real, if possible, than if I could have seen and touched Him naturally. I forgot I had eyes or ears; my spirit recognized Him. A heaven of divine love filled and thrilled my soul. Burning fire went through me. In fact, my whole being seemed to flow down before Him, like wax before the fire. I lost all consciousness of time or space, being conscious only of His wonderful presence. I worshiped at His feet. It seemed a veritable "Mount of transfiguration." I was lost in the pure Spirit.

For some time He remained with us. Then, slowly, He withdrew His presence. We would have been there yet had He not withdrawn. I could not doubt His reality after that experience. Brother Boehmer experienced largely the same thing. We had lost all consciousness of each other's presence while He remained with us. We were almost afraid to speak or breathe when we came back to our surroundings. The Lord had said nothing to us, but only overwhelmed our spirits by His presence. He had come to strengthen and assure us for His service. We knew now we were workers with Him, fellowshippers of His sufferings, in the ministry of "soul travail." Real soul travail is just as definite in the spirit as natural human birth pangs. The simile is almost perfect in its sameness. No soul is ever born without this. All true revivals of salvation come this way.

The sun was up the next morning before we left the hall. But the night had seemed but half an hour. With Him all is eternity. It is "eternal life." God knows no time. This element is lost in Heaven. This is the secret of time appearing to pass so swiftly in all nights of real prayer. Time is superseded. The element of eternity is there. For days that marvelous presence seemed to walk by my side. The Lord Jesus was so real. I could hardly take up with human conversation again. It seemed so crude and empty. Human spirits seemed so harsh, earthly fellowship a torment. How far we are naturally from the gentle Spirit of Christ!

I spent the following day in prayer, going to Smale's church in the evening, where I had a ministry in intercession. Heavenly peace and joy filled my soul. Jesus was so real. Doubts and fears cannot abide in His presence.

I wrote a number of articles to several papers, describing God's operations among us, and exhorting the saints everywhere to faith and prayer for a revival. The Lord used these articles greatly to bring faith and conviction. I was soon receiving quite a large correspondence from many places.

I wrote in my diary at this time the following observations: "We may cut ourselves off from God by our spiritual pride, while He may cause the weakest to repent, and go through to victory. The work in our own hearts must go deeper than we have ever experienced, deep enough to destroy sectarian prejudice, party spirit, etc., on all sides. God can perfect those whom He chooses."

THE SPIRIT OF REVIVAL SPREADS

The present worldwide revival was rocked in the cradle of little Wales. It was "brought up" in India, becoming full grown in Los Angeles later. I received from God early in 1905 the following keynote to revival: "The depth of revival will be determined exactly by the depth of the spirit of repentance." And this will hold true for all people, at all times.

The revival spirit at Brother Smale's rapidly spread its interest over the whole city, among the spiritual people. Workers were coming in from all parts, from various affiliations, uniting their prayers with us for a general outpouring. The circle of interest widened rapidly. We were now praying for California, for the nation, and also for a worldwide revival. The spirit of prophecy began to work among us for mighty things on a large scale. Someone sent me 5,000 pamphlets on "The Revival in Wales." These I distributed among the churches. They had a wonderful quickening influence.

I visited Smale's church again and started the meeting. He had not yet arrived. The meetings were getting wonderful by this time for their spontaneity. Our little Gideon's band was marching on to certain victory, led by the Captain of their salvation, Jesus. I was led to pray at this early date especially for faith, discernment of spirits, healing, and prophecy. I felt I needed more wisdom and love, also. I seemed to receive a real "gift of faith" for the revival at this time, with a spirit of prophecy to the same end, and began to prophesy of mighty things to come.

When we began to pray in the spring of 1905, no one seemed to have much faith for anything out of the ordinary. Pessimism in regard to the then present conditions seemed to be felt generally among the saints. But this attitude had changed. God Himself had given us faith for better things. There had been nothing in sight to stimulate us to this. It came from nothing. And can He not do the same today?

ARTICLE IN THE *DAILY NEWS*

I wrote an article at this time for the *Daily News* of Pasadena, describing what I saw in Brother Smale's church. It was published, and the manager himself came to see soon after. He was greatly convicted, came to the altar, and sought God earnestly. The article was copied in a number of Holiness papers throughout the country. It was entitled, "What I Saw in a Los Angeles Church." The following is an extract:

> "For some weeks special services have been held in the First Baptist Church, Lost [sic] Angeles. Pastor Smale had returned from Wales, where he was in touch with Evan Roberts and the revival. He registers his conviction that Los Angeles will soon be shaken by the mighty power of God.

> "The service of which I am writing began in an impromptu and spontaneous way some time before the pastor arrived. A handful of people had gathered early, which seemed to be sufficient for the Spirit's operation. The meeting started. Their expectation was from God. God was there, the people were there, and, by the time the pastor arrived, the meeting was in full swing. Pastor Smale dropped into his place, but no one

seemed to pay any special attention to him. Their minds were on God. No one seemed to get in another's way, although the congregation represented many religious bodies. All seemed to be in perfect harmony. The Spirit was leading.

"The pastor arose, read a portion of the Scripture, made a few well-chosen remarks full of hope and inspiration for the occasion, and the meeting passed again from his hands. The people took it up and went on as before. Testimony, prayer, and praise were intermingled throughout the service. The meeting seemed to run itself as far as human guidance was concerned. The pastor was one of them. If one is at all impressionable religiously, they must feel in such an atmosphere that something wonderful and imminent is about to take place. Some mysterious, mighty upheaval in the spiritual world is evidently at our doors. The meeting gives one a feeling of 'heaven on earth,' with an assurance that the supernatural exists, and that in a very real sense."

ARTICLE IN THE *WESLEYAN METHODIST*

I wrote another article for the *Wesleyan Methodist* at the same time, July 1905, of which the following is an extract:

"Mercy rejected means judgment, and on a corresponding scale. In all the history of God's world, there has always been first the offer of divine mercy, then judgment following. The prophets ceased not day and night to faithfully warn Israel, but their tears and entreaties for the most part proved in vain. The awful destruction of Jerusalem, in 70 a.d., which resulted in the extermination of a million Jews and the captivity of multitudes more, was preceded by the offer of divine mercy at the hands of the Son of God Himself.

"In 1859 a great revival wave visited our country, sweeping a half million souls into the fountain of salvation. Immediately the terrible carnage of 1861-1865 [the Civil War] followed. And so, as we anticipate the coming revival, which is already assuming rapidly world-wide proportions, we wonder if judgment will follow mercy, as at other times. And judgment in proportion to the mercy extended."

For *God's Revivalist*, I wrote: "Unbelief of every form has come in upon us like a flood. But lo, our God comes also! A standard is being raised against the enemy. The Lord is choosing out His workers. This is a time to realize the vision of service. 'The Lord hath spoken and called the earth from the rising of the sun unto the going down thereof. Our God shall come, and shall not keep silence, [saying…] Gather [My] saints together unto [Me], those who have made a covenant with [Me] by sacrifice' (Psalm 50 [see verses 1,3,5])."

PROMISE OF ABUNDANT HARVEST

I often used to declare during 1905 that I would rather live 6 months at that time than 50 years of ordinary time. It was a day of the beginning of great things. The grain of corn was willing to "fall into the ground and die," and there was promise of abundant harvest. But for spiritual "flappers," the whole matter was naturally foolishness.

I wrote another letter to Evan Roberts, asking for continued prayer for California. Thus we were kept linked up in prayer with Wales for the revival. In those days, real prayer was little understood. It was hard to find a quiet place where one would not be disturbed. Gethsemane experiences with Jesus were rare among the saints in those days.

At Smale's church one day, I was groaning in prayer at the altar. The spirit of intercession was upon me. A brother rebuked me severely. He did not understand it. The flesh naturally shrinks from such ordeals. The "groans" are no more popular in most churches than is a woman in birth pangs in the home. Soul travail does not make pleasant company for selfish worldlings. But we cannot have souls born without it. Childbearing is anything but a popular exercise, and so with a real revival of new born souls in the churches. Modern society has little place for a childbearing mother. They prefer society "flappers." And so with the churches regarding soul travail. There is little burden for souls. Men run from the groans of a woman in travail of birth. And so the church desires no "groans" today. She is too busy enjoying herself.

PRESSED FINANCIALLY

We were much pressed financially again, but the Lord delivered. We never made our wants known to anyone but God, and we never begged or borrowed, no matter how pressing the need might seem to be. We believed that if the saints were living closely enough to God, He would speak to them. We trusted Him fully, and went without if He did not send help. I wrote my first tract at this time. It was entitled, "Love Never Faileth." This was the beginning of a large tract ministry. I had to trust the Lord for the means, but He never failed me.

A friend paid our expenses at a camp meeting in the Arroyo for a few days, so we tented there. It was midsummer, and we enjoyed the change and outing. I spent most of my time on my face in the woods in prayer. In the moonlit evenings, I poured out my soul unto God, and He met me there. There was much "empty wagon" rattle in the camp. Most were seeking selfish blessings. They rushed to meetings, like a big sponge, to get more blessing. They needed stepping on.

I found my soul crying out for God far beyond the seeming aspirations of most of the Holiness people. I wanted to go deeper, beneath the mere emotional realm to something more substantial and lasting that would put a rock in my soul. I was tired of so much froth and foam, so much religious ranting and pretension. And the Lord did not long disappoint me.

The camp meeting committee got me on the carpet because of the tracts I was distributing in the camp. They thought I was attacking the Holiness movement, but I was only exhorting them to a deeper place in God. They needed more humility and love. My tract against sectarianism, "That They All May Be One," stirred the camp. Surely man-made movements need to be stirred. God has but one "movement"—that is His "one Body." This was the message at Azusa Mission in the beginning.

I received a second letter from Evan Roberts, which read as follows: "Loughor, Wales, July 1, 1905. Dear brother: I am very thankful to you for your thoughtful kindness. I was exceedingly pleased to learn the good news of how you are beginning to experience wonderful things. Praying God to continue to bless you, and with many thanks repeated for your good wishes, I am yours in the service. Evan Roberts."

THROWING GOD OUT

I went to Smale's church one night, and he resigned. The meetings had run daily in the First Baptist Church for 15 weeks. It was now September. The officials of the church were tired of the innovation and wanted to return to the old order. He was told to either stop the revival or get out. He wisely chose the latter. But what an awful position for a church to take—to throw God out. In this same way, they later drove the Spirit of God out of the churches in Wales. They tired of His presence, desiring to return to the old, cold ecclesiastical order. How blind men are! The most spiritual of Pastor Smale's members naturally followed him, with a nucleus of other workers who had gathered to him from other sources during the revival. They immediately contemplated organizing a New Testament church.

I had a feeling that at least for a time, perhaps the Lord was cutting Brother Smale loose for the evangelistic field to spread the fire in other places. But he did not see it so. I had a conference with him, with this object in view, and was able to arrange for him to speak at the Lake Avenue M.E. Church in Pasadena. This had been the storm center of the revival there.

The night before Brother Smale's services at Lake Avenue Church, two of us spent the night until after midnight in prayer. Brother Smale preached twice on Sunday. He was wonderfully anointed of God for the occasion. We spent the time between the services in prayer. His message was on the revival in Wales, and the people were greatly moved.

Brother Smale soon organized a New Testament Church. I became a charter member, as I felt I ought to stay with them, though I did not care very much for organization. He rented Burbank Hall and prepared to hold meetings there. In the meantime, I secured the Fourth Street Holiness Hall for him, until Burbank Hall was ready.

The Lord gave me another tract, entitled "Pray! Pray! Pray!" I took it to the printer in faith, and God sent the money on time. It was a strong exhortation to prayer. Like the prophets of old, we must pray for those who will not pray for themselves. We must confess the sins of the people for them.

PRAYER CHANGES THINGS

About this time, while Brother Boehmer and I prayed, the Spirit was poured out in a wonderful way in several meetings we were praying for. We felt we had hold of God for them. The reports proved our convictions. Prayer changes things. There is a wonderful power in the proper kind of prayer—Elijah on Mount Carmel, for instance, a man of "like passions" with us. "*The effectual fervent prayer of a righteous man availeth much*" (James 5:16 KJV). Confession may also be necessary in this connection, as the first part of that same verse says: *"Confess therefore your faults one to another."*

Almost every day in Los Angeles found me engaged in personal work, tract distribution, prayer, or preaching in some meeting. I was writing articles for the religious press continually. At one tent meeting in Pasadena, the Lord wonderfully anointed me in preaching, and 20 souls came to the altar. By this time the spirit of intercession had so possessed me that I prayed almost day and night. I fasted much also, until my wife almost despaired of my life at times. The sorrows of my Lord had gripped me. I was in Gethsemane with Him. The "travail of His soul" had fallen in a measure on me. At times I feared that I might not live to realize the answer to my prayers and tears for the revival. But He assured me, sending more than one angel to strengthen me. I felt I was realizing a little of what Paul meant about "filling up the cup of His sufferings" for a lost world. Some were even afraid that I was losing my mind. They could not understand my tremendous concern. Nor can very many understand these things today. *"The natural man receiveth not the things of the Spirit"; they are foolishness to him* (1 Cor. 2:14). Selfish spirits can never understand sacrifice. But "he that would save his life shall lose it" (see John 12:25). *"Except a grain of corn fall into the ground and die, it abideth alone: but if it die, it bringeth forth much fruit"* (John 12:24). Our Lord was a man of "sorrows" as well as of joy.

GOD PROVIDES

I frequently went to Pasadena having to trust God for carfare to get home. On one occasion, Brother Boehmer had an impression I was coming. He went to the little Peniel Mission and found me there. We spent several hours in prayer, then he paid my carfare home. We often spent whole nights together in prayer during those days. It seemed a great privilege to spend a whole night with the Lord. He drew so near. We never seemed to get weary on such occasions.

Boehmer worked at gardening. I never asked him for a penny, but he always gave me something. God finally got not only his money, but his life also, in His service. He was a wonderful man of prayer. God taught us what it means to "*know no man after the flesh*" (2 Cor. 5:16). He lifted us into such a high relationship that our fellowship seemed only in the Spirit. Beyond that we died to one another.

I wrote Evan Roberts a third time to have them continue to pray for us in Wales. In those days, after I had preached, I generally called the saints to their knees, and we would be in prayer for hours before we could get up. The Lord led me to write to many leaders throughout the country to pray for revival. The spirit of prayer was growing continually.

THE NEW TESTAMENT CHURCH

The New Testament Church, begun by Brother Smale, seemed to be losing the spirit of prayer as they increased their organization. They now tried to shift this ministry on a few of us. I knew God was not pleased with that and became much burdened for them. They had taken on too many secondary interests. It began to look as though the Lord would have to find another body. My hopes had been high for this particular company of people, but the enemy seemed to be sidetracking them, or at least leading them to miss God's best. They were now even attempting to organize prayer—an impossible thing. Prayer is spontaneous. I felt it were better not to have organized than to lose the ministry of prayer and spirit of revival as a body. It was for this they had been called in the beginning.

They had become ambitious for a church and organization. It seemed hard to them not to be "like the other nations (churches) around them." And right here they began to fail. As church work increased, they lost sight of the real issue. Human organization and human programs leave very little room for the free Spirit of God. It means much to be willing to be considered a failure, while we seek to build up a purely spiritual Kingdom. God's Kingdom cometh not "by observation." It is very easy to choose second best. The prayer life is needed much more than buildings or organizations. These are often a substitute for the other. Souls are born into the Kingdom only through prayer.

I feared the New Testament Church might develop a party (sectarian) spirit. A rich lady offered them the money to build a church edifice. The devil was bidding high. However, she soon withdrew her offer, and I confess I was glad she did. They would soon have had no time for anything but building. It would have been the end of their revival. We had been called out to evangelize Los Angeles, not to build up another sect or party spirit. We needed no more organization nor machinery than what was really necessary for the speedy evangelizing of the city. Surely we already had enough separate, rival church organizations on our hands, each working largely for its own interest, advancement, and glory.

The New Testament Church seemed to be drifting toward intellectualism. I became much burdened for it. During one meeting—it was so painful after what we had seen—I groaned aloud in prayer. One of the elders rebuked me severely for this. "How are the mighty fallen" kept ringing in my ears. A few of the most spiritual had the same burden with me. After this incident, prayer again seemed to prevail in a measure. We had a great meeting in the church one Sunday night, and 100 knelt at the altar.

CONSUMED BY PRAYER

I met with the Peniel boys in Pasadena for prayer, and we had a breaking through time. We felt the Lord would soon work mightily. At Brother Brownley's tent at Seventh and Spring

Streets, Los Angeles, we had a deep spirit of prayer and powerful altar services. There was a feeling that God was about to do something extraordinary. The spirit of prayer came more and more heavily upon us.

In Pasadena, before moving to Los Angeles, I would lie on my bed in the daytime and roll and groan under the burden. At night I could scarcely sleep for the spirit of prayer. I fasted much, not caring for food while burdened. At one time I was in soul travail for nearly 24 hours without intermission. It nearly used me up. Prayer literally consumed me. Sometimes I would groan all night in my sleep.

Prayer was not formal in those days. It was God-breathed. It came upon us and overwhelmed us. We did not work it up. We were gripped with real soul travail by the Spirit that could no more be shaken off than could the birth pangs of a woman in travail without doing absolute violence to the Spirit of God. It was real intercession by the Holy Spirit.

EVAN ROBERTS' TESTIMONY

For several days I had an impression that another letter was coming from Evan Roberts. It soon came and read as follows:

"Loughor, Wales, Nov. 14, 1905. My dear comrade: What can I say that will encourage you in this terrible fight? I find it is a most awful one. Praise God, the kingdom of the evil one is being besieged on every side. Oh, the millions of prayers—not simply the form of prayer—but the soul finding its way right to the White Throne! People in Wales have prayed during the last year. May the Lord bless you with a mighty down-pouring. In Wales it seems as if the Holy One rests upon the congregation, awaiting the opening of the hearts of the followers of Christ. We had a mighty downpouring of the Holy Spirit last Saturday night.

This was preceded by the correcting of the people's views of true worship. 1. To give unto God, not to receive. 2. To please God, not to please ourselves. Therefore, looking to God and forgetting the enemy, and also the fear of men, we prayed and the Spirit descended. I pray [to] God to hear your prayer, to keep your faith strong, and to save California. I remain, your brother in the fight. Evan Roberts."

This was the third letter I had received from Wales, from Evan Roberts, and I feel their prayers had much to do with our final victory in California.

Evan Roberts tells us of his own experience with God: "One Friday night last spring, while praying by my bedside before retiring, I was taken up to a great expanse, without time or space. It was communion with God. Before this I had had a far off God. I was frightened that night, but never since. So great was my shivering that I rocked the bed, and my brother, being awakened, took hold of me, thinking I was ill."

Evan Roberts experienced this every night for three months, from 1 A.M. until 5 A.M. He wrote a message to the world about this time, as follows:

"The revival in South Wales is not of men, but of God. He has come very close to us. There is no question of creed or of dogma in this movement. We are teaching no sectarian doctrine, only the wonder and beauty of Christ's love. I have been asked concerning my methods. I have none. I never prepare what I shall speak, but leave that to Him. I am not the source of this revival, but only one agent among what is growing to be a multitude. I wish not personal following, but only the world for Christ.

"I believe that the world is upon the threshold of a great religious revival, and I pray daily that I may be allowed to help bring this about. Wonderful things have happened in Wales in a few weeks, *but these are only a beginning.* The world will be swept by His Spirit as by a rushing, mighty wind. Many who are now silent Christians will lead the movement. They will see a great light and will reflect this light to thousands now in darkness. Thousands will do more than we have accomplished, as God gives them power."

THE SECRET OF ALL POWER

What beautiful humility! This is the secret of all power. An English eyewitness of the revival in Wales wrote: "Such real travail of soul for the unsaved I have never before witnessed. I have seen young Evan Roberts convulsed with grief and calling on his audience to pray. 'Don't sing,' he would exclaim, 'it's too terrible to sing.'" (Conviction has often been lifted from the people by too much singing.)

Another writer declared, "It was not the eloquence of Evan Roberts that broke men down, but his tears. He would break down, crying bitterly for God to bend them, in an agony of prayer, the tears coursing down his cheeks, his whole frame writhing. Strong men would break down and cry like children. Women would shriek. A sound of weeping and wailing would fill the air. Evan Roberts, in the intensity of his agony, would fall in the pulpit, while many in the crowd often fainted."

Of the later work in India we read:

"The girls in India were wonderfully wrought upon and baptized with the Spirit (in Ramabai Mission), under conviction of their need. Great light was given to them. When delivered, they jumped up and down for joy for hours without fatigue; in fact, they were stronger for it. They cried out with the burning that came into and upon them. Some fell as they saw a great light pass before them, while the fire of God burned the members of the body of sin—pride, anger, love of the world, selfishness, uncleanness, etc. They neither ate nor slept until the victory was won. Then the joy was so great that for two or three days after receiving the baptism of the Holy Spirit they did not care for food.

"About twenty girls went into a trance at one time and became unconscious of this world for hours; some for three or four days. During that time they sang, prayed, clapped their hands, rolled about, or sat still. When they became conscious, they told of seeing a throne in heaven, a white robed throng, and a glory so bright they could not bear it. Soon the whole place was aflame. School had to be suspended, they forgot to eat or sleep, and whole nights and days were absorbed in prayer. The Spirit was poured out upon one of the seeking girls in the night. Her companion sleeping next to her awoke, and seeing fire envelop her, ran across the dormitory and brought a pail of water to dash upon her. In less than an hour, nearly all the girls in the compound were weeping, praying and confessing their sins. Many of these girls were invested with a strange, beautiful and supernatural fire."

The spontaneous composition of hymns was a curious feature of some of the meetings in other parts of India. At Kara Camp, pictures appeared on the walls to a company of small girls in prayer, supernaturally depicting the life of Christ. The figures moved in the pictures and were in color. Each view would last from two to ten minutes, and then the light would gradually fade away, to reappear in a few moments with a new scene. These appeared for 12 hours and were not only seen by the native children of the orphanage and eight missionaries, but by native Christians living nearby. Even heathens came to see the wonderful sight. These pictures were all faithfully depicting the Bible narration and were entirely supernatural. They had a tremendous effect in breaking up the hard hearts of the heathen. In Wales, colored lights were often seen, like balls of fire, during the revival there.

I kept going day and night to different missions, exhorting continually to prayer and faith for the revival. One night at the New Testament Church, during a deep spirit of prayer on the congregation, the Lord came suddenly so near that we could feel His presence as though He were closing in on us around the edges of the meeting. Two-thirds of the people sprang to their feet in alarm, and some ran hurriedly out of the meeting, even leaving their hats behind them, almost scared out of their senses. There was no out-of-the-ordinary demonstration in the natural to cause this fright. It was a supernatural manifestation of His nearness. What would such do if they saw the Lord?

OBEY GOD RATHER THAN MEN

I started a little cottage prayer meeting where we could have more liberty to pray and wait on the Lord. The spirit of prayer was being hindered, at times, in the other meetings. The more spiritual were hungry for this opportunity. However, the leaders misunderstood and opposed me. Then our landlady got the devil in her and wanted to throw us out of our home. She was not right with God. Our rent was paid up, but the enemy tried to use her. The fight was on. They began to oppose my ministry at the New Testament Church. A sister tried to persuade me to discontinue the prayer meetings I had started. I asked the Lord to show me His will in the matter. He came and filled our little cottage with a cloud of glory until I could scarcely bear His presence. That settled it for me. "We ought to obey God rather than men."

I suffered much criticism. I think they were afraid I would start another church. But I had no such thought at that time. I only wanted to have freedom to pray. Many a mission and church have gone on the rocks opposing God.

I wrote more articles for the religious press during this time. Here is an excerpt from an article I wrote for the *Christian Harvester*:

> "Slowly but surely, the conviction is coming upon the saints of Southern California that God is going to pour out His Spirit here as in Wales. We are having faith for things such as we have never dreamed of, for the near future. We are assured of no less than a 'Pentecost' for this whole country. But we can never have pentecostal results without pentecostal demonstration. Few care to meet God face to face. Flesh and blood cannot inherit the Kingdom of God."

PENTECOST IS KNOCKING

In an article for the *Way of Faith*, November 16, 1905, I wrote:

> "The current of revival is sweeping by our door. Will we cast ourselves on its mighty bosom and ride to glorious victory? A year of life at this time, with its wonderful possibilities for God, is worth a hundred years of ordinary life. 'Pentecost' is knocking at our doors. The revival for our country is no longer a question. Slowly but surely, the tide has been rising until, in the very near future, we believe for a deluge of salvation that will sweep all before it. Wales will not long stand alone in this glorious triumph for our Christ. The spirit of reviving is coming upon us, driven by the breath of God, the Holy Spirit. The clouds are gathering rapidly,

big with a mighty rain, whose precipitation lingers but a little.

"Heroes will arise from the dust of obscure and despised circumstances, whose names will be emblazoned on heaven's eternal page of fame. The Spirit is brooding over our land again as at creation's dawn, and the decree of God goes forth—'*Let there be light!*' Brother, sister, if we all believed God, can you realize what would happen? Many of us here are living for nothing else. A volume of believing prayer is ascending to the throne night and day. Los Angeles, Southern California, and the whole continent shall surely find itself before long in the throes of a mighty revival, by the Spirit and power of God."

We had been for some time led to pray for a Pentecost. It seemed almost beginning. Of course we did not realize what a real "Pentecost" was. But the Spirit did, and led us to ask correctly. One afternoon, after a service in the New Testament Church, seven of us seemed providentially led to join hands and agree in prayer to ask the Lord to pour out His Spirit speedily, "*with signs following.*" Where we got the idea from at that time I do not know. He must have suggested it to us Himself. We did not have "tongues" in mind. I think none of us ever heard of such a thing. This was in February 1906.

While at a prayer meeting, on my knees, the Lord told me to get up and go to Brother Brownley's tent at Seventh and Spring Streets. He gave me a message for them. I went, greatly burdened, and after speaking we had a real "breaking up time," weeping before the Lord. I then wrote a moving tract on "Soul Travail." The Lord was dealing with me much also about His atoning blood. I spent another entire night in prayer with Brother Boehmer, and the Lord gave me a blessed ministry at Pasadena in different meetings. At one meeting, I lay for two hours helpless under a burden for souls. The battle was getting more and more earnest.

On March 26, I went to a cottage meeting on Bonnie Brae Street. Both white and black saints were meeting there for prayer. I had attended another cottage meeting shortly before this, where I first met a Brother Seymour. He had just come from Texas. He was a black man, blind in one eye, very plain, spiritual, and humble. He attended the meetings at Bonnie Brae Street.

At that time the Lord gave me another tract, entitled "The Last Call."

William Seymour posing with his Bible, (Used by permission, Flower Pentecostal Heritage Center).

This was used mightily to awaken the people. Here is an extract: "And now, once more, at the very end of the age, God calls. The Last Call, the Midnight Cry, is now upon us, sounding clearly in our ears. God will give this one more chance, the last. A final call, a worldwide Revival. Then Judgment upon the whole world. Some tremendous event is about to transpire."

CHAPTER TWO

THE FIRE FALLS AT AZUSA

I went to Burbank Hall, the New Testament Church, Sunday morning, April 15. A black sister was there and spoke in "tongues." This created a great stir. The people gathered in little companies on the sidewalk after the service inquiring what this might mean. It seemed like Pentecostal "signs." We then learned that the Spirit had fallen a few nights before, April 9, at the little cottage on Bonnie Brae Street. They had been tarrying very earnestly for some time for an outpouring. A handful of black and white saints had been waiting there daily, but for some reason I was not privileged to be present at that particular meeting. I went to the Bonnie Brae meeting in the afternoon, however, and found God working mightily. We had been praying for many months for victory. Jesus was now "showing Himself alive" again to many. The pioneers had broken through for the multitude to follow.

There was a general spirit of humility manifested in the meeting. They were taken up with God. Evidently the Lord had found the little company at last, outside as always, through whom He could have His way. God had not chosen an established mission where this could be done. They were in the hands of men; the Spirit could not work. Others far more pretentious had failed. That which man esteems had been passed by once more, and the Spirit was born again in a humble "stable," outside ecclesiastical establishments.

A body must be prepared, in repentance and humility, for every outpouring of the Spirit. The preaching of the Reformation was begun by Martin Luther in a tumbledown building in the midst of the public square in Wittenberg. In his book, *The Reformation of the Sixteenth Century*, Merle D'Aubigne describes it as follows:

> "In the middle of the square at Wittenberg stood an ancient wooden chapel, thirty feet long and twenty feet wide, whose walls, propped up on all sides, were falling into ruin. An old pulpit made of planks, and three feet high, received the preacher. It was in this wretched place that the preaching of the Reformation began. It was God's will that that which was to restore His glory should have the humblest surroundings. It was in this wretched enclosure that God willed, so to speak, that His well-beloved Son should be born a second time. Among those thousands of cathedrals and parish churches with which the world is filled, there was not one at that time which God chose for the glorious preaching of eternal life."

In the revival in Wales, the great expounders of England had to come and sit at the feet of crude, hard-working miners, and see the wonderful works of God. I wrote for the *Way of Faith* at this time: "The real thing is appearing among us. The Almighty will again measure swords with Pharaoh's magicians. But many will reject Him and blaspheme. Many will fail to recognize Him, even among His professed followers. We have been praying and believing for a 'Pentecost.' Will we receive it when it comes?"

The present worldwide Pentecostal manifestation did not break out in a moment, like a huge prairie fire, and set the world on fire. In fact, no work of God ever appears that way. There is a necessary time for preparation. The finished article is not realized at the beginning. Men may wonder where it came from, not being conscious of the preparation, but there is always such. Every movement of the Spirit of God must also run the gauntlet of the devil's forces. The dragon stands before the bearing mother, ready to swallow up her child (see Rev. 12:4).

THE COUNTERFEIT OF THE ENEMY

So it was with the present Pentecostal work in its beginning. The enemy did much counterfeiting. God kept the young child well hidden for a season from the Herods, until it could gain strength and discernment to resist them. The flame was guarded jealously by the hand of the Lord from the winds of criticism, jealousy, unbelief, etc. It went through about the same experiences that all revivals have. Its foes were both inside and out. Both Luther and Wesley experienced the same difficulties in their time. We have this treasure in "earthen vessels." Every natural birth is surrounded by circumstances not entirely pleasant. God's perfect work is wrought in human imperfection. We are creatures of "the fall." Then why expect a perfect manifestation in this case? We are coming *back* to God.

John Wesley writes of his time:

"Almost as soon as I was gone, two or three began to take their imaginations for impressions from God. Meantime, a flood of reproach came upon me from almost every quarter. Be not alarmed that Satan sows tares among the wheat of Christ. It has ever been so, especially on any remarkable outpouring of the Spirit, and ever will be, until the devil is chained for a thousand years. Till then he will always ape and endeavor to counteract the work of the Spirit of Christ."

D'Aubigne has said: "A religious movement almost always exceeds a just moderation. In order that human nature may make one step in advance, its pioneers must take many."

Another writer says:

"Remember with what accompaniments of extravagance and fanaticism the doctrine of justification by faith was brought back under Luther. The wonder was, not that Luther had the courage to face pope and cardinals, but that he had the courage to endure the contempt which his own doctrines brought upon him, as espoused and paraded by fanatical advocates. Recall, too, the scandal and offense which attended the revival of piety under Wesley. What we denounce as error may be the 'refraction of some great truth below the horizon.'"

John Wesley himself once prayed, after the revival had about died out for the time: "Oh, Lord, send us the old revival, without the defects; but if this cannot be, send it with all its defects. We must have the revival!"

Adam Clarke, in his Bible commentary, said: "Nature, along with Satan, will always mingle themselves, as far as they can, in the genuine work of the Spirit in order to discredit and destroy it. In great revivals of religion, it is almost impossible to prevent wild-fire from getting in among the true fire."

Dr. Seiss says: "Never, indeed, has there been a sowing of God on earth but it has been oversown by Satan; or a growth for Christ, which the plantings of the wicked one did not mingle with and hinder. He who sets out to find a perfect church, in which there are no unworthy elements and no disfigurations, proposes to himself a hopeless task."

Still another writer says:

"In the various crises that have occurred in the history of the Church, men have come to the front who have manifested a holy recklessness that astonished their fellows. When Luther nailed his theses to the door of the cathedral at Wittenberg, cautious men were astonished at his audacity. When John Wesley ignored all church restrictions and religious propriety and preached in the fields and byways, men declared his reputation was ruined. So it has been in all ages. When the religious condition of the times called for men who were willing to sacrifice all for Christ, the demand created the supply, and there have always been found a few who were willing to be regarded reckless for the Lord. An utter recklessness concerning men's opinions and other consequences is the only attitude that can meet the needs of the present times."

God found His Moses, in the person of Brother Smale, to lead us to the Jordan crossing. But He chose Brother Seymour for our Joshua, to lead us over.

THE SAN FRANCISCO EARTHQUAKE

Sunday, April 15, the Lord called me to ten days of special prayer. I felt greatly burdened but had no idea of what He had particularly in mind. He had a word for me and wanted to prepare me for it.

Wednesday, April 18, the terrible San Francisco earthquake came, which also devastated the surrounding cities and country. No less than 500 people lost their lives in San Francisco alone. I felt a deep conviction that the Lord was answering our prayers for a revival in His own way.

"When Thy judgments are in the earth, the inhabitants of the world will learn righteousness" (Isa. 26:9 KJV). A tremendous

burden of prayer came upon me that the people might not be indifferent to His voice.

Thursday, April 19, while sitting in the noon meeting at Peniel Hall, 227 South Main Street, the floor suddenly began to move with us. An unusual tremor ran through the room as Los Angeles was hit with a small earthquake. We sat in awe. Many people ran into the middle of the street, looking up anxiously at the buildings, fearing they were about to fall. It was an earnest time.

I went home and, after a season of prayer, was impressed of the Lord to go to the meeting that had been removed from Bonnie Brae Street to 312 Azusa Street. Here they had rented an old frame building in the center of the city, a building that was formerly a Methodist church but had been long out of use for meetings and had become a receptacle for old lumber, plaster, etc. The people had cleared space enough in the surrounding dirt and debris to lay some planks on top of empty nail kegs, with seats enough for possibly 30 people, if I remember rightly. The makeshift pews were arranged in a square, facing one another.

THE ARK MOVED TO AZUSA

I was under tremendous pressure to get to the meeting that evening. It was my first visit to Azusa Mission. Mother Wheaton, a wonderful woman of God who was living with us, was going with me. She was so slow that I could hardly wait for her. We finally reached Azusa and found about a dozen saints there, some white, some black. Brother Seymour was there, in charge. The "Ark of God" moved off slowly, but surely, at Azusa. It was carried on the shoulders of His own appointed priests in the beginning. We had no "new cart" in those days to please the carnal, mixed multitude. We had the devil to fight, but the Ark was not drawn by oxen (dumb beasts). The priests were "alive unto God," through much preparation and prayer.

Discernment was not perfect, and the enemy got some advantage, which brought reproach to the work, but the saints soon learned to "take the precious from the vile." The combined forces of hell were set determinedly against us in the beginning. It was not all blessing. In fact, the fight was terrific. As always, the devil combed the country for crooked spirits to destroy the work if possible. But the fire could not be smothered. Gradually the tide arose in victory. But from a small beginning, a very little flame.

Asuza Street Mission, April 1906, (Used by permission, Flower Pentecostal Heritage Center).

I gave a message at my first meeting at Azusa. Two of the saints spoke in tongues. Much blessing seemed to attend the utterance. It was soon noised abroad that God was working at Azusa, and all kinds of people began to come to the meetings. Many were curious and unbelieving, but others were hungry for God. The newspapers began to ridicule and abuse the meetings, thus giving us much free advertising. This brought the crowds.

The devil overdid himself again. Outside persecution never hurt the work. We had the most to fear from the working of evil spirits within. Even spiritualists and hypnotists came to investigate, and to try their influence. Then all the religious soreheads, crooks, and cranks came, seeking a place in the work. We had the most to fear from these. But this is always the danger to every new work; they had no place elsewhere. This condition cast a fear over many, which was hard to overcome. It hindered the Spirit much. Many were afraid to seek God for fear the devil might get them.

We found out early in the Azusa work that when we attempted to steady the Ark, the Lord stopped working. We dared not call the attention of the people too much to the working of the evil one. Fear would follow. We could only pray—then God gave victory. There was a presence of God with us, through prayer, that we could depend on. The leaders had limited experience, and the wonder is that the work survived at all against its powerful adversaries. But it was of God. That was the secret.

A certain writer has well said: "On the day of Pentecost, Christianity faced the world, a new religion without a college, a people, or a patron. All that was ancient and venerable rose up before her in sold opposition, and she did not flatter or conciliate any one of them. She assailed every existing system and every bad habit, burning her way through innumerable forms of opposition. This she accomplished with her 'tongue of fire' alone."

Another writer has said: "The apostasy of the early Church came as a result of a greater desire to see the spread of its power and rule than to see new natures given to its individual members. The moment we covet a large following and rejoice in the crowd that is attracted by our presentation of what we consider truth, and have not a greater desire to see the natures of individuals changed according to the divine plan, we start to travel the same road of apostasy that leads to Rome and her daughters."

DID GOD DO THAT?

I found that the earthquake had opened many hearts. I was especially distributing my most recent tract, "The Last Call." It seemed very appropriate after the earthquake. Sunday, April 22, I took 10,000 of these to the New Testament Church. The workers seized them eagerly and scattered them quickly throughout the city.

Nearly every pulpit in the land was working overtime to prove that God had nothing to do with earthquakes and thus allay the fears of the people. The Spirit was striving to knock at hearts with conviction through this judgment. I felt indignation that the preachers should be used of satan to drown out His voice. Even the teachers in the schools labored hard to convince the children that God was not in earthquakes. The devil put out much propaganda on this line.

I had been in prayer since the earthquake and had slept little. After the earthquake in Los Angeles, the Lord told me that He definitely had a message to give me for the people. On the Saturday after, He gave me a part of it. On Monday the rest was given. I finished writing it at 12:30 A.M. on Tuesday, and it was ready for the printer. I kneeled before the Lord, and He met me in a powerful way, a powerful witness that the message was from Him. I was to have it printed in the morning. From that time until 4 A.M., I was wonderfully taken up in the spirit of intercession. I seemed to feel the wrath of God against the people and to withstand it in prayer. He showed me He was terribly grieved at their obstinacy in the fact of His judgment on sin. San Francisco was a terribly wicked city.

He showed me that all hell was being moved to drown out His voice in the earthquake. The message He had given me was to counteract this influence. Men had been denying His presence in the earthquake. Now He would speak. It was a terrific message He had given me. I was to argue the question with no man, but simply give them the message. They would answer to Him. I felt all hell against me in this, and so it proved. I went to bed at 4 o'clock, arose at 7, and hurried with the message to the printer.

The question in almost every heart was, "Did God do that?" But instinct taught men on the spot that He had. Even the wicked were conscious of the fact. The tract was set up quickly. That same day it was on the press, and the next noon I had my first consignment of the tracts. I was impressed that I must hasten and get them to the people as quickly as possible. I was reminded that the ten days I was called by the Lord to prayer ended the very day I received the first of the tracts. I understood it all now.

I distributed the message speedily in the missions, churches, saloons, business houses, and in fact, everywhere, both in Los Angeles and Pasadena. In addition, I mailed thousands to workers in nearby towns for distribution. The whole undertaking was a work of faith. I began without a dollar, but He supplied the money as needed. I worked hard every day. Brother and Sister Otterman distributed them in San Diego. It required courage. Many raved at the message. I went with them through all the dives in Los Angeles. All hell was stirred.

God sent Brother Boehmer from Pasadena to help me. He stood outside and prayed while I went into the saloons with them. They were mad enough to kill me in some instances. Business was at a standstill after the news came from San Francisco. The people were paralyzed with fear. This accounted to some extent for the influence of my tract. The pressure against me was terrific. All hell was surging around me to stop the message. But I never faltered. I felt God's hand upon me continually in the matter. The people were appalled to see what God had to say about earthquakes. He sent me to a number of meetings with a solemn exhortation to repent and seek Him. At Azusa Mission we had a powerful time. The saints humbled themselves. A black sister both spoke and sang in tongues. The very atmosphere of Heaven was there.

Sunday, May 11, I had finished my "Earthquake" tract distribution. Then the burden suddenly left me. My work was done. Seventy-five thousand had been published and distributed in Los Angeles and Southern California in less than three weeks' time. At Oakland, Brother Manley, of his own volition, had printed and distributed 50,000 more in the Bay Cities in about the same space of time.

The San Francisco earthquake was surely the voice of God to the people on the Pacific Coast. It was used mightily in conviction for the revival that the Lord graciously brought afterward. In the early Azusa days, both Heaven and hell seemed to have come to town. Men were at the breaking point. Conviction was mightily on the people. They would fly to pieces even on the street, almost without provocation. A very "blood line" seemed to be drawn around Azusa Mission by the Spirit. When people came within two or three blocks of the place, they were seized with conviction.

The work was getting clearer and stronger at Azusa. God was working mightily. It seemed that everyone had to go to Azusa. Missionaries were gathered there from Africa, India, and the islands of the sea. Preachers and workers had crossed the continent and come from distant lands with an irresistible drawing to Los Angeles. *"Gather My saints together"* (Ps. 50:5 KJV). They had come up for "Pentecost," though they little realized it. It was God's call.

Holiness meetings, tents, and missions began to close up for lack of attendance. Their people were at Azusa. Brother and Sister Garr closed the Burning Bush Hall, came to Azusa, received the baptism in the Spirit, and were soon on their way to India to spread the fire. Even Brother Smale had to come to Azusa to look up his members. He invited them back home, promised them liberty in the Spirit, and for a time God wrought mightily at the New Testament Church, also.

PERSECUTION DRAWS CROWDS

There was much persecution, especially from the press. They wrote us up shamefully, but this only drew the crowds. Some gave the work six months to live. Soon the meetings were running day and night. The place was packed out nightly. The whole building, upstairs and down, had now been cleared and put into use. There were far more white people than black people coming. The "color line" was washed away in the blood. A.S. Worrell, translator of the New Testament, declared the Azusa work had rediscovered the blood of Christ to the Church at that time. Great emphasis was placed on Christ's blood, for cleansing, etc. A high standard was held up for a clean life. *"When the enemy shall come in like a flood, the Spirit of the Lord shall lift up a standard against him"* (Isa. 59:19).

Divine love was wonderfully manifest in the meetings. They would not even allow an unkind word to be said against their opposers or the churches. The message was the love of God. It was a sort of "first love" of the early Church returned. The baptism of the Holy Spirit, as we received it in the beginning, did not allow us to think, speak, or hear evil of any man. The Spirit was very sensitive, tender as a dove. The Holy Spirit is symbolized as a dove. We knew the moment we had grieved the Spirit by an unkind thought or word. We seemed to live in a sea of pure divine love. The Lord fought our battles for us in those days. We committed ourselves to His judgment fully in all matters, never seeking to even defend the work or ourselves. We lived in His wonderful, immediate presence. And nothing contrary to His pure Spirit was allowed there.

TARRYING IN THE UPPER ROOM

The false was sifted out from the real by the Spirit of God. The Word of God itself decided absolutely all issues. The hearts of the people, both in act and motive, were searched to the very bottom. It was no joke to become one of that company. No man "durst join himself to them" unless he meant business. It meant a dying out and cleaning up process in those days to receive the baptism. We had a "tarrying" room upstairs for those especially seeking God for the Holy Spirit baptism, though many got it in the main assembly room also. In fact, they often got it in their seats in those days.

The Spirit wrought very deeply in the "tarrying" room. An unquiet spirit or a thoughtless talker was immediately reproved by the Spirit. We were on "holy ground." This atmosphere was unbearable to the carnal spirit. They generally gave this room a wide berth unless they had been thoroughly subdued and burned out. Only honest seekers sought it, those who really meant business with God. It was no place to throw fits or blow off steam. Men did not "fly to their lungs" in those days. They flew to the mercy seat. They took their shoes off, figuratively speaking. They were on "holy ground."

Arthur Booth-Clibborn has written the following weighty words:

"Any cheapening of the price of Pentecost would be a disaster of untold magnitude. The company in the upper room, upon whom Pentecost fell, had paid the highest price for it. In this they approached as near as possible to Him who had paid the supreme price in order to send it. Do we ever really adequately realize how utterly lost to this world, how completely despised, rejected and outcast was that company? Their master and leader had just passed through the 'hangmen's rope,' so to speak, at the hands of the highest civilization of the day. Their Calvary was complete, and so a complete Pentecost came to match it. The latter will resemble the former in completeness. We may, therefore, each of us say to ourselves: As your cross, so will your Pentecost be. God's way to Pentecost be. God's way to Pentecost was via Calvary. Individually it must be so today also. The purity and fullness of the individual Pentecost must depend upon the completeness of the individual Calvary. This is an unalterable principle."

GIFT OF SONG

Friday, June 15, at Azusa, the Spirit dropped the "heavenly chorus" into my soul. I found myself suddenly joining the rest who had received this supernatural "gift." It was a spontaneous manifestation and rapture that no earthly tongue can describe.

In the beginning, this manifestation was wonderfully pure and powerful. We feared to try to reproduce it, as with the tongues also. Now many seemingly have no hesitation in imitating all the "gifts," causing them to lose their power and influence. No one could understand this "gift of song" but those who had it. It was indeed a "new song" in the Spirit. When I first heard it in the meetings, a great hunger entered my soul to receive it. I felt it would exactly express my pent-up feelings.

I had not yet spoken in tongues, but the "new song" captured me. It was a gift from God of high order. No one had preached it. The Lord had sovereignly bestowed it, with the out-pouring of the "residue of oil," the "Latter Rain" baptism of the Spirit. It was exercised as the Spirit moved the possessors, either in solo fashion or by the company. It was sometimes without words, other times in tongues. The effect was wonderful on the people. It brought a heavenly atmosphere, as though the angels themselves were present and joining with us. And possibly they were. It seemed to still criticism and opposition and was hard for even wicked men to gainsay or ridicule.

Some have condemned this "new song" without words. But was not sound given before language? And is there not intelligence without language also? Who composed the first song? Must we necessarily always follow some man's composition before us? We are too much worshipers of tradition. The speaking in tongues is not according to man's wisdom or understanding; then why not a "gift of song"? It is certainly a rebuke to the "jazzy" religious songs of our day. And possibly it was given for that purpose. Yet some of the old hymns are very good to sing also. We need not despise them or treat them lightly. Someone has said that every fresh revival brings in its own hymnology. And this one surely did.

In the beginning in Azusa, we had no musical instruments. In fact, we felt no need for them. There was no place for them in our worship—all was spontaneous. We did not even sing from hymnbooks. All the old, well-known hymns were sung from memory, quickened by the Spirit of God. "The Comforter Has Come" was possibly the one most sung. We sang it from a fresh, powerful heart experience. Oh, how the power of God filled and thrilled us. Then the songs of Christ's blood were very popular. "The life is in the blood." Sinai, Calvary, and Pentecost, all had their rightful place in the Azusa work. But the "new song" was altogether different, not of human composition. It cannot be successfully counterfeited. The crow cannot imitate the dove. But they finally began to despise this gift, when the human spirit asserted itself again. They drove it out by hymnbooks and selected songs by readers. It was like murdering the Spirit, and was most painful to some of us, but the tide was too strong against us.

Hymnbooks today are too largely a commercial proposition, and we would not lose much without most of them. Even the old tunes are often violated by change, and new styles must be gotten out every season for added profit. There is very little real spirit of worship in them. They move the toes, but not the hearts of men. The spirit of song given from God in the beginning was like the Aeolian harp in its spontaneity and sweetness. In fact, it was the very breath of God, playing on human heartstrings, or human vocal cords. The notes were wonderful in sweetness, volume, and duration. In fact, they were often humanly impossible. It was indeed "singing *in the Spirit.*"

ALL WERE ON ONE LEVEL

Brother Seymour was recognized as the nominal leader in charge. But we had no pope or hierarchy. We were brethren. We had no human program; the Lord Himself was leading. We had no priest class, nor priest craft. These things have come in later, with the apostasizing of the movement. We did not even have a platform or pulpit in the beginning. All were on one level. The ministers were servants, according to the true meaning of the word. We did not honor men for their advantage in means or education, but rather for their God-given "gifts." *He* set the members in the Body. Now "*A wonderful and horrible thing is committed in the land; the prophets prophesy falsely, and the priests bear rule by their means; and My people love to have it so: and what will ye do in the end thereof?*" (Jer. 5:30-31 KJV). Also, "*As for My people, children are their oppressors* [sometimes grown-up ones], *and women rule over them* (Isa. 3:12 KJV).

William Seymour posing with his Bible, (Used by permission, Flower Pentecostal Heritage Center).

Brother Seymour generally sat behind two empty boxes, one on top of the other. He usually kept his head inside the top one during the meeting, in prayer. There was no pride there. The services ran almost continuously. Seeking souls could be found under the power almost any hour of the day or night. The place was never closed nor empty. The people came to meet God— He was always there. Hence a continuous meeting. The meeting did not depend on the human leader. God's presence became more and more wonderful. In that old building, with its low rafters and bare floors, God broke strong men and women to pieces, and put them together again for His glory. It was a tremendous overhauling process. Pride and self-assertion, self-importance, and self-esteem could not survive there. The religious ego preached its own funeral sermon quickly.

No subjects or sermons were announced ahead of time, and no special speakers for such an hour. No one knew what might be coming, what God would do. All was spontaneous, ordered by the Spirit. We wanted to hear from God, through whomever He might speak. We had no respect of persons. All were equal. No flesh might glory in His presence. He could not use the self-opinionated. Those were Holy Spirit meetings, led of the Lord. It had to start in poor surroundings to keep out the selfish, human element. All came down in humility together at His feet. They all looked alike and had all things in common, in that sense at least. The rafters were low; the tall must come down. By the time they got to Azusa, they were humbled, ready for the blessing. The fodder was thus placed for the lambs, not for giraffes. All could reach it.

AFTER THE FLESH NO MORE

We were delivered right there from ecclesiastical hierarchism and abuse. We wanted God. When we first reached the meeting, we avoided human contact and greeting as much as possible. We wanted to meet God first. We got our head under some bench in the corner in prayer, and met men only in the Spirit, knowing them "after the flesh" no more. The meetings started themselves, spontaneously, in testimony, praise, and worship. The testimonies were never hurried by a call for "popcorn." We had no prearranged program to be jammed through on time. Our time was the Lord's. We had real testimonies, from fresh heart-experience. Otherwise, the shorter the testimonies, the better. A dozen might be on their feet at one time, trembling under the mighty power of God. We did not have to get our cue from some leader; yet we were free from lawlessness. We were shut up to God in prayer in the meetings, our minds on Him.

All obeyed God, in meekness and humility. In honor we "preferred one another." The Lord was liable to burst through anyone. We prayed for this continually. Someone would finally get up, anointed for the message. All seemed to recognize this and gave way. It might be a child, a woman, or a man. It might be from the back seat or from the front. It made no difference. We rejoiced that God was working. No one wished to show himself. We thought only of obeying God. In fact, there was an atmosphere of God there that forbade anyone but a fool from attempting to put himself forward without the real anointing—and such did not last long. The meetings were controlled by the Spirit, from the throne. Those were truly wonderful days. I often said that I would rather live 6 months at that time than 50 years of ordinary life. But God is just the same today. Only we have changed.

Someone might be speaking. Suddenly the Spirit would fall upon the congregation. God Himself would give the altar call. Men would fall all over the house, like the slain in battle, or rush for the altar en masse to seek God. The scene often resembled a forest of fallen trees. Such a scene cannot be imitated. I never saw an altar call given in those early days. God Himself would call them. And the preacher knew when to quit. When He spoke, we all obeyed. It seemed a fearful thing to hinder or grieve the Spirit. The whole place was steeped in prayer. God was in His holy temple. It was for man to keep silent. The shekinah glory rested there. In fact, some claim to have seen the glory by night over the building. I do not doubt it. I have stopped more than once within two blocks of the place and prayed for strength before I dared go on. The presence of the Lord was so real.

Presumptuous men would sometimes come among us, especially preachers who would try to spread themselves in self-opinionation. But their effort was short lived. The breath would be taken from them. Their minds would wander, their brains reel. Things would turn black before their eyes. They could not go on. I never saw one get by with it in those days. They were up against God. No one cut them off; we simply prayed—the Holy Spirit did the rest. We wanted the Spirit to control. He wound them up in short order. They were carried out dead, spiritually speaking. They generally bit the dust in humility, going through the process we had all gone through. In other words, they died out, and came to see themselves in all their weakness. Then, in childlike humility and confession, they were taken up of God and transformed through the mighty baptism in the Spirit. The "old man" died with all his pride, arrogance, and good works.

In my own case, I came to abhor myself. I begged the Lord to drop a curtain so close behind me on my past that it would hit my heels. He told me to forget every good deed as though it had never occurred, as soon as it was accomplished, and go forward again as though I had never accomplished anything for Him, lest my good works become a snare to me.

STRONG MEN DIE HARD

We saw some wonderful things in those days. Even very good men came to abhor themselves in the clearer light of God. Often, it was hardest for preachers to die to self. They had so much to die to. So much reputation and good works. But when God got through with them, they gladly turned a new page and chapter. That was one reason they fought so hard. Death to self is not at all a pleasant experience. And strong men die hard.

Brother Ansel Post, a Baptist preacher, was sitting on a chair in the middle of the floor one evening in the meeting. Suddenly the Spirit fell upon him. He sprang from his chair, began to praise God in a loud voice in tongues, and ran all over the place, hugging all the brethren he could get hold of. He was filled with divine love. He later went to Egypt as a missionary. Let us have his own testimony, as it was printed in *Way of Faith*:

> "As suddenly as on the day of Pentecost, while I was sitting some twelve feet right in front of the speaker, the Holy Spirit fell upon me and filled me literally. I seemed to be lifted up, for I was in the air in an instant, shouting, 'Praise God,' and instantly I began to speak in another language. I could not have been more surprised if at the same moment someone had handed me a million dollars."

After Brother Smale had invited his people back and promised them liberty in the Spirit, I wrote the following in *Way of Faith*, June 1906:

"The New Testament Church received her 'Pentecost' yesterday. We had a wonderful time. Men and women were prostrate under the power all over the hall. A heavenly atmosphere pervaded the place. Such singing I have never heard before, the very melody of heaven. It seemed to come directly from the throne."

In the *Christian Harvester* I wrote on the same date:

"At the New Testament Church, a young lady of refinement was prostrate on the floor for hours, while at times the most heavenly singing would issue from her lips. It would swell as though reaching the throne and then die away in an almost unearthly melody. She sang, 'Praise God! Praise God!' All over the house men and women were weeping. A preacher was flat on his face on the floor, dying to himself. 'Pentecost' has fully come."

We had several all-night prayer sessions at the New Testament Church. But Pastor Smale never received the baptism of the Spirit with the speaking in tongues. He was in a trying position. It was all new to him, and the devil did his worst to bring the work into disrepute and destroy it. He sent wicked spirits among us to frighten the pastor and cause him to reject it.

But Brother Smale was God's Moses, to lead the people as far as the Jordan, though he himself never got across. Brother Seymour led them over. And yet, strange to say, Seymour did not speak in tongues himself until some time after Azusa had been opened. Many of the saints entered in before him. All who received this baptism of the Spirit spoke in tongues.

GOD CAN NEVER WAIT
FOR A PERFECT INSTRUMENT

Many stumbled in the beginning at Azusa because of the nature of the instruments first used. I wrote in *Way of Faith* as follows:

> "Someone has said, it is not the man who can build the biggest brush heap, but rather the one who can set his heap on fire that will light up the country. God can never wait for a perfect instrument to appear. If so, He would certainly be waiting yet. Luther himself declared he was but a rough woodsman, to fell the trees. Pioneers are of that nature. God has more polished servants to follow up and trim and shape the timber symmetrically. A charge of dynamite does not produce the finished product, but it does set loose the stones that later stand as monuments under the sculptor's skilled hand. Many high dignitaries of the Roman Church in Luther's time were convinced of the need for reformation, and they knew that he was on the right track. But they declared, in so many words, that they could never consent that this new doctrine should issue from 'such a corner.' That it should be a monk, a poor monk, who presumes to reform us all is what we cannot tolerate, they said. 'Can any good thing come out of Nazareth?'"

Fallen humanity is such a peculiar thing at its best, so shattered that it is very imperfect. "We have this treasure in earthen vessels." In the embryonic stage of all new experiences much allowance must be made for human frailty. There are always many coarse, impulsive, imperfectly balanced spirits among those first reached by a revival. Then, our understanding of the Spirit of God is so limited that we are always liable to make a mistake, failing to recognize all that may be really of God. We can understand fully only in the measure that we ourselves possess

63

the Spirit. Snap judgment is always dangerous. "Judge nothing before the time." The company used at Azusa Mission to break through were the "Gideon's band" that opened the way to victory for those to follow.

I wrote further in *Way of Faith*, August 1, 1906:

"'Pentecost' has come to Los Angeles, the American Jerusalem. Every sect, creed, and doctrine under heaven is found in Los Angeles, as well as every nation represented. Many times I have been tempted to wonder if my strength would hold out to see it. The burden of prayer has been very great. But since the spring of 1905, when I first received this vision and burden, I have never doubted the final outcome of it. Men are now troubled in soul everywhere, and the revival with its unusual phenomena is the topic of the day. There is terrible opposition manifested also. The newspapers here are very venomous and most unfair and untrue in their statements. The pseudo systems of religion are fighting hard also. But, 'the hail shall sweep away the refuge of lies.' Their 'hiding places' are being uncovered. A cleansing stream is flowing through the city. The Word of God prevails.

"Persecution is strong. Already the police have been asked to break up the meetings. The work has been hindered much also by fanatical spirits, of which the city has far too many. It is God and the devil, a battle royal. We can do little but look on and pray. The Holy Spirit Himself is taking the lead, setting aside all human leadership largely. And woe to the man who gets in His way, selfishly seeking to dictate or control. The Spirit will not tolerate interference of this kind. The human instruments are largely lost sight of. Our hearts and minds are directed to the Lord. The meetings are crowded out. There is great excitement among the unspiritual and unsaved.

"Every false religion under heaven is found represented here. Next to old Jerusalem there is nothing like it in the world. It is on the opposite side, nearly halfway around the world, with natural conditions very similar also. All nations are represented as at Jerusalem. Thousands are here from all over the Union and from many parts of the world, sent of God for 'Pentecost.' These will scatter the fire to the ends of the earth. Missionary zeal is at white heat. The 'gifts' of the Spirit are being given, the Church's armor restored. Surely we are in the days of restoration, the 'last days,' wonderful and glorious days. But awful days for those who refuse God's call. They are days of privilege, responsibility, and peril.

"Demons are being cast out, the sick healed, many blessedly saved, restored, and baptized with the Holy Spirit and power. Heroes are being developed, the weak made strong in the Lord. Men's hearts are being searched as with a light candle. It is a tremendous sifting time, not only of actions, but of inner secret motives. Nothing can escape the all-searching eye of God. Jesus is being lifted up, His blood magnified, and the Holy Spirit honored once more. There is much 'slaying power' manifest—and this is the chief cause of resistance on the part of those who refuse to obey. It is real business. God is with us

Leaders of the Azusa Street Mission: Seated (L-R) sister Evans, Hiram Smith, William Seymour, Clara Lum. Standing (L-R) Unidentified woman, Brother Evans, Jenny Moore (Seymour's future wife), Glenn Cook, Florence Crawford, unidentified man, Sister Prince. Florence Crawford's daughter is sitting on Hiram Smith's lap. (Used by permission, Flower Pentecostal Heritage Center)

in great earnestness; we dare not trifle. Strong men lie for hours under the mighty power of God, cut down like grass. The revival will be a world-wide one, without doubt."

IT IS REAL BUSINESS

Some time later the pastor of the Trinity Church, M.E. South, of Los Angeles, uttered the following words: "Here on the Pacific Coast, where the sons of men meet from every quarter of the globe, prophetic souls believe the greatest moral and spiritual battles are to be fought—the Armageddon of the world."

Evan Roberts's "Message to the Churches" was voiced by him in the following lines of an old poem:

While the fire of God is falling,

While the voice of God is calling,

Brothers, get the flame.

While the torch of God is burning,

Men's weak efforts overturning,

Christians, get the flame.

While the Holy Ghost is pleading,

Human methods superseding,

He himself the flame.

While the power hard hearts are bending,

Yield thy own, to Him surrendering,

All to get the flame.

For the world at last is waking,
And beneath His spell is breaking,
Into living flame.
And our glorious Lord is seeking,
Human hearts, to rouse the sleeping,
Fired with heavenly flame.

If in utter self-surrender,
You would work with Christ, remember,
You must get the flame.
For the sake of bruised and dying,
And the lost in darkness lying,
We must get the flame.

For the sake of Christ in glory,
And the spreading of the story,
We must get the flame.
Oh, my soul, for thy refining,
And thy clearer, brighter shining,
Do not miss the flame.

On the Holy Ghost relying,
Simply trusting and not trying,
You will get the flame.

Brothers, let us cease our dreaming,

And while God's flood-tide is streaming,

We will have the flame.

THE OPPORTUNITY OF A LIFETIME

I wrote a little tract in June 1906, of which the following is an extract:

"Opportunity once passed is lost forever. There is a time when the tide is sweeping by our door. We may then plunge in and be carried to glorious blessing, success, and victory. To stand shivering on the bank, timid or paralyzed with stupor at such a time, is to miss all, and most miserably fail, both for time and for eternity. Oh, our responsibility! The mighty tide of God's grace and favor is even now sweeping by us in its prayer-directed course. 'There is a river (of salvation), the streams whereof make glad the city of God (Psalm 46:4). It is time to 'get together' and plunge in, individually and collectively. We are baptized 'by one Spirit, into one body' (1 Corinthians 12:13). Let us lay aside all carnal contentions and divisions that separate us from each other and from God. If we are of His body, we are 'one body.' The opportunity of a lifetime—of centuries—is at our door, to be eternally gained or lost. There is no time to hesitate. Act quickly, lest another take thy crown. Oh, Church of Christ, awake! Be baptized with power. Then fly to rescue others, and to meet your Lord."

A.J. Gordon, in his book, *The Ministry of Healing* (1882), said: "If anti-Christ is about to make his mightiest and most malignant demonstration, ought not the Church to confront him with mighty displays of the Spirit's saving [power]?"

A.B. Simpson said:

"We are to witness, before the Lord's return, a real missionary 'tongues' like those of Pentecost, through which the heathen world shall hear in their own language 'the wonderful works of God,' and this perhaps on a scale whose vastness we have scarcely dreamed. Thousands of missionaries will go forth in one last mighty crusade from a united body of believers and at home to bear swift witness of the crucified and coming Lord to all nations."

Arthur T. Pierson has said:

"The most alarming peril of today is naturalism—the denial of all direct divine agency and control. Science is uniting with unbelief, wickedness and worldliness, skepticism and materialism, to rule a personal God out of the universe. This drift toward materialism and naturalism demands the supernatural as its only corrective. In Enoch's time human sin was fast making atheists, and God 'took him,' spirit, soul, and body, that men might be startled with the proof of a Divine Being and an invisible world. In Elijah's day, general apostasy was rebuked by the descent of horses and chariots of fire. And if ever men needed to be confronted with fruits of power above nature—a living God back of all the forces and machinery He controls, who does answer prayer, guide by His providences, and convert by His grace—it is now."

Oh, our weakness! Oh, our unbelief! May the Lord help us get back to Pentecostal experiences. *"When the Son of Man cometh, shall He find faith on the earth?"* (Luke 18:8 KJV).

Hear Spurgeon's dying appeal:

"The presence of God in the Church will put an end to infidelity. Men will not doubt His Word when they feel His Spirit. For a thousand reasons, we need that Jehovah should come into the camp, as aforetimes He visited and delivered His people from bondage in Egypt."

CHAPTER THREE

DEEPER YET

August 8, 1906, I rented a church building at the corner of Eighth and Maple Streets for a Pentecostal mission. I was led to this church in February while it was still occupied by the "Pillar of Fire" people. I had been impressed to pray for a building for services after I found the New Testament Church not going ahead, but I had not even known of the existence of this building. One day, unexpectedly, I was passing by and saw it for the first time. I noticed it had been a German church and was out of regular use. Through curiosity I opened the door, which was unlocked, and entered. I found out that the "Pillar of Fire" had it. Kneeling at the altar for a season of prayer, the Lord spoke to me, and I received a wonderful witness of the Spirit. In a moment I was walking the aisles claiming it for "Pentecost." Over the door was a large motto painted, "Gott ist die Liebe" (God is Love). This was two months before the Azusa work began.

I looked no further for a building, knowing that God had spoken. One night, six months later, in August, I was passing that way and saw a sign, "For Rent," on the church. It had just been vacated. The Lord spoke to me: "There is your church."

"The Pillar of Fire" had gone up in smoke, not being able to raise the rent. They had been the most bitter opposers of the Azusa work. The Lord had vacated the building for us. The next day, I was led to tell our landlord, Brother Fred Shepard, of the situation. I did not ask him to help me, but the Lord had sent me to him. He asked how much the rent was, went into another room, and returned quickly with a check for 50 dollars. This was the first month's rent, and I secured the place at once.

THE CURSE OF THE SECTARIAN SPIRIT

The truth must be told. Azusa began to fail the Lord early in her history. God showed me one day that they were going to organize, though not a word had been said in my hearing about it. The Spirit revealed it to me. He had me warn them against making a "party" spirit of the Pentecostal work. The "baptized" saints were to remain "one Body," even as they had been called, and to be free as His Spirit was free, not "entangled again in a yoke of (ecclesiastical) bondage." The New Testament Church saints had already arrested their further progress in this way. God wanted a revival company, a channel through whom He could evangelize the world, blessing all people and believers. He could naturally not accomplish this with a sectarian party. That spirit has been the curse and death of every revival body sooner or later. History repeats itself in this matter.

Sure enough, the very next day after I had spoken this warning in the meeting, I found a sign outside the building reading "Apostolic Faith Mission." The Lord said: "That is what I told you." They had done it. Surely a "party spirit" cannot be "Pentecostal." There can be no divisions in a true Pentecost. To formulate a separate body is but to advertise our failure as a people of God. It proves to the world that we cannot get along together, rather than causing them to believe in our salvation. *That they all may be one...that the world may believe"* (John 17:21 KJV).

From that time the trouble and division began. It was no longer a free Spirit for all as it had been. The work had become one more rival party and body, along with the other churches and sects of the city. No wonder the opposition steadily increased from the churches. We had been called to bless and serve the whole Body of Christ everywhere. Christ is one, and His Body can be but "one." To divide it is but to destroy it, just as with the natural body. In "*one Spirit are we all baptized* [organized] *into one body*" (1 Cor. 12:13). The Church is an organism, not a human organization.

They later tried to pull the work on the whole coast into this organization, but miserably failed. The work had spread as far as Portland and Seattle. God's people must be free from hierarchism. They are "blood-bought," and not their own. An earlier work in Texas later tried to gather in the Pentecostal missions on the Pacific Coast and Los Angeles, but they also failed. Why should they claim authority over us? The revival in California was unique and separate as to origin. It came from Heaven, even Brother Seymour not receiving the baptism until many others had entered in here. He did not arrive in Los Angeles until the eleventh hour. The great battle from the beginning, both in Los Angeles and elsewhere, has been the conflict between the flesh and the Spirit, between Ishmael and Isaac.

GOD RAN THE MEETINGS

At Eighth and Maple Streets, the Spirit was mightily manifest from the very first meeting. He was given complete control. The atmosphere was heavy with God's presence. One had to get right in order to remain at Eighth and Maple. "Fearfulness" truly "surprised the hypocrites." For some days we could do little but lie before the Lord in prayer.

The atmosphere was almost too sacred and holy to attempt to minister. Like the priests in the Tabernacle of old, we could not minister because the glory was so great. In spite of this, however, we had terrible battles with fleshly professors and deceivers, and the Spirit was much grieved by contentious spirits. But God gave the victory. The atmosphere at Eighth and Maple was for a time even deeper than at Azusa. God came so wonderfully near us that the very atmosphere of Heaven seemed to surround us. Such a divine "weight of glory" was upon us that we could only lie on our faces. For a long time we could hardly even remain seated. All would be on their faces on the floor, sometimes during the whole service. I was seldom able to keep from lying full length on the floor on my face. There was a little rise of about a foot, for a platform, when we moved into the church. On this I generally lay, while God ran the meetings. They were *His* meetings. Every night the power of God was powerfully with us. It was glorious! The Lord seemed almost visible; He was so real.

We had the greatest trouble with strange preachers who wanted to preach. Of all people, they seemed to have the least sense and did not know enough to keep still before Him. They liked to hear themselves. But many a preacher died to self in these meetings. The city was full of them, just as today. They rattled like a last year's bean pod. We had a regular "dry bone" yard.

We always recognized Azusa as having been the mother mission, and there was never any friction or jealousy between us. We visited back and forth. Brother Seymour often met with us. I wrote in the *Christian Harvester* at that time, as follows:

"The meetings at Eighth and Maple are marvelous. We had the greatest time yesterday that I have ever seen. All day long the power of God swept the place. The church was crowded. Mighty conviction seized the people. The Spirit ran the meeting from start to finish. There was no program, and hardly a chance for even necessary announcements. No attempt was made to preach. A few messages were given by the Spirit. Everybody was free to obey God. The altar was full of seeking souls all day. A Free Methodist preacher's wife came through to a mighty baptism, speaking something like Chinese. All who received the baptism of the Spirit spoke in tongues. There were at least six Holiness preachers, some of them gray-headed, honored, and trusted for fruitful service for years, seeking the baptism most earnestly. They simply threw up their hands in the face of this revelation from God and stopped to tarry for their 'Pentecost.' The president of the Holiness Church of Southern California was one of the first at the altar, seeking earnestly."

Again I wrote in the same paper:

"The Spirit allows little human interference in the meetings, generally passing mistakes by unnoticed, or moving them out of the way Himself. Things that ordinarily we would feel must be corrected are often passed over, and a worse calamity averted thereby. To draw attention to them brings the spirit of fear on the saints, and they stop seeking. The Spirit is hindered from working. He moves them out of the way. There are greater issues at stake at present. We try to keep them from magnifying Satan's power. We are preaching a big Christ instead. And God is using babes.

"The enemy is moving hell to break up our fellowship through doctrinal differences, but we must preserve the unity of the Spirit by all means. Some things can be adjusted later. They are much less important. God will never give this work into the hands of men. If it ever gets under man's control, it is done. Many would join themselves to us if they did not need to 'lose their heads,' and get small."

IT SEEMED A PERFECT LANGUAGE

On the afternoon of August 16, at Eighth and Maple, the Spirit manifested Himself through me in tongues. There were seven of us present at the time. It was a weekday. After a time of testimony and praise, with everything quiet, I was softly walking the floor, praising God in my spirit. All at once I seemed to hear in my soul (not with my natural ears), a rich voice speaking in a language I did not know. I have later heard something similar to it in India. It seemed to envelop and fully satisfy the pent-up praises in my being.

In a few moments I found myself, seemingly without volition on my part, enunciating the same sounds with my own vocal organs. It was an exact continuation of the same expression that I had heard in my soul a few moments before. It seemed a perfect language. I was almost like an outside listener. I was fully yielded to God and simply carried by His will, as on a divine stream. I could have hindered the expression but would not have done so for worlds. A heaven of conscious bliss accompanied it. It must be experienced to be appreciated. There was no effort made to speak on my part and not the least possible struggle. The experience was most sacred, the Holy Spirit playing on my vocal chords, as on an Aeolian harp. The whole utterance was a complete surprise to me. I had never really been solicitous to speak in tongues. Because I could not understand it with my natural mind, I had rather feared it.

I had no desire at the time to even know what I was saying. It seemed a spiritual expression purely, outside the realm of the natural mind or understanding. I was truly "sealed in the forehead," ceasing from the works of my own natural mind fully. I wrote my experience for publication later in the following words:

"The Spirit had gradually prepared me for this culmination in my experience, both in prayer for myself, and others. I had thus drawn nigh to God, my spirit greatly subdued. A place of utter abandonment of will had been reached, in absolute consciousness of helplessness, purified from natural self-activity. This process had been cumulative. The presence of the Spirit within had been as sensitive to me as the water in the glass indicator of a steam boiler. My mind, the last fortress of man to yield, was taken possession of by the Spirit. The waters that had been gradually accumulating went over my head. I was possessed of Him fully. The utterance in tongues was without human mixture, 'as the Spirit gave utterance.'"

Oh, the thrill of being fully yielded to Him! My mind had always been very active. Its natural workings had caused me most of my trouble in Christian experience: "Casting down reasonings" (see 2 Cor. 10:5). Nothing hinders faith and the operation of the Spirit so much as the self-assertiveness of the human soul, the wisdom, strength, and self-sufficiency of the human mind. This must all be crucified, and here is where the fight comes in. We must become utterly undone, insufficient, and helpless in our own consciousness, thoroughly humbled, before we can receive full possession of the Holy Spirit. We want the Holy Spirit, but the fact is that *He* is wanting possession of us.

In my case, in the experience of speaking in tongues, I reached the climax in abandonment. This opened the channel for a new ministry of the Spirit in service. From that time, the Spirit began to flow through me in a new way. Messages would come, with anointing, in a way I had never known before. The spontaneous inspiration and illumination was truly wonderful, attended with convincing power. The full Pentecostal baptism spells complete abandonment, or possession by the Holy Spirit, of the whole man with a spirit of instant obedience. I had known much of the power of God for service for many years before this, but I now realized a sensitivity to the Spirit, a yieldedness, that made it possible for God to possess and work in new ways and channels, with far more powerful, direct results.

In the experience, I also received a new revelation of His sovereignty, both in purpose and actions, such as I had never known before. I found I had often charged God with seeming lack of interest or tardiness of action, when I should have yielded to Him, in faith, that He might be able to work through me His sovereign will. I went into the dust of humility at this revelation of my own stupidity and His sovereign care and desire. I saw that the little bit of desire I possessed for His service was only the little bit that He had been able to get to me of His great desire and interest and purpose. His Word declares it. All there was of good in me, in thought or action, had come from Him.

Like Hudson Taylor, I now felt that He was asking me simply to go with Him to help in that which He alone had purposed and desired. I felt very small in the light of this revelation and my past misunderstanding. He had existed, and had been working out His eternal purpose, long before I had ever been thought of—and will be long after I am gone.

There was no strain or contortions. No struggle in an *effort* to get the baptism. With me it was simply a matter of yielding. In fact, it was the opposite of struggle. There was no swelling of the throat, no "operation" to be performed on my vocal organs. I had not the slightest difficulty in speaking in tongues. And yet I can understand how some may have such difficulties. They are not fully yielded to God. With me the battle had been long drawn out. I had already worn myself out and fully yielded.

God deals with no two individuals alike. I was not really seeking the baptism when I got it. And in fact, I never actually sought it as a definite experience. I wanted to be yielded fully to God, but beyond that I had no real definite expectation or desire. I wanted more of *Him*, that was all.

NATURAL BIRTHS ARE BETTER

There was no shouting crowd around me to confuse or excite me. No one was suggesting tongues to me at the time, either by argument or imitation. Thank God, He is able to do His work without such help, and often far better without it. I do not believe in dragging the child forth, spiritually speaking, with instruments. I do believe in sane, earnest prayer-help in the Spirit. Too many souls are dragged from the womb of conviction by force and have to be incubated ever after. As with nature, so in grace. It is best to dispense as far as possible with the doctors and old midwives. The child is almost killed at times through their unnatural violence. A pack of jackals over their prey could hardly act more fiercely than we have witnessed in some cases. In natural childbirth, it is generally best to let the mother alone as far as possible. We should teach and stand by to encourage, but not force the deliverance. Natural births are better.

I had been shut up largely to a ministry of intercession and prophecy before I reached this condition of utter abandonment to the Spirit. I was now to go forth again in the service. My day of "Pentecost" was fully come. The door of my service sprang open at the touch of the hand of a sovereign God. The Spirit began to operate within me in a new and mightier way. It was a distinct, fresh climax and development, an epochal experience for me.

I now knew that I had tasted that for which we had been shut up as a company. In fact, this has proven an epoch in the history of the Church just as distinct and definite as the Spirit's action in the time of Luther and Wesley, and with far greater portend. And it is not yet all history. We are too close to it yet to understand or appreciate it fully. But we have made another step back on the way to the restoration of the Church as in the beginning. We are completing the circle. Jesus will return for a perfect Church, "without spot or wrinkle." He is coming for "one Body," not a dozen. He is the Head, and as such He is no monstrosity, with a hundred bodies. *"That they all may be one...that the world may believe"* (John 17:21 **KJV**). This, *after all, is the greatest "sign" to the world. "Though we speak with the tongues of men and of angels, and have not love..."* (1 Cor. 13).

I felt after the experience of speaking in tongues that languages would come easy to me. And so it has proven. Also, I have learned to sing in the Spirit, although I never was a singer and do not know music.

I never sought tongues. My natural mind resisted the idea. This phenomenon necessarily violates human reason. It means abandonment of this faculty for the time. And this is "foolishness" and a stone of stumbling to the natural mind or reason. It is supernatural. We need not expect anyone who has not reached this depth of abandonment in their human spirit, this death to their own reason, to either accept or understand it. The natural reason must be yielded in the matter. There is a gulf to cross between reason and revelation, and it is this principle in experience which leads to the Pentecostal baptism. It is the underlying principle of this baptism. This is why the simple people usually get in first, though perhaps not always so well-balanced or capable otherwise. They are like the little boys going swimming—to use a homely illustration. They get in first because they have the least clothes to divest themselves of. We must all come "naked" into this experience.

The early Church lived in this as its normal atmosphere. Hence its abandonment to the working of the Spirit, its supernatural gifts, and its power. Our "wiseacres" cannot reach this. Oh, to become a fool, to know nothing in ourselves that we might receive the mind of Christ.

NOTHING LEFT BUT GOD

I do not mean to say we must talk in tongues continually. The baptism is not all tongues. We can live in this place of illumination and abandonment and still speak in our own language. The Bible was not written in tongues. We may surely live in the Spirit *at all times*. Oh, the depth of abandonment—all self gone—conscious of knowing nothing, except as the Spirit will teach and impart to us. This is the true place of power in the ministry of service. There is nothing left but God, the pure Spirit. Every hope or sense of capability in the natural is gone.

We live by His breath, as it were. The "wind" on the day of Pentecost was the breath of God (see Acts 2:2). But what more can we say? It must be experienced to be understood. It cannot be explained. We have certainly had a measure of the Spirit before without this. To this fact all history testifies, but we cannot have the "Pentecostal" baptism without it. The apostles received it suddenly and in full. Only simple faith and abandonment can receive, for human reason can find all kinds of flaws and apparent foolishness in it.

I spoke in tongues possibly for about 15 minutes on this first occasion. Then the immediate inspiration passed away, for the time. I have spoken at times since also; but I never try to reproduce it. It would be foolishness and sacrilege to try to imitate it. The experience left behind it the consciousness of a state of utter abandonment to the Lord, a place of perfect rest from my own works and activity of mind. It left with me a consciousness of utter God-control, and of His presence naturally in corresponding measure. It was a most sacred experience.

Many have trifled foolishly with this principle and possession. They have failed to continue *in the Spirit* and have caused others to stumble. This has brought about great harm. But the experience still remains as a fact, both in history and in present-day realization. The greater part of most Christians' knowledge of God is and has always been, since the loss of the Spirit by the early Church, an intellectual knowledge. Their knowledge of the Word and principles of God is an intellectual one, through natural reasoning and understanding largely. They have little revelation, illumination, or inspiration directly from the Spirit of God.

The famous commentators, Conybeare and Howson, write:

"This gift [speaking in tongues] was the result of a sudden influx of the supernatural to the believer. Under its influence, the exercise of the understanding was suspended while the spirit was wrapped in a state of sheer joy by the immediate communication of the Spirit of God. In this joyful state, the believer was constrained by irresistible power to pour forth his feelings of thanksgiving and rapture in words not his own. He was usually even ignorant of their meaning."

James Stalker, in his book, *Life of Paul* (page 102), has the following to say:

"It [speaking in tongues] seems to have been a kind of utterance in which the speaker poured out an impassioned rhapsody, by which his religious faith received both expression and exaltation. Some were not able to tell others the meaning of what they were saying, while others had this additional power; and there were those who, though not speaking in tongues themselves, were able to interpret what the inspired speakers were saying. In all cases, there seems to have been a kind of immediate inspiration, so that what they did was not the effect of calculation or preparation, but of a strong present impulse.

"These phenomena are so remarkable that, if narrated in a history, they would put a severe strain on Christian faith. They show with what mighty force, at its first entrance into the world, Christianity took possession of the spirits it touched."

He also added, "The very gifts of the Spirit were perverted into instruments of sin; for those possessed of the more showy gifts, such as miracles and tongues, were too fond of displaying them, and turned them into grounds of boasting." There is always danger attached to privileges. Children frequently cut themselves with sharp knives, when they are given the freedom to use them. However, we are certainly in more danger from remaining in stagnation, where we are, than in going ahead trustingly for God.

EMPTY-HANDED

Describing some of my personal experiences, previous to experiencing this baptism, I wrote the following in *Christian Harvester*:

"My own heart was searched until I cried out under the added light, 'God deliver me from my religious self-consciousness!' Seldom have I suffered in humility, shame and reproach, as at this vision of my very best in the sight of God. My religious comeliness was indeed turned into corruption. I felt that I could not bear to hear, or even to think of it again. I felt I would be glad to forget even my own name and identity. So with extreme satisfaction, I destroyed records of my past achievements for God, upon which my eyes had loved to linger. I now abhorred them, as a temptation from the devil to self-exaltation. Letters of commendation for religious services rendered, literary works of seeming excellence to me, and sermons which to me had seemed wonderful in knowledge and construction, now actually nauseated me, because of the element of self-pride detected in them. I found I had come to rest on these for expected divine favor and reward. '*Nothing but the blood of Jesus*' had at least partially been lost sight of. I was depending also on these other things to recommend me to God. In this lay great danger; so I destroyed these treasured documents, false evidences, as I would a viper, lest they tempt me from the sufficiency of His merits alone. It meant a deep heart searching.

"Past services now became a complete blank to me, and with the greatest relief on my part. I began again for God, as though I had never accomplished anything. I felt that I stood before Him empty-handed. The fire of testing seemed to sweep away all of my religious doings. God did not want me to rest in these. For the future I was to forget all that I might ever do for God as quickly as it was accomplished, so that it might not prove a further snare to me, and go on as though I had never done a thing for God. This was my safety."

Without a doubt, even the least self-satisfaction in one's religious service is a great hindrance to the blessing and favor of God. It must be shunned as we would a serpent.

We continued to have wonderful meetings at Eighth and Maple. The Lord showed me that He wanted this work to go deeper yet than anything we had attained at that time. He was not satisfied fully with the Azusa work, deep as it had gone. There was still too much of the self-life, the religious self, among us. This naturally meant war, hard and bitter, from the enemy. Ours was to be a sort of "clearing station," where fleshly exercises, false manifestations, and the religious self in general should be dealt with. We were after real experience, permanent and established, with God-like character and no relapses.

I was greatly tested financially again. One day I had to walk 25 blocks to town, not having even carfare. A brother almost as poor as myself gave me a nickel to ride home. At the same time we were having glorious meetings. Many were prostrated under the power.

JUDGMENT BEGINS
AT THE HOUSE OF GOD

The devil sent two strong characters one night to sidetrack the work. A spiritualist woman put herself at the head, like a drum major, to lead the singing. I prayed her out of the church. The other was a fanatical preacher with a voice that almost rattled the windows. I had to rebuke him openly. He had taken over the whole meeting. Conceit fairly stuck out of him. The Spirit was terribly grieved; God could not work. I had suffered too much for the work to turn things over to the devil so easily. Besides, I was responsible for souls, and for the rent.

We had a fierce battle with such spirits. They would have ruined everything. The devil has no conscience, and the "flesh" has no sense. The very first time I opened the church for meetings, I found one of the worst fanatics and religious crooks in town sitting on the steps waiting for me. He was a preacher and wanted to run things. I chased him from the place like Nehemiah did the son of Joiada (see Neh. 13:28). I had never dreamed there was so much of the devil in so many people. The town seemed full of them. He tempted the saints to fight and hindered the Spirit. These crooks and cranks were the first at the meeting. We had a great clearing-up time. There was much professional, religious quackery. Judgment had to "begin at the house of God."

Martin Luther was greatly troubled with willful, religious fanatics in his day. From the Wartburg, where he was then concealed, he wrote to Melancthon at Wittenberg, giving a test-stone for these fanatics: "Ask these prophets whether they have felt those spiritual torments, those creations of God—that death and hell—which accompany a real separation." When he returned to Wittenberg and they tried their sorcery on him, he met them with these crude words: "I slap your spirit on the snout!" They acted like devils at that challenge. But it broke their spell.

We were obliged to deal firmly with the extreme cases, but in the main, the Spirit passed over and moved out of the way irregularities without further advertising them. Many have declared that we cannot throw our meetings open today. But if that is true, then we must shut God out also. What we need is more of God controlling the meetings. He must be left free to come forth at all costs. The saints themselves are too largely in confusion and rebellion. Through prayer and self-abasement, God will undertake for the meetings.

This was the secret in the beginning. We held together in prayer, love, and unity, and no power could break this. But self must be burned out. Meetings must be controlled by way of the throne. A spiritual atmosphere must be created, through humility and prayer, that satan cannot live in. And this we realized in the beginning. It was the very opposite of religious zeal and carnal, religious ambition. We knew nothing about present day "pep" and "make it snappy" methods. That whole system is an illegitimate product, as far as "Pentecost" is concerned. It takes time to be holy. The world rushes on. It gets us nowhere with God.

FIRST LOVE LOST

One reason for the depth of the work at Azusa was the fact that the workers were not novices. They were largely called and prepared for years from the Holiness ranks and from the mission field, etc. They had been burnt out, tried, and proven. They were largely seasoned veterans. They had walked with God and learned deeply of His Spirit. These were pioneers, "shock troops," the Gideon's 300, to spread the fire around the world, just as the disciples had been prepared by Jesus. We have now taken on a "mixed multitude," and the seeds of apostasy have had time to work. "First love" has been largely lost. The dog had "returned to his vomit" in many cases—i.e., to

Babylonian doctrines and practices. An enfeebled mother can hardly be expected to bring forth healthy children.

The Spirit dealt so deeply, and the people were so hungry in the beginning, that the carnal, human spirit injected into the meetings was discerned easily. It was as though a stranger had broken into a private, select company. The presence was painfully noticeable. Men were after God. He was in His holy temple; earth (the human) must keep silence before Him. It only caused grief and pain. Our tarrying and prayer rooms today are but a shadow of the former ones, too often a place to blow off steam in human enthusiasm, or become mentally intoxicated, supposedly from the Holy Spirit. This should not be. It is simply fanaticism.

In the early days, the "tarrying room" was the first thought and provision for a Pentecostal Mission. It was held sacred, a kind of "holy ground." There was mutual consideration also. There men sought to become quiet from the activities of their own too active mind and spirit, to escape from the world for the time, and get alone with God. There was no noisy, wild spirit there. That, at least, could be done elsewhere. The claims and confusion of an exacting world were shut out. It was a sort of "city of refuge" from this sort of thing, a "haven of rest," where God could be heard and talk to their souls. Men would spend hours in silence there, searching their own hearts in privacy, and securing the mind of the Lord for future action. This sort of thing seems well nigh impossible today amid present surroundings. We die out to self by coming into His presence. And this requires great quietness of spirit. We need a "holy of holies." What Jew of old would have dared to act in God's temple as we do today in the missions? It would have meant death to him. We are full of foolishness and fanatical self-assertion. Even the formal Romanists have more reverence on the whole than we.

Sunday, August 26, Pastor Pendleton and about 40 of his members came into Eighth and Maple to worship with us. They had received the baptism and spoken in tongues in their church.

The denomination had thrown them out of their own building for this "unpardonable" crime. When I heard the church was going to try him for heresy, I invited them to come in with us if they were thrown out. Two days later they were expelled and accepted my invitation. Brother Pendleton declared after this experience that he would never build another doctrinal roof over his head. He was determined to go on for God.

Multitudes are shut up in ecclesiastical systems, within sectarian boundaries, while God's great, free pasture lies out before them, only limited by the encircling Word of God. "*There shall be one flock, and one shepherd*" (John 10:16). *Traditional theology, partial truth and revelation, soon become law.* The conscience is utterly bound, like Chinese footbinding, shut up against further progress.

Sunday, September 9, was a wonderful day. Several were stretched out under the power for hours. The altar was full all day, with scarcely any cessation to the services. Several received the baptism. In those days we preached but little. The people were taken up with God. Brother Pendleton and I could generally be found lying full length on the low platform on our faces, in prayer, during the services. It was almost impossible to stay off our faces in those days. The presence of the Lord was so real. And this condition lasted for a long time. We had but little to do with guiding the meetings. Everyone was looking to God alone. We felt almost like apologizing when we had to claim attention from the people for announcements. It was a continuous sweep of victory—God had their attention. At times the audience would be convulsed with penitence. God dealt deeply with sin in those days. It could not remain in the camp.

The New Testament Church had a split about this time. I was glad I had nothing to do with that. Brother Smale had forced the Spirit-baptized saints to the wall, having finally rejected their testimony. A brother, Elmer Fisher, then started another mission at 327 South Spring Street, known as the

Upper Room Mission. Most of the white saints from Azusa went with him, with the baptized ones from the New Testament Church. This later became for a time the strongest mission in town. Both Azusa and the New Testament Church had by this time largely failed God. I soon after turned Eighth and Maple over to Brother Pendleton, as I was too worn to continue longer in constant service in the meetings. I had been for a long time under constant strain in prayer and meetings and needed a rest and change.

JESUS, THE CENTRAL THEME

In the beginning of the Pentecostal work, I became very much exercised in the Spirit that Jesus should not be slighted, "lost in the temple," by the exaltation of the Holy Spirit and of the gifts of the Spirit. There seemed to be a great danger of losing sight of the fact that Jesus was "all, and in all." I endeavored to keep Him as the central theme and figure before the people. Jesus will always be the center of our preaching. All comes through and in Him. The Holy Spirit is given to "show the things of Christ." The work of Calvary, the atonement, must be the center of our consideration. The Holy Spirit never draws our attention from Christ to Himself, but rather reveals Christ in a fuller way. We are in the same danger today.

There is nothing deeper nor higher than to know Christ. Everything is given by God *to that end.* The "one Spirit" is given to that end. Christ is our salvation and our all. That we might know *"the breadth, and length, and depth, and height...[of] the love of Christ"* (Eph. 3:18-19 KJV), having a *"spirit of wisdom and revelation in the knowledge of Him"* (Eph. 1:17 KJV). It was *"to know Him* [Christ]," for which Paul strove.

I was led to suddenly present Jesus one night to the congregation at Eighth and Maple. They had been forgetting Him in their exaltation of the Holy Spirit and the gifts. Now I introduced Christ for their consideration. They were taken completely by surprise and convicted in a moment. God made me do it. Then they saw their mistake and danger. I was preaching Christ one night at this time, setting Him before them in His proper place, when the Spirit so witnessed of His pleasure that I was overpowered by His presence, falling helplessly to the floor under a mighty revelation of Jesus to my soul. I fell like John on the Isle of Patmos, at His feet.

I wrote a tract at this time, of which the following is an extract:

> "We may not even hold a doctrine, or seek an experi-
> ence, except in Christ. Many are willing to seek power
> from every battery they can lay their hands on in order
> to perform miracles, draw the attention and adoration
> of the people to themselves, thus robbing Christ of His
> glory and making a fair showing in the flesh. *The great-*
> *est religious need of our day would seem to be that of true*
> *followers of the meek and lowly Jesus.* Religious enthusi-
> asm easily goes to seed. The human spirit so predomi-
> nates the show-off, religious spirit. But we must stick to
> our text—Christ. He alone can save. The attention of
> the people must be first of all, and always held to Him.
> A true 'Pentecost' will produce a mighty conviction for
> sin, a turning to God. False manifestations produce
> only excitement and wonder. Sin and self-life will not
> materially suffer from these. We must get what our
> conviction calls for. Believe in your own heart's hunger
> and go ahead with God. Don't allow the devil to rob
> you of a real 'Pentecost.' Any work that exalts the Holy
> Spirit or the gifts above Jesus will finally end up in
> fanaticism. Whatever causes us to exalt and love Jesus
> is well and safe. The reverse will ruin all. The Holy
> Spirit is a great light, but will always be focused on
> Jesus for His revealing."

A.S. Worrell, translator of the New Testament, was an earnest friend of Pentecost and a seeker after the baptism. He wrote the following in the *Way of Faith*:

> "The blood of Jesus is exalted in these meetings as I have rarely known elsewhere. There is a mighty power manifest in witnessing for Jesus, with a wonderful love for souls. There is also a bestowal of 'gifts of the Spirit.' The places of meeting are at Azusa Street, at the New Testament Church, where Joseph Smale is pastor (some of his people were among the first to speak with tongues, but most have withdrawn because they felt restraint in his church), and at Eighth and Maple Streets, where Pastors Bartleman and Pendleton are the principal leaders."

A LAYMEN'S REVIVAL

In September 1906, the following letters appeared in the *Way of Faith*, from the pen of Dr. W.C. Dumble of Toronto, Canada, who was visiting Los Angeles at this time:

> "Possibly some of your readers may be interested in the impressions of a stranger in Los Angeles. A similar gracious work of the Spirit to that in Wales is in progress here. But while that is mostly in the churches, this is outside. The churches will not have it, or up to the present have stood aloof in a critical and condemnatory spirit. Like the work in Wales, this is a laymen's revival, conducted by the Holy Spirit and carried on in halls and old tumble-down buildings, whatever can be gotten for the work.

> "This is a remarkable movement, that may be said to be peculiar by the appearance of the gift of tongues. There are three different missions where one may hear these strange tongues. I had the rare joy of spending last

evening at Pastor Bartleman's meeting, or more correctly, at a meeting where he and Pastor Pendleton are the nominal leaders, but *where the Holy Spirit is actually in control.* Jesus is proclaimed the Head, and the Holy Spirit His executive. Hence, there is no preaching, no choir, no organ, no collection, except what is voluntarily placed on the table or put in the box on the wall.

"God was mightily present last night. Someone begins to sing: three or four hymns may be sung, interspersed with hallelujahs and amens. Then some overburdened soul rises and shouts, 'Glory to Jesus!' and amid sobs and tears tells of a great struggle and a great deliverance. Then three or four are on the floor with shining faces. One begins to praise God, and then breaks out with uplifted hands into a tongue. Pastor Pendleton now tells how he felt the need, and sought the baptism, and God baptized him with such an experience of the divine presence and love and boldness as he had never had before. The officials of his church therefore desired him to withdraw, and a number of his people went with him and joined forces with Pastor Bartleman. Then a sweet-faced, old, German Lutheran lady told how she wondered when she heard the people praising God in tongues and began to pray to be baptized with the Spirit. After she had gone to bed, her mouth went off in a tongue, and she praised the Lord through the night to the amazement of her children.

"Next, an exhortation in tongues comes from Pastor Bartleman's lips in great sweetness, and one after another make their way to the altar quickly, until the rail is filled with seekers. Whatever criticism may be said of this work, it is very evident that it is divinely endorsed and the Lord is 'adding to them daily such as are being saved.' It is believed that this revival is but in its infancy and that we are in the evening of this dispensation. The burden of the tongues is, 'Jesus is coming soon.'"

Dr. Dumble wrote again, for the same paper:

"At Pastor Bartleman's church, meetings are held every night, all day Sundays, and all night every Friday. There is no order of services; they are expected to run in the divine order. The blessed Holy Spirit is the executive in charge. The leaders, or pastors, will be seen most of the time on their faces on the floor, or kneeling in the place where the pulpit commonly is, but there is neither pulpit, nor organ, nor choir.

"A young lady, for the first time in one of these meetings, came under the power of the Spirit, and lay for half an hour with beaming face lost to all about her, beholding visions unutterable. Soon she began to say, 'Glory! Glory to Jesus!' and spoke fluently in a strange tongue. On the last Sabbath, the meeting continued from early morning to midnight. There was no preaching, but prayer, testimony, praise, and exhortation."

THE KINGS CAME BACK

It is a fact that in the beginning platforms and pulpits were as far as possible removed out of the way. We had no conscious need of them. Priest class and ecclesiastical abuse were entirely swept away. We were all brethren. All were free to obey God. He might speak through whom He would. He had poured out His Spirit "on all flesh," even on "His servants and handmaidens" (Acts 2). We honored men for their God-given "gifts" and offices only. As the movement began to wane, platforms were built higher, coattails were worn longer, choirs were organized, and string bands came into existence to "jazz" the people. The kings came back once more to their thrones, restored to sovereignty. We were no longer brethren. Then the divisions multiplied. While

Brother Seymour kept his head inside the old empty box in Azusa, all was well. They later built a throne for him also. Now we have not one hierarchy, but many.

I wrote the following for *Apostolic Light*, another religious paper, in 1906:

"Cursed with unbelief, we are struggling upward—with the utmost difficulty—for the restoration of that glorious light and power, once so bountifully bestowed on the Church, but long since lost. Our eyes have been so blinded by the darkness of unbelief into which we were plunged by the Church's fall, that we fight the light, for our eyes are weak. So far had we fallen as a Church that when Luther sought to restore the truth of 'justification by faith' it was fought and resisted by the Church of his day as the utmost heresy, and men paid for it with their lives. And it was much the same in Wesley's time. Now, here we are with the restoration of the very experience of 'Pentecost'—with the 'latter rain,' a restoration of the power, in greater glory—to finish up the work begun. We shall yet again be lifted to the Church's former level, to complete her work, begin where they left off when failure overtook them, and, speedily fulfilling the last great commission, open the way for the coming of the Christ.

"We are to drop out the centuries of the Church's failure, the long, dismal 'dark ages,' and telescoping time, be now fully restored to pristine power, victory, and glory. We seek to pull ourselves, by the grace of God, out of a corrupt, backslidden, spurious Christianity. The synagogues of a proud, hypocritical Church are arrayed against us, to give us the lie. The 'hirelings' thirst for our blood. The scribes and pharisees, chief priests, and rulers of the synagogues are all against us and the Christ.

"Los Angeles seems to be the place and this the time, in the mind of God, for the restoration of the Church to her former place, favor, and power. The fullness of time seems to have come for the Church's complete restoration. God has spoken to His servants in all parts of the world and has sent many of them to Los Angeles, representing every nation under heaven. Once more, as of old, they are come up for 'Pentecost,' to go out again into all the world with the glad message of salvation. The base of operations has been shifted, from old Jerusalem to Los Angeles for the latter 'Pentecost.' And there is a tremendous, God-given hunger for this experience everywhere. Wales was but intended as the cradle for this world-wide restoration of power of God. India but the Nazareth where He was 'brought up.'"

GET GOD TO THE PEOPLE

Again I wrote in the same paper:

"If ever men shall seek to control, corner, or own this work of God, either for their own glory or for that of an organization, we shall find the Spirit refusing to work. The glory will depart. Let this be one work where God shall be given His proper place, and we shall see such a work as men have never yet dreamed of. It would be a fearful thing if God were obliged to withdraw His blessed Spirit from us, or withhold it at such a time as this, because we tried to corner it. All our business is to get God to the people. Let us yield ourselves for this, and this alone.

"Some of the 'canker worms' of past experience have been party spirit, sectional difference, prejudices, etc., which are all carnal, contrary, and destructive to the law of love, to the 'one body' of Christ. 'For by one Spirit are we all baptized into one body' (1 Corinthians

12:13). Self-satisfaction will always cause defeat. Oh, brother! Cease traveling round and round your old habit-beaten path, on which all grass has ceased to grow. Strike out into pastures green, beside the living waters!"

In the *Way of Faith,* I wrote the following:

"We are coming back from the 'dark ages' of the Church's backsliding and downfall. We are living in the most momentous moments of the history of our time. The Spirit is brushing aside all our plans, our schemes, our strivings, and our theories, and is Himself acting again. Many who have feathered their nests well are fighting hard. They cannot face the sacrifice involved in rising to meet these conditions.

"The precious ore of truth, the Church's emancipation from the bondage of man's rule, has been brought about in a necessarily crude form at first, as rough ore. It has been surrounded, as in nature, by all kinds of worthless, hurtful elements. Extravagant violent characters have sought to identify themselves with the work. A great truth is struggling in the bowels of the earth, entombed by the landslide of retrograding evil in the Church's history. But it is bursting forth, soon to shake itself free from the objectionable matter yet clinging to it. Christ is at last proclaimed the Head. The Holy Spirit is the life. The members are in principle all 'one body.'"

WHAT MEANETH THIS?

Again, here is an extract from an article in the *Way of Faith* in early 1907:

"We detect in these present-hour manifestations the rising of a new order of things out of the chaos and failure of the past. The atmosphere is filled with inspiring expectation of the ideal. But unbelief retards our progress. Our preconceived ideas betray us in the face of opportunity. They lead to loss and ruin. But the world is awakening today, startled from her guilty slumber of ease and death. Letters are pouring in from every side, from all parts of the world, inquiring feverishly, 'what meaneth this?' And, we have the pulse of humanity, especially in the Church of today. There is a mighty expectation. And these hungry, expectant children are crying for bread. Cold, intellectual speculation has had nothing but denials for them. The realm of the Spirit cannot be reached alone by the intellect. The miraculous has again startled us into a realization of the fact that God still lives and moves among us.

"Old forms are breaking up, passing away. Their death knell is being sounded. New forms, a new order and life, are appearing. There is naturally a mighty struggle. Satan moves the hosts of hell to hinder. But we shall conquer! The precious ore must be refined after it has been mined. The 'precious' must be taken 'from the vile.' Rough pioneers have cleared the way for our advance, but purer forms will follow. Heroic, positive spirits are necessary for this work.

"Men have been speaking through the ages, but the voice of God the Spirit is calling us today. Since the early Church lost her power and place with God, we have been struggling back. Up through 'its' and 'isms,' theories, creeds, doctrines, and schisms; issues and movements, blessings, experiences, and professions, we have come. The stream could rise no higher than its source. We need no more theology or theory. Let the devil have them. *Let us get to God.* Many are cramped up in present experiences. They are actually afraid to seek more of God for fear the devil will get them. Away with such foolish bondage! Follow your heart! Believe in your own heart's hunger, and go ahead for God. We are sticking to the bottom. We need the fire of God. Straight-jacket methods and religious rules have well-nigh crushed out our spiritual life altogether. We had better grieve all men rather than God."

Before the Azusa outpouring everything had settled down in concrete form, bound by man. Nothing could move for God. Dynamite—the power of the Holy Spirit—was necessary to free this mass. And this God furnished. The whole mass was set free once more. Our "year of Jubilee" had come. The last one had been realized in the great revival of 1859, 50 years before.

CHAPTER FOUR

TRAVELING MINISTRY

The latter part of March 1907, I received an invitation to come to Conneaut, Ohio, with a check enclosed for 50 dollars. They wanted Pentecostal meetings there. The leader wrote me that they were hungry for Pentecost. I felt it was a call from God to go east but could not help wondering if they really knew what they were inviting for themselves. The letter seemed full of enthusiasm, the very thing John Wesley so strongly discouraged. Wesley's definition of "fanaticism" was, "expecting the end without the means."

I did not cash the check, fearing lest they might be disappointed when they got through with me. They had to learn that Pentecost meant the dying out to the self-life, carnal ambition, pride, etc. It meant for them to enter into the "fellowship of His sufferings," not simply to have a popular, good time. This I felt they did not realize. A real Christian means a martyr, unavoidably, in one way or another. Few people are willing to pay the price to become a real Christian, to accept the ostracism, false accusation, and condemnation of others. But God has only one standard. Present-day profession is for the most part a mere sham. Only a small percentage of it is real.

A man once asked Luther to recommend a book that was both agreeable and useful. "Agreeable and useful!" replied Luther, "Such a question is beyond my ability. The better things are, the less they please."

"Except a man forsake *all*," said Jesus, "*he cannot be My disciple*" (see Luke 14:33). This may require some qualification, or explanation, as to positive action, but the principle remains the same for all. The Church, since her fall in the early centuries, has had an altogether mistaken conception of her calling and salvation. All believers are called to a 100 percent consecration. God doesn't have two standards of consecration—one for the foreign missionary, and another for the Christian at home. We cannot find it in the Bible. One is called to consecrate their all as well as the other. One goes, one prays, and one gives. It takes three to make a missionary. "This is a hard saying. Who can hear it?"

God has had but one purpose and interest since the fall. That has been to bring man back to Himself. The whole old dispensation, with its providential dealings, was unto this one end. God had one recognized people, the Jews. He had one purpose in this nation. All their operations were to one end. All their worship pointed to that one end—to bring the nations to the true knowledge of God and to bring in the Messiah of the world. Jesus Christ had but one interest in coming to this earth. His second coming waits for this one thing also. When this gospel shall have been preached in all the world "then shall the end come," the "curse" be lifted.

Is the Church working, with all her resources, for this one purpose and to this one end? That certainly does not mean the selfish heaping up of property and riches, more than we really need. It does not mean getting all we want for ourselves and then tossing the Lord a dollar we do not need. We have had the order totally reversed since the early Church's fall. God requires of everyone exactly the same consecration.

Here is where the Ananias and Sapphira business has come in. Not "one-tenth" in this dispensation, but "all." Our bodies are the temple of the Holy Spirit, and we are supposed to be 100 percent for Him at all times. We belong to Him. He has created us and bought us back, redeemed us after we had mortgaged His property, not ours, to the devil. In no sense are we our own. We are redeemed back with the blood. How long would it take, or have taken, to evangelize the world under this rule? Think on these things! Is the Church moving normally, in divine order? The politico-religious system, since the early Church, and today, is largely a hybrid, mongrel institution. It is full of selfishness, disobedience, and corruption. Its kingdom has become "of this world," rather than a "heavenly citizenship," with spiritual weapons.

TIMES MAKE THE MEN

The doctrinal issue has also been a great battle. Many were too dogmatic at Azusa. Doctrine, after all, is but the skeleton of the structure. It is the framework of the "body." We need flesh on the bones, the Spirit within, to give life. What the people need is a living Christ, not dogmatic, doctrinal contention. Much harm was done the work in the beginning by unwise zeal. The cause suffered most from those within its own ranks, as always. But God had some real heroes He could depend upon. Most of these sprang from the deepest obscurity into sudden prominence and power, and then as quickly retired again, when their work was done. Someone has well said: "Men, like stars, appear on the horizon at the command of God." This is a true evidence of a real work of God. Men do not make their times, as someone has also truly said, but the times make the man. Until the time, no man can produce a revival. The people must be prepared, and the instrument likewise.

The historian D'Aubigne has well said: "God draws from the deepest seclusion the weak instruments by which He purposes to accomplish great things; and then, when He has permitted them to glitter for a season with dazzling brilliancy on an illustrious stage, He dismisses them again to deepest obscurity." Again he says: "God usually withdraws His servants from the field of battle only to bring them back stronger and better armed." And this was the case with Luther, shut up in the Wartburg, after his glittering triumph over the great ones of earth at Worms.

D'Aubigne writes again:

"There is a moment in the history of the world, as in the lives of such men as Charles II or Napoleon, which decides their career and their renown. It is that in which their strength is suddenly revealed to them. An analogous moment exists in the life of God's heroes, but it is in a contrary direction. It is that in which they first recognize their helplessness and nothingness. From that hour they receive the strength of God from on high. A great work of God is never accomplished by the natural strength of man. It is from among the dry bones, the darkness, and the dust of death that God is pleased to select the instruments through whom He designs to scatter over the earth His light, regeneration, and life.

"Strong in frame, in character, and in talents, Zwingle had to see himself prostrated, that he might become such an instrument as God loves. He needed the baptism of adversity and infirmity, of weakness and pain. Luther had received it in that hour of anguish when his cell and the long galleries of the convent at Erfurth reechoed with his piercing cries. Zwingle was appointed to receive it by being brought into contact with sickness and death."

Men must come to know their own weakness before they can hope to know God's strength. The natural strength and ability of man are always the greatest hindrance to the work of God, and to God's working. That is why we had such a deep dying out, especially for the workers and preachers, in the early days of Azusa Mission. God was preparing His workers for their mission.

BARTLEMAN TRAVELS EAST

In answer to prayer, the Lord opened the way for me to take my family with me when I went east. I preached in Denver at the Holiness headquarters, where we had been members and labored before we came to California. We had a powerful time. Several souls were saved, among them one whole family, and the saints were wonderfully built up. Some received the baptism of the Spirit. I had three meetings in all.

God wonderfully used two little girls there. They both had the baptism and a real ministry of prayer. Their pleadings with the unsaved broke up the house, while their freedom from self-consciousness was a powerful lesson to us all. It was a strange work and ministry of God. Heartfelt conviction was upon the unsaved. "Except ye become as a little child," we learned anew. Evidently modern evangelistic methods are not altogether essential for the salvation of souls. We had better stick to our peculiar gift, though it be a "strange work." We will succeed better at that. Let God have His way. In those days the power and presence of God among us often converted sinners in their seats. We did not have to drag them to the altar and fight with them to get them saved. They did not come to the altar to fight God. There was much of the "signing in the Spirit" at Denver, as at Azusa. This particular gift seemed to accompany the work wherever it broke out.

We finally reached, Conneaut, Ohio, on April 30 in a snow-storm. The presence of the Lord was with us from the start. It was a Holiness mission. We really had little to do in the main but look on and see God work. The Spirit took the meetings. In fact, we were on our faces most of the time in prayer. I could hardly keep off my face; the battle was the Lord's. And no one else could have fought it there, for we came up against most stubborn resistance. The Lord had warned me of this condition before we left Los Angeles. The leader who had written inviting me had not the slightest idea what a Pentecost meant, just as I had feared. He wanted a big time, with a big increase in the mission, to build up the work in numbers, etc.

GOD REMOVES THE HINDRANCE

The meetings had not gone far until we found him wedged squarely in the way. One sister prayed without ceasing under a travail of soul for him. He was fleshly, proud, and self-important, and would not let the meetings go deeper. We could go no further. He did not seem to have the least idea of humbling himself along with the rest of us. But he *had* to come down. God showed me that I must deal with him. I had to obey or quit. There was no use going any further. We were eating at his table and sleeping in his beds. It was a hard thing to have to do, but I went after him. We locked horns, and he resisted me fiercely. God, however, brought him down. The Spirit convinced him, and he fell in a heap. He almost jarred the building when he fell. He lay under a bench for five hours and began to see himself as God saw him. The Spirit took him all to pieces and showed him his pride, ambition, etc. Finally, he got up without a word and went home. There he locked himself in his room and remained until God met him. He came out from that interview as meek as a little lamb and confessed his shortcomings. The hindrance was out of the way, and the meetings swept on in power. He got the baptism himself some time later, after we had gone.

The Lord wrought very deeply. Several were under the power all night on one occasion. There was no closing at nine o'clock sharp, as the preachers must do today in order to keep the people. We wanted God in those days. We did not have a thousand other things we wanted before Him. And He did not disappoint us. One sister sat and spoke in tongues for five full hours. Souls were saved, and the saints wonderfully built up and strengthened by the presence of the Lord. A number received the baptism, and the mission became full-fledged for Pentecost.

One Sunday night the hall was packed out, clear to the middle of the street. I went to the hall in the morning to look up the folks who had not come home. Several had stayed all night. I found them lost to all but God. They could not get away. A very shekinah glory filled the place. It was awesome, but glorious.

SCARCELY A SOUND WAS UTTERED

Our next meeting was at Youngstown, Ohio. Here I preached for the Christian Missionary Alliance. Some nights we were held in the hall until daylight. We could not leave. God was so near that no one felt tired or sleepy. I had much real soul travail here. In some meetings, suppressed groans were about all one could hear. Much prayer characterized the services. The Spirit was waited upon for every move, and He took complete control. No two services were alike. In one meeting, the very silence of Heaven took possession of us for about four hours. Scarcely a sound was uttered. The place became so steeped in prayer and sacred that we closed the door softly, and walked the same, scarcely speaking to one another, and then only in whispers. Another night, we were held in adoration and praise for hours. We seemed to be looking into the very face of God. There was no boisterousness in these meetings.

Another night we were all broken up by the love of God. We could do nothing but weep for a whole hour. Every meeting was different, and each seemed to go deeper. Two or three whole nights were spent in prayer. One night the Spirit fell upon us like an electric shower. Several went over on the floor, and God was master for the time. Such singing in the Spirit, the "heavenly chorus," I have seldom heard. A number came through speaking in tongues. But again our battle was with the leader. He opposed me fiercely. He was not right with God and would not yield. His wife was now under the power, seeking the baptism, but he carried on in the flesh until the Spirit was terribly grieved. The devil often gets into a preacher's coat. Satan used him persistently in the beginning of the meetings, but God finally got the victory, in spite of him. He did not yield. It is amazing the hold the devil has on some preachers.

I preached one night at Akron, Ohio, with much blessing. We then had five services at New Castle, Pennsylvania, with the C.M.A. again. God greatly blessed there also. Then we went to Alliance, Ohio, for the Pentecostal camp meeting. It was June 13. We had a wonderful camp. It was the first one of its kind in the Northeast. I led the preachers' meetings. The first Sunday morning I was given a message, but the leader asked me to speak in the afternoon instead. I said nothing, but prayed. In a few minutes he came back and told me to preach in the morning. In those days men did not get far without God. I preached with great help from the Lord on, "Jesus Christ in Worldwide Evangelism in the Power of the Holy Ghost." Everything centers around Jesus. We may not put the power, gifts, the Holy Spirit, or in fact anything ahead of Jesus. Any mission that exalts even the Holy Spirit above the Lord Jesus Christ is bound for the rocks of error and fanaticism.

PREFERRING ONE ANOTHER

This was a very important camp in the inception of the work in that part of the country. We remained two weeks, and I preached 11 times in all. We had a powerful time and a large, representative attendance. Four hundred camped on the grounds. Often meetings lasted all night. Missionary enthusiasm ran high. Meals were on the free-will offering plan. God bountifully provided and a precious spirit of unity prevailed. We were "brethren," baptized in "one Spirit," into "one Body." Thus Jesus' prayer was answered, *"that they all may be one"* (John 17:21). The harmony between the preachers was especially blessed. Such a spirit of love we have seldom seen displayed. Those were wonderful days. It could be truly said that in honor we preferred one another.

No organ or hymnbooks were used. The Spirit conducted the services, and there seemed no place for them. Hundreds met God. Many received a call to foreign fields, to prove God along real faith lines. The rapid evangelism of the world, on real apostolic lines, was the goal set. The present generation must be reached by the present generation. The altars were seldom empty of seekers day or night. Men who had been in both the Wales and India revivals declared this to be the deepest work of all. We determined to fight nothing but sin and to fear nothing but God.

I asked the Lord for a certain amount of money, which we needed to continue eastward. The committee gave me exactly the amount I had prayed for, without a single hint from me. God did it. Praise Him!

At 42nd Street Mission, New York City (Glad Tidings Hall), we had powerful times. A young girl came under the power, and her spirit was caught up to the throne. She sang a melody, without words, that was so heavenly that it seemed to come from within the veil. It seemed to come from another world. I have never heard its equal before or since.

A.B. Simpson was there himself that night and was tremendously impressed by it. He had been much opposed to the Pentecostal work. Doubtless God gave it as a witness for him. Several were slain under the power. Toward morning, the presence of the Lord was simply wonderful. I went to leave the hall just at daybreak and shook hands with a sister hungry for the baptism. The Spirit came upon her, and I could not turn her loose until she fell at the altar and came through speaking in tongues. I shook hands with another hungry sister as I started to leave the hall again. The Spirit fell upon her also, and she received the baptism right there on her feet, speaking in tongues before I could turn her loose. That was a wonderful night.

RETURNING TO CALIFORNIA

It was now time for us to start for California again. The Lord blessed me much at Indianapolis. I was so glad I had obeyed Him and gone there. I was there by His invitation purely, but I seldom, if ever, had felt such a wonderful flow of the Spirit before. The message seemed to be actually pulled out of me in preaching. In fact, I felt almost drawn off the platform by the hungry desire of the people. I could not speak as rapidly as the thoughts came to me and almost fell over myself trying to speak fast enough. At one meeting, when I was through speaking, the "slain of the Lord" lay all over the floor. I looked for the preachers behind me, and they lay stretched out on the floor, too. One of them had his feet tangled up in a chair, so I knew they had gone down under the power of God. I stepped over near the piano, among the people. My body began to rock under the power of God, and I fell over onto the piano and lay there. It was a cyclonic manifestation of the power of God.

At Colorado Springs I preached six times. The Spirit flowed like oil. I have seldom found such liberty anywhere. Oh, the possibilities that exist where purity and unity reign!

We had sent our trunks on to Los Angeles, not knowing where we would find our next home. But before reaching Pasadena, the Lord showed me we should get off there. We did not expect anyone to meet us, though I had written Brother Boehmer that we would get back on that train. When we reached Pasadena, with no place to go, we found Brother Boehmer at the depot waiting for us. He took us to a mission home on Mary

Street, which had just been opened in connection with the Alley Mission. So God had it all arranged for us, without our knowledge. We were weary pilgrims indeed, needing rest. We arrived December 5, 1907.

FLESH AND FANATICISM

I found that the work had fallen back considerably. The saints were badly split up. The Spirit was bound also. The outside opposition had become much more settled and determined. It was the same condition in Los Angeles. The saints at the Alley Mission had suffered greatly under the tyranny of a leader who did not himself have the baptism. I now helped them to pray him out of the mission and the home, and they were delivered. He had imposed himself on the work. He was a regular "dog in the manger." A larger mission was opened on Colorado Street, and I had some ministry there also. I found the power had been greatly dissipated. There was much empty manifestation. A great deal of it was simply froth and foam. This burdened me deeply. The spirit of prayer had been largely lost. In consequence, much flesh and fanaticism had crept in. Prayer burns out the proud flesh. It must be crucified.

We now moved into a little cottage next door to Brother Boehmer. The ministry of intercession was heavy upon me. I preached a number of times at Hermon, Eighth and Maple, and at Azusa Street. One evening at Azusa Mission the spirit of prayer came upon me as a rushing, mighty wind. The power ran all through the building. I had been burdened for the deadness that had crept in there. The temporary leaders were frightened and did not know what to do. They telephoned for help. They had not been with us in the beginning. Brother Seymour was out of town.

I was upstairs in the hallway. Others joined me in prayer. We went downstairs, and the fire broke out in the meeting. But the leaders in charge were not spiritual. Other rulers had arisen who "knew not Joseph." They did not understand it. God was trying to come back. They seemed afraid someone might steal the mission. The Spirit could not work. Besides, they had organized now, and I had not joined their organization. And so it is largely today. Sign on the dotted line or we cannot trust you. We affiliate only with those carrying our papers. Pentecost took that out of us! Why go back to it? All who belong to the different divisions in the Pentecostal work today do not have the spirit of division, but God would hold us to the ideal of the "one Body."

FEAR NOTHING BUT GOD

The Lord showed me my place of hiding. I determined to follow Him. That is the place of power. Fear nothing but God, and obey Him. I spoke many times at Eighth and Maple, at Azusa, and also at the Alley Mission in Pasadena, exhorting them to more earnestness and to walk in the Spirit. I had suffered much in prayer in the bringing forth of this work and I felt I had a right to admonish them. Our great battle from the beginning was with fleshly religious fanatics, purporting to be of the Spirit of God.

On March 11, 1908, I received a letter from Brother Sawtelle, leader of the Christian Alliance work in Portland, Oregon. He asked me to come north and hold some meetings for them. God had shown me that we would be called out again, and I recognized His call. We were to go north and east again. Brother Boehmer had received the baptism by this time and decided to go with us in the work. I felt we had come back to the coast largely to get him out. I was exhorting the saints all winter to push out in the spring for God. About a dozen followed us to different points as we started out again. I began to feel the worldwide call heavily upon me, also. The Lord seemed to show me the oceans must yet be crossed for Him. And this we realized later on. Like Peter the Hermit, I felt at times like stirring all Christendom with my cry for a revival.

[Brother Bartleman spent the year of 1908 ministering again throughout the United States. In 1909 he made a trip to the Hawaiian Islands.]

HOW ARE THE MIGHTY FALLEN

The work had gotten into a bad condition generally by the time we returned to Los Angeles (from the Hawaiian Islands). The missions had fought each other almost to a standstill. Little love remained. There was considerable rejoicing, but in the "flesh." A cold, hard-hearted zeal had largely taken the place of the divine love and tenderness of the Spirit. The missions, I found, were very zealous for doctrine, as usual. I began to preach at Eighth and Maple, Azusa Mission, and Hermon. Azusa had lost out greatly since we left. "How are the mighty fallen," came to me most forcibly. But the Spirit came upon three of us mightily in prayer one evening there. He assured us He was going to bring the power back to Azusa Mission again as at the beginning. We felt we had prayed through. (And the answer came a little over a year later when Brother Durham came from Chicago. The place was then once more filled with the saints and with the glory of God, although only for a short time.)

But at this time old Azusa Mission became more and more in bondage. The meetings had to run in appointed order. The Spirit tried to work through some poor, illiterate Mexicans, who had been saved and baptized in the Spirit, but the leader deliberately refused to let them testify, crushing them ruthlessly. It was like murdering the Spirit of God. Only God knows what this meant to those poor Mexicans. Personally, I would rather die than to have assumed such a spirit of dictatorship. Every meeting was now programmed from start to finish. Disaster was bound to follow, and it did so.

AROUND THE WORLD

I now began to feel that the Lord was calling me to girdle the globe on a missionary trip for Him. It was to be by faith, and I had not a cent in sight. I had really felt the call to make this trip for years, and the time had now come. It looked like madness to attempt such a thing in the natural, as I was just at that time up against a very severe test both physically and financially. However, the conviction became an assurance. After a time, in which it seemed almost impossible to get even as much as a dime, the Lord opened the way for me to start. I believe God allowed me to be thus tested in order to prove me for the journey. It looked almost like actual starvation faced us just before the way finally opened up.

I left home March 17, 1910, and circled the entire globe by faith, visiting Europe and most of the principal mission fields. I spent six delightful weeks in Palestine, returning home by way of Egypt, India, Ceylon, China, and Japan, and across the Pacific, via Honolulu. I was gone 11 months and 1 week. My family trusted God fully and were better cared for than they had ever been while I was with them. I returned with about one dollar in my pocket. My wife had 50 dollars in the bank. *"Faithful is He that calleth you, who also will do it"* (1 Thess. 5:24 KJV).

CHAPTER FIVE

THE WAVE CONTINUES

Just about one week before I arrived home, Brother Durham began meetings at old Azusa Mission. He was sent of the Lord from Chicago. The Upper Room Mission refused him a hearing, so he went to Azusa Street. Brother Seymour was absent in the east. Brother Durham started meetings, and the saints flocked back to the old place and filled it again with the high praises of God. This was what the Lord had witnessed to three of us while in prayer more than a year before. God had gathered many of the old Azusa workers back to Los Angeles from many parts of the world, evidently for this. It was called by many the second shower of the Latter Rain. On Sunday the place was crowded, and 500 were turned away. The people would not leave their seats between meetings for fear of losing them.

With this, the bottom dropped out of Upper Room Mission overnight. The leader had abused his privilege, and also the saints. He had failed God in other ways also. The Lord will spare any man or mission if there is repentance. We cannot persistently abuse our privilege, destroy the prophets of God, and finally get away with it. Great was the fall of Upper Room Mission. The leader had at one time been much used of God, but God had another place, man, and message ready. He never deserts His true flock. The "cloud" moved on and moved the saints with it.

The fire began to fall at old Azusa as at the beginning. I attended these meetings with great interest and joy. The Lord also blessed me much at Eighth and Maple, which was still running in spite of the outstanding meetings at Azusa.

GOD LOCKED OUT

Then, on May 2, I went to Azusa Street and to everyone's surprise found the doors all locked, with chain and padlock. Brother Seymour had hastened back from the east and, with his trustees, decided to lock Brother Durham out. It was his message they objected to. But they locked God and the saints out from the old cradle of power also.

In a few days, Brother Durham rented a large building at the corner of Seventh and Los Angeles Streets. Approximately 1,000 people attended the meetings there on Sundays and about 400 on weeknights. Here the "cloud" rested, and God's glory filled the place. Azusa became deserted. The Lord was with Brother Durham in great power, for God sets His seal especially on "present truth" that needs to be established. He preached a gospel of salvation by faith and was used mightily to draw anew a clear line of demarcation between salvation by works and faith, between law and grace. This had become very much needed, and it is certain that such a revelation and reformation are needed in the churches today almost as badly as in Luther's day.

"Learn from me," said Luther, "how difficult a thing it is to throw off errors which have been confirmed by the example of all the world, and which, through long habit, have become second nature to us."

"Men were astonished that they had not earlier acknowledged truths that appeared so evident in Luther's mouth," says the historian, D'Aubigne. And so with Durham's message. But it received great opposition also. Some abused the message, as they do every message sent of God, going to the extreme of declaring that because the work of redemption was fully accomplished on the cross, it was of necessity finished in us also, the moment we believed. This was a great error and hindered the message and work considerably.

Man always adds to the message God has given. This is satan's chief way to discredit and destroy it. Both Luther and Wesley had the same difficulties to contend with. And so has every God-given revival. Men are creatures of extremes. The message generally suffers more from its friends than from its foes. We have this treasure in "earthen vessels." The truth can always be abused. Some even went so far as to fight the principle of holiness itself, pretending to justify themselves by Durham's message. But they had either misunderstood it, or more likely seized a pretended opportunity to fight the principle that their own hearts refused to yield to.

CALLED TO HUMILITY

We had a wonderful year in Los Angeles in 1911. The battle was clearly between works and faith, between law and grace. Much of the old-time power and glory of the Azusa Mission days returned to us. I had much liberty and joy in Brother Durham's mission, especially in the beginning. God had prepared me beforehand for the message. I had been brought completely to the end of self-dependence. Works had no further place with me in meriting any phase of salvation. *"For we are **His** workmanship, created in Christ Jesus unto good works"* (Eph. 2:10 KJV). We were called to humility again, that the power of God might rest upon us.

So determined was I to take no chances of "self" surviving in my life, that I burned no less than 500 personal letters I had received in the early Azusa days from leading preachers and teachers all over the world inquiring anxiously about the revival that was then in our midst. Some of these inquirers were in very high positions officially. They had read my reports of the revival in various papers. I was afraid these letters might some day prove a temptation to me to imagine that I had been a person of some importance, since many begged an interest in my prayers. I almost wish at times that I had kept these letters, as they would be of much interest now as historical evidence to the widespread influence of the revival. No doubt the Lord could have kept me humble without this sacrifice, but at the time I was determined to take no chances.

We feared nothing more in those days than to seek our own glory, or that the Pentecostal experience should become a matter of past history. In fact, we hoped and believed that the revival would last without cessation until Jesus should come. It doubtless would, and should, if men would not fail God, but we drift back continually into the old ecclesiastical concepts, forms, and ceremonies. Thus history sadly repeats itself. Now we must work up an annual revival. We go to church on Sundays, etc., just "like the nations (churches) 'round about us." But in the beginning it was not so. In the early Azusa days, you could hardly keep the saints off their knees. Whenever two saints met, they invariably went to prayer. Today we can hardly be dragged to prayer. Some make as much fuss about it as the old camel does in the east in kneeling to receive his load. He fusses and bites and groans before the driver can bring him down.

I am glad I did not destroy my diary, however, nor the articles I wrote all through those early Pentecostal days. I have preserved between 500 and 600 separate, printed articles, besides more than 100 different tracts. From these I have been able to draw a large amount of reliable information for the present book. Had I destroyed these, the book would probably never have been written.

DURHAM STEPS DOWN

The opposition against Brother Durham was tremendous, and he was finally tempted to strike back. This I felt was not the Spirit of Christ, though he had great provocation. Possibly few have been able to stand such a test successfully. I left the platform finally, not willing to stand for a spirit of retaliation. I felt I must keep clear of carnal strife and controversy. However, the Lord had wonderfully used dear Brother Durham. He was sent of God to Los Angeles and possibly his work was done. To have remained much longer might have destroyed his victory, for his word was coming to be almost law in the Pentecostal missions, even as far as the Atlantic Coast. Too much power is unsafe for any one man. The paper he instituted in connection with his work began to take on the nature of a carnal controversy, fighting the old "second work of grace" theory. The Lord showed me that He was about to stop this spirit.

Brother Durham wrote the following observations on the work some time before he died. They are of such importance that we feel led to reproduce them, as follows:

"A great crisis is now on. Men do not see the plan of God in the present Pentecostal movement. Such a complete revolution is necessary that it staggers them. They are unwilling to see that which they have labored so hard to build up thrown down; but before God's plans can be carried out, man's plans must be set aside. They fail to see that God, having set aside all the plans of man, is begging to work after His own plan. He is revealing His real plan to so many that they will never consent to having the present work turned into a sect. God's people are simply not going to be led into the snare of human organization again.

"The Father has poured out His Spirit again that Jesus may be glorified. All past movements have resulted in

117

the promotion to positions of honor for one or more men. The present movement will honor and exalt Jesus Christ. The Holy Spirit always exalts Jesus and His precious blood. As He is exalted and faithfully preached, God is restoring the old time power. But it is not all restored yet. Not seeing the plan of God, men have not met the conditions, and therefore have not received all that God has for them. Many have run ahead of God.

"Shortly after God filled me, His Spirit rested mightily upon me one morning, and He said to me: 'If you were only small enough, I could do anything with you.' A great desire to be little, yea, to be nothing, came into my heart. But it has been oh so hard to keep low enough for Him to really work through me. And He only really uses me when I am little in my own eyes and really humble at His feet. When I feel that I must do something, He always lets me fail. But when I stay at His feet and feel that I am nothing, and that He is all, and so just trust Him, He does His work in such a beautiful way that it is wonderful to me.

"God is not trying to build up something else, or to do something for men that will make them great and mighty, but rather to bring all men to naught, and do the work through the power of the Holy Ghost. The call of God to His people now is to humble themselves, to recognize their weakness and lack of power, to get down before Him, and wait till His power is restored. The great question is, will men see the plan of God and yield to it? Will men get down in humility at Jesus' feet and pray and wait till He restores His full Pentecostal power? Or will they continue to run ahead of Him and fail in the end?

"Let God's people everywhere begin to seek in deep, true humility. Then He will reveal Himself and His plan to them. One man with the real power of God upon him can do more than a thousand who go on their own account. Only those who are true and loyal to God and His present day message will share in this great victory. The people who really humble themselves, and stand the test, God will use to do His work."

The fact is that when a man gets to the place where he really loves obscurity, where he does not care to preach, and where he would rather sit in the back seat than on the platform, then God can lift him up and use him, and not very much before.

The old Upper Room, 327 South Spring Street, was opened up again about this time under the leadership of Brother Warren Fisher, Brother Manley, and Brother Allen. I delivered a message there one Sunday, and two received the "baptism." God wonderfully anointed me. The presence of the Lord was very near. I had asked Him for a witness, so I now shifted my ministry to the Upper Room Mission.

After I left Brother Durham's platform, he seemed to mistrust me. Perhaps he thought I would work against him. I spoke many times now at Upper Room Mission where the Lord greatly blessed me. Soon after this, Brother Durham went to Chicago to hold a convention where he was wonderfully used of God. It was in the winter, and he contracted a cold, which led to his death soon after returning to Los Angeles.

DRAWN TO EUROPE

By this time, the Lord was speaking loudly to me about getting out into the field again. I felt strongly drawn to Europe. I had had conviction of this when passing through Europe in

1910. The time had come, and the Lord began to touch hearts in a marked way on our behalf.

We left Los Angeles and started to work our way across the continent once more, this time en route for Europe. The account of our "Two Years Mission Work in Europe," with labors in England, Scotland, Wales, Holland, Switzerland, France, Germany, Norway, Sweden, Finland, and old Russia itself—where I had to preach in secret, although almost under the Czar's nose—was published in a separate booklet. We did not want to return to America so soon, but were obliged to for the safety of the family, because of the war.

Besides, the whole effort of the nations now became one of filling their people's hearts with hate and murder. There seemed no place for the spirit of the gospel. People are expected to do all they can to hate, curse, or kill the enemy in wartime, certainly not to love him. Let others do this, however, if they will; but as for me, the gospel is just the same in peace or war. *"Jesus Christ is the same yesterday and today and forever"* (Heb. 13:8).

RUINED FOR LACK OF LOVE

In all my writings, for at least 25 years, I have labored for the unity of the Body of Christ. Everything I've written is full of the sentiment of John 17:21. Dr. Philip Schaff, the well-known scholar, has happily declared:

> "The divisions of Christendom will finally be over-ruled for a deeper and richer harmony, of which Christ is the keynote. In Him and by Him all problems of theology and history will be solved. In the best case, a human creed is only an approximate and relatively correct expression of revealed truth and may be improved by the progressive knowledge of the Church."

The editor of *The Friend of Russia* writes:

"God's people can never get together on human creeds and disciplines. They are too narrow and changeable. We have a foundation that is broad enough to hold all. Christ Himself is this foundation. In Christ, all God's people are one, irrespective of race, color, social standing, or creed."

A certain preacher of standing in a prominent church outside the Pentecostal ranks, while addressing the baptized saints not long ago, said:

"As we look upon the Church divided, upon the sect-ridden multitude, none of whom can see alike, how our tried souls cry out for that original love. And we will never win the world on any other plain. It was said of the early Christians, by the heathen themselves, 'Behold how these Christians love one another!' While we are breaking up into sects, creeds, isms, and doctrines, our love is dying. Our churches will be empty and our people lost. Your beautiful Pentecostal work, so full of promise, where God has designed to come in and fill souls and wonderfully baptize them in the Holy Spirit, is broken and peeled and ruined for lack of love."

Someone has recently written as follows: "It is a common thing to read in the daily papers such words as these, 'Only union men need apply.' And it is becoming a common thing to read in church papers: 'Affiliating brethren are invited.' What is the difference? No difference, except one is a secular union, the other is a religious union."

Every fresh division or party in the Church gives the world a contradiction as to the oneness of the Body of Christ and the truthfulness of the gospel. Multitudes are bowing down and burning incense to a doctrine rather than Christ. The many sects in Christendom are, to say the least, evidence to the world that Christians cannot get along together. Written creeds only serve to publish the fact that we cannot understand the Word of God alike and get together on it. Is the Word of God, then, so hard to understand? They who establish a fixed creed bar the way to further progress.

It is said of the mighty evangelist, Charles G. Finney, that he "forged his theology on the anvil of prayer in his own heart." He was not bound by the systems of his day.

THE ONE BODY OF CHRIST

The Spirit is laboring for the unity of believers today—for the "one Body"—that the prayer of Jesus may be answered, *"that they all may be one...that the world may believe"* (John 17:21 KJV). But the saints are ever too ready to serve a system or party, to contend for religious, selfish, party interests. God's people are shut up in denominational coops. As someone once said, "Error always leads to militant exclusion. Truth evermore stoops to wash the saints' feet." Yet the Bible says, *"By one Spirit are we all baptized into one body"* (1 Cor. 12:13 KJV). We should be as one family, which we are, at home in God's house anywhere.

We belong to the whole Body of Christ, both in Heaven and on earth. God's Church is one. It is a terrible thing to go about dismembering the Body of Christ. How foolish and wicked the petty differences between Christians will appear in the light of eternity. Christ is the "issue," not some doctrine about Him. The gospel leads to Him. It exalts Christ, not some particular doctrine. To "know Christ" is the alpha and the omega of the Christian faith and practice.

"The Church was in the beginning a community of brethren guided by a few of the brethren," wrote D'Aubigne. *"One is your Master, even Christ; and all ye are brethren"* (Matt. 23:8 KJV). We have too many who have a "leadership" spirit. These divide the Body, separate the saints.

Now, however, we are coming around the circle, from the early Church's fall back to primitive love and unity, in the "one Body" of Christ. This is doubtless the Church for which Christ is coming, "[without] *spot, or wrinkle, or any such thing*" (Eph. 5:27 KJV).

T H E   D E E P E R
S I G N I F I C A N C E   O F   P E N T E C O S T

[Frank Bartleman was a man of passion and deep burden. His prayers literally opened the heavens, and his messages were withering to all that was of the flesh. Everything that stood as an obstruction to the full exaltation of Jesus Christ as "Lord of all" became the object of his travailing prayer and was ruthlessly exposed by his fearless pen and tongue.

But Frank Bartleman was more than an intercessor and more than a dauntless revivalist. He was a man of vision—a prophet! He perceived the deeper significance of what the Holy Spirit was after in revival and called upon God's people to go on to that ultimate. His voice, although so long silent, now once again goes forth. The following message was delivered in about 1925 shortly before Mr. Bartleman's death.]

The world is the field; the true Church is the treasure—like a kernel in a shell. But the great nominal Church, the ecclesiastical Body in each generation, is also like a field in which the true mystical Church—the *living* Church—like a treasure, is hidden.

But even this true, mystical Church is far from being the treasure of divine life and power originally planned and provided for in the purpose of God. Ever since the early Church fell from New Testament purity and life, she has been like a backslider, fallen from the summit of apostolic days—though destined to return and yet enter into the full blessing of the Father's house.

I refer to the true, mystical Body of Christ. It is a "prodigal son," wandered from the Father's house, but since the Reformation gradually returning. Nearly five centuries have now passed since the Reformation. The route back has been devious and long, with many a dark valley, as well as many a glorious summit. But steadily, relentlessly, the mighty Spirit of God has been moving on, restoring that which was lost and heading things up toward that great prophetic revelation of the Body of Christ in unity and fullness—even one Body, fully matured *"unto the measure of the stature of the fulness of Christ"* (Eph. 4:13 KJV)!

Beloved, unless we understand this, we will not be able to move on with God and understand the different stages, experiences, and various standards and operations in the Church's history during this dispensation. That is why most Christians have failed to move on with God and to accept His cumulative unfoldings in the restoration of revelation, light, and experience, once lost, but now being restored to the true Church.

If you do not fully see this, or if it seems to differ from your present conception of things, do bear with me. Before I am finished, I believe you will understand; and, if so, it may well transform your life, giving new and vital direction to your prayers and ministry.

THE HEART OF OUR TROUBLE

The human soul is ever lazy toward God, and no one generation has seemed to be able to travel very far on its way back to God and His standard from which the early Church fell. It is true that human error or conceit continually satisfies itself with a part instead of the whole, but the real fact is that men are not willing to pay the full price to come back fully to God's standard, to be *all* the Lord's.

The early Church came forth from the "upper room" fresh in her "first love," baptized with the Holy Spirit, filled with God, possessing both the graces and gifts of the Spirit, and with a 100 percent consecration for God. This was the secret of her power. She was all for God, and God was all for her. This principle will apply in all ages, both individually and collectively. No sacrifice on the altar means no fire. The fire of God never falls on an empty altar. The greater the sacrifice, the more the fire.

When the prodigal gets home, and the Church becomes 100 percent for God again, we will have the same power, the same life—and the same persecution from the world. The reason we have so little persecution now is that the Spirit cannot press the claims of God home on the world through us. When that happens, men must either surrender or fight.

"Jesus Christ is the same yesterday and today and forever" (Heb. 13:8)! God never changes. *We* have changed. We are not waiting for God. God is waiting for us. The Holy Spirit is given; we are still in the dispensation opened on the day of Pentecost. But God can only work when we are willing, yielded, and obedient. We tie God's hands.

The history of the Church has been the same. Each company that has come forth in the line of restoration has run the same course. That is human, fallen nature. It is human failure, not God's. When everything dries up and dies out, we call upon God. This alone makes it possible for God to come. *He must have someplace to put His Spirit, and only empty vessels can be filled.*

When we are filled with our own ways, think ourselves rich and increased in goodness spiritually, God can give us nothing.

"To the hungry soul every bitter thing is sweet" (Prov. 27:7 KJV). The crumbs tasted good to the Syrophoenician woman, but well-fed children despise even dainties. They will throw the food across the table at one another. Like the children of Israel, they despise even "angels' food."

The best preacher in the land cannot preach with liberty when his message is not desired or received. The oil ceases to flow as soon as there are no more empty vessels to be filled. This will often explain why good preachers sometimes have liberty and at other times have no anointing. Criticism will stop the flow of oil through any preacher. Oil will not flow when frozen.

HOW IT ALL BEGAN

The early Church ran well for a season. Everything went down before it. But by the third or fourth century, they had compromised to escape the cross. They sold out to the devil, backslid, and went down into the "Dark Ages." They lost the Holy Spirit anointing, the gifts, the life, the power, the joy—*everything*. The Church became a prodigal, left the Father's house, and went to feeding swine.

The devil found he could not stamp out the early Church by killing them. For every one he killed, two sprang up. Like the children of Israel, *"the more they afflicted them, the more they multiplied and grew"* (Exod. 1:12 KJV). The early Christians vied with one another for a martyr's crown. They exposed themselves purposely, recklessly, for this reward. Someone has said the greatest call that ever came to man is the call to suffer in a noble cause.

Heaven was real to the early Church—far more real than earth. In fact, they seem to have lived only for the next age. That was their longing, their goal, to be delivered from this present evil world. It was the sole relief they looked forward to. This present life, after all, is the true saint's purgatory. It is the sinner's heaven—his only heaven—and that is said beyond words to express! But, glory to God, it is our only hell! We are in the enemy's country, running the gauntlet, with foes lined up on all sides—but we're just passing through.

Without question, it was God's desire to restore the backslidden, prodigal Church at once, when she fell, just as He must have desired at once to restore the human race in the beginning, when they fell. But He could not. Human, fallen nature was too weak.

God also wanted to take the children of Israel right into Canaan from Kadesh-Barnea when He brought them out of Egypt. It was only a short journey, but they frustrated His purpose and desire. "They grieved God and *limited* the Holy One of Israel" (see Ps. 78:41) just as it has ever been. In consequence, they stopped going forward, went to "milling around," and "their carcasses fell in the wilderness" (see Heb. 3:17).

Beloved, whenever we stop going forward, we go to "milling around." When an individual stops going forward for God, he begins to go in a circle, just as a man when lost in a forest ceases to go straight forward but wanders in a circle.

So it was with the early Church. When they ceased to go forward, they started wandering in a circle and became lost in the Dark Ages. The devil had found that he could not destroy them or stop their march by persecuting and killing them; so he removed the cross, offering them titles, positions, honor, salaries, profits of every kind—and they fell for it.

They no longer needed to look to God for their protection and support. They were "like the nations round about them," just as the children of Israel when they rejected God as their King. And it is so with our great church bodies of today. History repeats itself in every movement through human weakness and failure.

THE REFORMATION AND SUBSEQUENT HISTORY

Out of the Dark Ages came the great politico-religious, ecclesiastical, Roman hierarchy, which in time dominated the whole world, both political and religious. And the same condition has developed out of every fallen movement. An illegitimate, hybrid monster has come forth.

This was the condition of the formal church in Martin Luther's time. However, the living seed of the true Church had remained buried in this mass, even through those long, dark centuries. This seed now began to spring up and germinate—the Church within the Church. The prodigal backslider began to come to himself at last and desire to return home. The Church had fed on swine long enough!

Through the labors of such men as Huss, Wycliffe, Luther, Foxe, Wesley, Darby, Muller, Moody, Evan Roberts, Wigglesworth, and a host of others, the prodigal Church has been coming home. But each company that God has been able to bring forth and give a fresh deposit of the Spirit and of the truth once lost, has sooner or later stopped short of the full goal. Although often gaining much ground and experiencing tremendous blessing, each group has ceased to go forward as a body and completely return to the early New Testament standard and realization.

Again and again the Church climbed from the depths of some sectarian stranglehold, with its various stages of formalism and spiritual darkness, only to fall again, within perhaps only a generation, into sometimes an even worse state. Fortunately, each time, some new light and understanding of truth and God's ways was given upon which the next revival company could build. But in it all, it is the failure of man, not God's failure. Each company has only gone so far. It was certainly God's desire to fully restore the early Church to her first estate and love at once, as it is true with every backslider. To think otherwise is to charge God with sin. But the Church would not.

A backslider does not get back to God in a moment. He generally has more or less of a battle to get back, according to the light and experience that he has sinned against. The early Church had great light and experience. If it were too easy to be fully restored, it would be too easy to backslide.

There is a natural law that is similar to this. Faith has been broken down. It is like a tubercular case, where the tissues of the lungs have been destroyed. It is a hard fight back, even under favorable circumstances of rest and climate. To return to the "lowlands" generally means a return of the disease. So it is with the restored backslider. He must keep away from temptation ground and aggressively walk in obedience.

Today we can look back and see the different companies that, in the line of restoration, God has brought out in the Church since the Middle Ages. We can see where they ceased to go forward with God, where they began to mill around in a circle, and where their carcasses fell in the wilderness as a body—Lutherans, Anglicans, Congregationalists, Methodists, Salvation Army, and so forth. They ceased to be a forward company.

Whenever we cease to go forward and keep on the offensive for God, we stop and die as a people. *In fact, a movement is no longer a movement when it stops moving—be it the Holiness movement, the Pentecostal movement, or any other movement.* It may continue to increase both in numbers and in wealth, but that is not necessarily a sign of life and power with God. All anti-Christian movements can show that kind of growth. No movement has ever recovered itself, as a body, when it has once gone on the skids.

GOD'S MOVEMENT

We do not have to leave movements. *We simply move on with God!* As long as a movement moves, we move with it. The different movements in the history of the Church, although part of His true restoration, are only incidental with God. God has one great movement we should all belong to, and that has *never* ceased moving. It is God's move through the ages to redeem a fallen, lost world and carry that great blood-washed assembly on to His eternal purpose. It began when the Lamb was slain before the foundation of the world and will end when the last saint gets safely home to glory.

We must work for the Kingdom of God as a whole, not for some pet individual party, organization, or movement. That has been the curse and cause of hindrance to our going on with God to full restoration in all generations. We have worshiped certain doctrines, party standards, partial experiences, and blessings, all fine as far as they go, but abnormal in themselves and *only a part of the whole.*

Most of these have been unbalanced, exaggerated misstatements of truth at best. In the end, they have generally brought bondage in place of blessing. They have broken fellowship, divided the children of God, and put the Church in bondage to men and their ideas, standards, understandings, and opinions.

We must keep moving! *The clearest light on truth and experience has not yet come.* We will wait for the full restoration of the "pattern shown in the mount," that of the early New Testament Apostolic Church as a whole.

The great mistake has been to stop with sectarian, partial, abnormal revelations. We must keep our eyes on God, not on a party. Keep free from party spirit. That is respect of persons. Seek only God and His plan *as a whole,* His Church as a *whole.*

Every company, in time, repeats the experience of the early Church. They compromise to escape the cross and accept positions, salaries, titles, and ecclesiastical power. An ecclesiastical hierarchy arises, just as it did in the early Church during the second and third centuries.

The backslidden Church is still in an abnormal condition. It will continue to be so until it becomes fully restored to the first standard of apostolic Christianity from which it fell. No experience or revelation in the line of gradual restoration has been perfect in itself. All is abnormal, both in understanding and experience, until the perfect *whole* is realized and restored.

We need a readjustment of all our doctrines to the full, clear light of God in the Word. All past experiences must be examined and redefined in the light of the perfect whole.

Someone has said that every reformation is at its best and highest tide when it first comes forth. This would seem to be so, but at the same time the true Church is ever moving on to maturity. I speak of the Church within the Church, the kernel in the shell, not the surrounding movement. Just as the individual believer who goes on with God gradually matures, so the Church within the Church is maturing toward the end of the age when she will be a full-grown Church. The goal is not just the standard lost by the early Church but that toward which they themselves were pressing: "*fully matured man,*" even "*the measure of the stature of the fulness of Christ*" (Eph. 4:13 KJV).

APOSTASY AND RECOVERY

As with Israel in the Exodus, the "mixed multitude," the exterior shell of every movement with which it loads itself and in which it later becomes buried, falls to lusting for "flesh." One can usually judge the progress of this process by the things the movement comes to demand. Instead of delight in the pure Word, prayer and worship, a love for souls and zeal for good works, there comes entertainment, programs, musicals, sensationalism, and oratory. These things have no place in essential, true Christianity, but are professionalism—flesh! Oh, God, deliver us from fleshly substitutes for the Spirit.

Most meetings can only be kept alive now by continuous entertainment, professional evangelism, and a strong social spirit. And this is all too true in Pentecostal, Holiness, and interdenominational circles, as well as in the older denominations. Where is the *Life itself* to draw the people and bring God to them as in the beginning? This is not New Testament. It is abnormal, grieving and limiting the Holy One in Israel in our midst.

Each movement seems to run its course faster than the one before it. Like the Niagara River, it flows downward more swiftly as it approaches the falls, the end of time. These are the last days of apostasy.

The fight gets harder as we get higher up in our restoration from the early Church's fall. When Adam fell, the satanic powers intervened between the fallen race and God. God removed the seat of His presence with man from earth to Heaven. So when the early Church fell, she again lost the image of God that had, in a sense, been restored in New Testament days when the body of believers became the Temple of the Holy Spirit. In a higher sense than Adam had known, the *"spiritual wickedness in high places"* (Eph. 6:12 KJV) intervened between the Church and God again. Now, the prodigal Church, coming up out of the Dark Ages, has had to fight her way back through these evil powers. Each movement, as we go higher toward full restoration, has to meet a higher order of these wicked, spiritual powers and intelligences and hence must fight harder.

Each step forward requires of necessity a deeper preparation and greater spiritual equipment for a greater measure of restoration.

It was never God's decree that the experience of the Church should be so long and drawn out in recovering the normal standard and going on to fullness. But we have ever sought to call our present abnormal understanding and experience normal. We must see that all has been abnormal since the early Church's fall. *Experiences, understanding—everything has been partial, unbalanced, and abnormal. Nothing has been perfectly understood, and all the different truths and experiences have only been parts of the whole.*

We have not understood these truths and experiences, just as no machine is properly and clearly understood in detail except as we understand the whole. We have been recovering the whole in parts, without seeing the whole—thus we so often distort and overemphasize the truth or experience that our particular movement has recovered. I trust that you grasp this, for it is very important.

The New Testament Church in the Book of Acts entered normally into the fullness of the Spirit immediately at its inception, as for instance at Cornelius' household in the tenth chapter of Acts. The different phases of our salvation were all viewed as just so many parts of one glorious, normal whole. But all the various movements in the restoration, since the early reformers, have ceased in their turn to go forward to full realization. They have established their party standard of a partial, abnormal revelation, putting a part for the whole. Then, in human conceit, they have each contended they had it all.

This is sectarianism, and it is like a lot of dams holding back God's people from flowing on toward the vast ocean of God's fullness. God cares little for these partial standards of men—their names, sects or parties, slogans or standards. All is only partial, distorted *light that finally becomes the enemy of the real truth as the Lord marches on to glory.*

Each oncoming wave of the sea toward high tide must fight its way through the last receding one. So it is with the different movements toward a final restoration of the Church. The immediately receding one especially hates and opposes the next oncoming one. What fools the devil has made of us! Oh, that we might see it! However real and good, as far as they have gone, these past revivals and movements are each but faltering, uncertain steps toward the final goal.

LET'S GO ON!

God has but one Church, whether in Heaven where most of it is, or here on earth. And there is yet very much land to be possessed before we realize the divine purpose to which we are destined. We must recognize the whole Body of Christ. In our human conceits, we fail to recognize God when we meet Him. Those who dare to go further with God toward the full restoration are denounced and opposed by others as if they were of the devil. And this was not just true of Luther and the Catholic Church; it was also true of Wesley and the Anglican Church, of Booth and the Methodist Church, etc. And it is still true today. But, beloved, we must face it: The backslider has not yet been fully restored; the prodigal has not yet reached home. We must keep moving on!

Elijah's rain came out of a clear sky, without even the sign of a cloud to begin with—the result of faith alone. So the Pentecostal outpouring came in 1906. And this has been the case with every revival. Revival is the property of *faith*, not sight. There is nothing for sight to see in fallen nature but hopelessness. Revival and restoration must come from God, out of a clear sky. We are earthly and fleshly, but God is Spirit. God's Word is "spirit and life," and faith in that Word brings the living God on the scene regardless of circumstances or outward prospects.

Will God visit His people again? Why not? As surely as He has done it in the past, He will do it again. God's skies are full of Pentecosts. He only waits for us to claim them. Do we not need one? Then we can have it, when we are willing to pay the price of obedient faith.

The Church is not fully restored. No past group, after it has waned, has had the faith and vision to move God to visit them again. If they had, they would not be strewn along the way as more or less dead movements, their bones bleaching in the wilderness. None of them had future faith. They stopped short of the goal. None of them went clear through. "They limited the Holy One of Israel," just as we do today. They would not pay the price. That was the trouble. *But worse than this, they justified themselves in their abnormal standards and opposed and condemned others who would go further.* And still they do so.

The sin of the Jewish high church in Jesus' time was the same. They refused to go further themselves, and set themselves in their backslidden condition to oppose all who wished to go forward. That spelled their doom, and it will bring down the judgments of God on any denomination, movement, or group who follow in their steps.

But a Gideon's band is forming again today. Faith is rising. Another visitation from God is coming. It is only the Gideon's band that can ever bring or receive it—only a praying, consecrated, pilgrim band. They of the "mixed multitude" will not be in it, for they are too many and too fleshly. "**Upon the flesh of man,**" the Lord said of the precious anointing oil in the tabernacle, "*it shall not be poured*" (see Exod. 30:32). God usually has to work with the little things, the weak things—the small, consecrated groups.

"*I will pour water upon him that is thirsty, and floods upon the dry ground*" (Isa. 44:3 KJV). Dryness is a condition that invites rain. At such times men cry for rain. It is a cause for encouragement when we thirst for God. Blessed are they that hunger and thirst, for they shall be filled (see Matt. 5:6). It was after an awful drought that Elijah's rain came. The rain is ready,

Beloved—*when we want it, and when we are in a condition to receive it.*

We must have the spirit of Caleb and Joshua, a different spirit from the multitude. They "followed the Lord wholly" (see Josh. 14:8,14); therefore, they entered Canaan with the next company to go forward. They had their portion in it, while the old crowd died in the wilderness. No movement, as a movement, has ever gone all the way through to full restoration for the reasons we have explained. *Hence, we must never become the property of, or limit ourselves to, a party or a movement. Worship only God.* Join God in *His* great movement. Keep moving!

THE END IS NEARING

We are rounding the corner toward complete recovery. God is again pressing His full claims upon His Church and upon the world in this, the end of the age. But the devil is also pressing his claims with great vigor. Whom will we serve? It is either 100 percent for God or for the devil—there is no neutral ground. We are nearing the awesome climax of this deadly war between the Kingdom of God and the kingdom of satan. Each must be at his best for his side.

A normal Church is always 100 percent for God. There can be no flirting with the enemy. The Church has no other business than to carry the gospel to the world and press the claims of God upon His own. All its energies and resources should be used with that one object in view—*"Then shall the end come"* (Matt. 24:14 KJV). God waits for this.

Nothing but the zeal and the 100 percent consecration of the early Church, both in laboring for the salvation of the nations and in building up the one true worldwide Church, will or can satisfy God. He will accept no substitutes or compromise with our ideas and fleshly plans. There simply must be an utter abandonment to His full will and His great eternal purpose in His own children! Nothing short of this can clear our conscience and responsibility in the day of judgment. We could have done this long ago—if we had willed to do so—but we have not. Oh, let us not delay longer, but at once go right up and storm the enemy's citadels, vowing never to withdraw our sword until Jesus comes and *the whole land is ours!*

We are rapidly approaching the last days. I am convinced that God is going to put the Church through the fire to destroy the dross. Judgment begins at the house of God. And, believe me, nothing but 100 percent reality will remain! A theoretical salvation will not do.

We are reaching the culmination of this age, and nothing but a practical application of the gospel can hope to survive. All else will be destroyed by the fires of worldwide persecution. God can only defend obedience to His Word. Never fear—He is going to have a Church without spot or wrinkle. But do you and I want to have a part in it? A sectarian, competitive, selfish, self-seeking Church cannot survive. The Church must return to the spirit of the early Church in the Book of Acts. She must yield to God and press into His "present truth" for this last hour—or perish in the fires of persecution and in her own blood. *Our God is a consuming fire!*

Let us go on!

ENDNOTES

FRANK BARTLEMAN'S
AZUSA STREET

1. Robert Anderson, *Visions of the Disinherited* (Peabody, MA: Hendrickson Publishers, 1979), 103.

2. http://www.sendrevival.com/history/azusa_street/azusa_street_bartleman_vinson_3_leaders.htm

3. Frank Bartleman, *Azusa Street*.

4. Ibid.

APPENDIX

THE APOSTOLIC FAITH NEWSPAPERS

THE APOSTOLIC FAITH

"Earnestly contend for the faith which was once delivered unto the saints."—Jude 3.

Vol. 1, No. 1 | Los Angeles, Cal., September, 1906 | Subscription Free

Pentecost Has Come

Los Angeles Being Visited by a Revival of Bible Salvation and Pentecost as Recorded in the Book of Acts

The power of God now has this city agitated as never before. Pentecost has surely come and with it the Bible evidences are following, many being converted and sanctified and filled with the Holy Ghost, speaking in tongues as they did on the day of Pentecost. The scenes that are daily enacted in the building on Azusa street and at Missions and churches in other parts of the city are beyond description, and the real revival is only started, as God has been working with His children mostly, getting them through to Pentecost, and laying the foundation for a mighty wave of salvation among the unconverted.

The meetings are held in an old Methodist church that had been converted in part into a tenement house, leaving a large, unplastered, barn-like room on the ground floor. Here about a dozen congregated each day, holding meetings on Bonnie Brae in the evening. The writer attended a few of these meetings and being so different from anything he had seen and not hearing any speaking in tongues, he branded the teaching as third-blessing heresy and thought that settled it. It is needless to say the writer was compelled to do a great deal of apologizing and humbling himself to get right with God.

In a short time God began to manifest His power and soon the building could not contain the people. Now the meetings continue [illegible] into the night and the fire is kindling all over the city and surrounding towns. Proud, well-dressed preachers come in to "investigate." Soon their high looks are replaced with wonder, then conviction comes, and very often you will find them in a short time wallowing on the dirty floor, asking God to forgive them and make them as little children.

It would be impossible to state how many have been converted, sanctified and filled with the Holy Ghost. They have been and are daily going out to all points of the compass to spread this wonderful gospel.

BRO. SEYMOUR'S CALL.

Bro. W. J. Seymour has the following to say in regard to his call to this city:

"It was the divine call that brought me from Houston, Texas, to Los Angeles. The Lord put it in the heart of one of the saints in Los Angeles to write to me that she felt the Lord would have me come over here and do a work, and I came, for I felt it was the leading of the Lord. The Lord sent the means, and I came to take charge of a mission on Santa Fe Street, and one night they locked the door against me, and afterwards got Bro. Roberts, the president of the Holiness Association, to come down and settle the doctrine of the Baptism with the Holy Ghost, that it was simply sanctification. He came down and a good many holiness preachers with him, and they stated that sanctification was the baptism with the Holy Ghost. But yet they did not have the evidence of the second chapter of Acts, for when the disciples were all filled with the Holy Ghost, they spoke in tongues as the Spirit gave utterance. After the president heard me speak of what the true baptism of the Holy Ghost was, he said he wanted it too, and told me when I had received it to let him know. So I received it and let him know. The beginning of the Pentecost started in a cottage prayer meeting at 214 Bonnie Brae."

LETTER FROM BRO. PARHAM.

Bro. Chas. Parham, who is God's leader in the Apostolic Faith Movement, writes from Tonganoxie, Kansas, that he expects (D. V.) to be in Los Angeles Sept. 15. Hearing that Pentecost had come to Los Angeles, he writes, "I rejoice in God over you all, my children, though I have never seen you; but since you know the Holy Spirit's power, we are baptised by one Spirit into one body. Keep together in unity till I come, then in a grand meeting let all prepare for the outside fields I desire, unless God directs to the contrary, to meet and see all who have the full Gospel when I come."

THE OLD-TIME PENTECOST.

This work began about five years ago last January, when a company of people under the leadership of Chas. Parham, who were studying God's word, tarried for Pentecost in Topeka, Kan. After searching through the country everywhere, they had been unable to find any Christians that had the true Pentecostal power. So they laid aside all commentaries and notes and waited on the Lord, studying His word, and what they did not understand they got down before the bench and asked God to have wrought out in their hearts by the Holy Ghost. They had a prayer tower from which prayers were ascending night and day to God. After three months, a sister who had been teaching sanctification for the baptism with the Holy Ghost, one who had a sweet, loving experience and all the carnality taken out of her heart, felt the Lord lead her to have hands laid on her to receive the Pentecost. So when they prayed, the Holy Ghost came in [illegible] and she commenced speaking in an unknown tongue. This made all the Bible school hungry, and three nights afterward, twelve students received the Holy Ghost, and prophesied, and cloven tongues could be seen upon their heads. They then had an experience that measured up with the second chapter of Acts, and could understand the first chapter of Ephesians.

Now after five years something like 13,000 people have received this gospel. It is spreading everywhere, until churches who do not believe backslide and lose the experience they have. Those who are older in this movement are stronger, and greater signs and wonders are following them.

The meetings in Los Angeles started in a cottage meeting, and the Pentecost fell there three nights. The people had nothing to do but wait on the Lord and praise Him, and they commenced speaking in tongues, as they did at Pentecost, and the Spirit sang songs through them.

The meeting was then transferred to Azusa Street, and since then multitudes have been coming. The meetings begin about ten o'clock in the morning and can hardly stop before ten or twelve at night, and sometimes two or three in the morning, because so many are seking, and some are slain under the power of God. People are seeking three times a day at the altar and row after row of seats have to be emptied and filled with seekers. We cannot tell how many people have been saved, and sanctified, and baptised with the Holy Ghost, and healed of all manner of sicknesses. Many are speaking in new tongues, and some are on their way to the foreign fields, with the gift of the language. We are going on to get more of the power of God.

Many have laid aside their glasses and had their eye sight perfectly restored. The deaf have had their hearing restored.

A man was healed of asthma of twenty years standing. Many have been healed of heart trouble and lung trouble.

Many are saying that God has given the message that He is going to shake Los Angeles with an earthquake. First, there will be a revival to give all an opportunity to be saved. The revival is now in progress.

The Lord has given the gift of writing in unknown languages, also the gift of playing on instruments.

A little girl who walked with crutches and had tuberculosis of the bones, as the doctors declared, was healed and dropped her crutches and began to skip about the yard.

All over this city, God has been setting homes on fire and coming down and melting and saving and sanctifying and baptizing with the Holy Ghost.

Many churches have been praying for Pentecost, and Pentecost has come. The question is now, will they accept it? God has answered in a way they did not look for. He came in a humble way as of old, born in a manger.

The secular papers have been stirred and published reports against the movement, but it has only resulted in drawing hungry souls who understand that the devil would not fight a thing unless God was in it. So they have come and found it was indeed the power of God.

Jesus was too large for the synagogues. He preached outside because there was not room for him inside. This Pentecostal movement is too large to be confined in any denomination or sect. It works outside, drawing all together in one bond of love, one church, one body of Christ.

A Mohammedan, a Soudanese by birth, a man who is an interpreter and speaks sixteen languages, came into the meetings at Azusa Street and the Lord gave him messages which none but himself could understand. He identified, interpreted and wrote a number of the languages.

A brother who had been a spiritualist medium and who was so possessed with demons that he had no rest, and was on the point of committing suicide, was instantly delivered of demon power. He then sought God for the pardon of his sins and sanctification, and is now filled with a different spirit.

A little girl about twelve years of age was sanctified in a Sunday afternoon children's meeting, and in the evening meeting she was baptized with the Holy Ghost. When she was filled those standing near remarked, "Who can doubt such a clear case of God's power."

In about an hour and a half, a young man was converted, sanctified, and baptized with the Holy Ghost, and spoke with tongues. He was also healed from consumption, so that when he visited the doctor he pronounced his lungs sound. He has received many tongues, also the gift of prophecy, and writing in a number of foreign languages, and has a call to a foreign field.

Many are the prophesies spoken in unknown tongues and many the visions that God is giving concerning His soon coming. The heathen must first receive the gospel. One prophecy given in an unknown tongue was interpreted, "The time is short, and I am going to send out a large number in the Spirit of God to preach the full gospel in the power of the Spirit."

About 150 people in Los Angeles, more than on the day of Pentecost, have received the gift of the Holy Ghost and the Bible evidence, the gift of tongues, and many have been saved and sanctified, nobody knows how many. People are seeking at the altar three times a day and it is hard to close at night on account of seekers and those who are under the power of God.

When Pentecostal lines are struck, Pentecostal giving commences. Hundreds of dollars have been laid down for the sending of missionairies and thousands will be laid down. No collections are taken for rent, no begging for money. No man's silver or gold is coveted. The silver and the gold are His own to carry on His own work. He can also publish His own papers without asking for money or subscription price.

In the meetings, it is noticeable that while some in the rear are opposing and arguing, others are at the altar falling down under the power of God and feasting on the good things of God. The two spirits are always manifest, but no opposition can kill, no power in earth or hell can stop God's work, while He has consecrated instruments through which to work.

Many have received the gift of singing as well as speaking in the inspiration of the Spirit. The Lord is giving new voices, he translates old songs into new tongues, he gives the music that is being sung by the angels and has a heavenly choir all singing the same heavenly song in harmony. It is beautiful music, no instruments are needed in the meetings.

A Nazarene brother who received the baptism with the Holy Ghost in his own home in family worship, in trying to tell about it, said, "It was a baptism of love. Such abounding love! Such compassion seemed to almost kill me with its sweetness! People do not know what they are doing when they stand out against it. The devil never gave me a sweet thing, he was always trying to get me to censuring people. This baptism fills us with divine love."

The gift of languages is given with the commission, "Go ye into all the world and preach the Gospel to every creature." The Lord has given languages to the unlearned Greek, Latin, Hebrew, French, German, Italian, Chinese, Japanese, Zulu and languages of Africa, Hindu and Bengali and dialects of India, Chippewa and other languages of the Indians, Esquimaux, the deaf mute language and, in fact the Holy Ghost speaks all the languages of the world through His children.

A minister says that God showed him twenty years ago that the divine plan for missionaries was that they might receive the gift of tongues either before going to the foreign field or on the way. It should be a sign to the heathen that the message is of God. The gift of tongues can only be used as the Spirit gives utterance. It cannot be learned like the native tongue, but the Lord takes control of the organs of speech at will. It is emphatically God's message.

During a meeting at Monrovia, a preacher who at one time had been used of God in the Pentecost Bands under Vivian Dake, but had cooled off, was reclaimed, sanctified and filled with the Holy Ghost. When the power of God came on him his eight-year-old son was kneeling behind him. The boy had previously sought and obtained a clear heart, and when the Holy Ghost fell on his father, He also fell on him and his hands began to shake and he sang in tongues.

Bro. Campbell, a Nazarene brother, 83 years of age, who has been for 53 years serving the Lord, received the baptism with the Holy Ghost and gift of tongues in his own home. His son, who was a physician, was called and came to see if he was sick, but found him only happy in the Lord. Not only old men and old women, but boys and girls, are receiving their Pentecost. Viola Price, a little orphan colored girl eight years of age, has received the gift of tongues.

Mrs. Lucy F. Farrow, God's anointed handmaid, who came some four months ago from Houston, Texas, to Los Angeles, bringing the full Gospel, and whom God has greatly used as she laid her hands on many who have received the Pentecost and the gift of tongues, has now returned to Houston, en route to Norfolk, Va. This is her old home which she left as a girl, being sold into slavery in the south. The Lord, she feels, is now calling her back. Sister Farrow, Bro. W. J. Seymour and Bro. J. A. Warren were the three that the Lord sent from Houston as messengers of the full gospel.

THE APOSTOLIC FAITH

"Earnestly contend for the faith which was once delivered unto the saints."—Jude 3.

Vol. 1, No. 2 | Los Angeles, Cal., October, 1906 | Subscription Free

The Pentecostal Baptism Restored

The Promised Latter Rain Now Being Poured Out on God's Humble People.

All along the ages men have been preaching a partial Gospel. A part of the Gospel remained when the world went into the dark ages. God has from time to time raised up men to bring back the truth to the church. He raised up Luther to bring back to the world the doctrine of justification by faith. He raised up another reformer in John Wesley to establish Bible holiness in the church. Then he raised up Dr. Cullis who brought back to the world the wonderful doctrine of divine healing. Now He is bringing back the Pentecostal Baptism to the church.

God laid His hand on a little crippled boy seven years of age and healed him of disease and made him whole except his ankles. He walked on the sides of his ankles. Then, when he was fourteen years of age, he had been sent to college and God had called him to preach. One day as he was sitting reading his Bible, a man came for him to go and hold a meeting. He began to say to the Lord: "Father, if I go to that place, it will be necessary for me to walk here and yonder. just put strength into these ankle joints of mine." And immediately he was made whole and leaped and praised God, like the man at the beautiful gate. He has since been in evangelistic work over the United States, seeing multitudes saved, sanctified and healed.

Five years ago, God put it into this man's heart (Bro. Charles Parham) to go over to Topeka, Kansas, to educate missionaries to carry the Gospel. It was a faith school and the Bible was the only text book. The students had gathered there without tuition or board, God sending in the means to carry on the work. Most of the students had been religious workers and said they had received the baptism with the Holy Ghost a number of years ago. Bro. Parham became convinced that there was no religious school that tallied up with the second chapter of Acts. Just before the first of January, 1901, the Bible School began to study the word on the Baptism with the Holy Ghost to discover the Bible evidence of this baptism that they might obtain it.

The students kept up continual prayer in the praying tower. A company would go up and stay three hours, and then another company would go up and wait on God, praying that all the promises of the Word might be wrought out in their lives.

On New Year's night, Miss Agnes N. Ozman, one who had had for years "the anointing that abideth," which she mistook for the baptism, was convinced of the need of a personal Pentecost. A few minutes before midnight, she desired hands laid on her that she might receive the gift of the Holy Ghost. During prayer and invocation of hands, she was filled with the Holy Ghost and spake with other tongues as the Spirit gave utterance.

This made all hungry. Scarcely eating or sleeping, the school with one accord waited on God. On the 3rd of January, 1901, Bro. Parham being absent holding a meeting at the time, while they all waited on God to send the baptism of the Spirit, suddenly twelve students were filled with the Holy Ghost and began to speak with other tongues, and when Bro. Parham returned and opened the door of the room where they were gathered, a wonderful sight met his eyes. The whole room was filled with a white sheen of light that could not be described, and twelve of the students were on their feet talking in different languages.

He said they seemed to pay no attention at all to him, and he knelt in one corner and said: "O, God, what does this mean?" The Lord said: "Are you able to stand for the experience in the face of persecution and howling mobs?" He said: "Yes, Lord, if you will give me the experience, for the laborer must first be partaker of the fruits." Instantly the Lord took his vocal organs, and he was preaching the Word in another language.

This man has preached in different languages over the United States, and men and women of that nationality have come to the altar and sought God. He was surely raised up of God to be an apostle of the doctrine of Pentecost.

This Pentecostal Gospel has been spreading ever since, but on the Pacific coast it has burst out in great power and is being carried from here over the world. We are expecting Bro. Parham to visit Los Angeles in a few days and for a mightier tide of salvation to break out.

FIRE STILL FALLING.

The waves of Pentecostal salvation are still rolling in at Azusa Street Mission. From morning till late at night the meetings continue with about three altar services a day. We have made no record of souls saved, sanctified and baptized with the Holy Ghost, but a brother said last week he counted about fifty in all that had been baptized with the Holy Ghost during the week. Then at Eighth street and Maple avenue, the People's church, Monrovia, Whittier, Hermon, Sawtelle, Pasadena, Elysian Heights, and other places the work is going on and souls are coming through amid great rejoicing.

Four of the Holiness preachers have received the baptism with the Holy Ghost. One of them, Bro. Wm. Pendleton, with his congregation, being turned out of the church, are holding meetings at Eighth street and Maple avenue. There is a heavenly atmosphere there. The altar is filled with seekers, people are slain under the power of God, and rising in a life baptized with the Holy Ghost.

The fire is spreading. People are writing from different points to know about this Pentecost, and are beginning to wait on God for their Pentecost. He is no respecter of persons and places. We expect to see a wave of salvation go over this world. While this work has been going on for five years, it has burst out in great power on this coast. There is power in the full Gospel. Nothing can quench it.

Missionaries for the foreign fields, equipped with several languages, are now on their way and others are only waiting for the way to open and for the Lord to say: "Go." We are on our faces before God. Let a volume of prayer go up from all the Lord's people. Awake! Awake! There is but time to dress and be ready, for the cry will soon go forth. "The Bridegroom cometh."

Eight missionaries have started to the foreign field since this movement began in Los Angeles a few months ago. About thirty workers have gone out into the field.

The brother at Elysian Heights who received his eyesight after being blind for a year and a half, is a living witness of the power of God. Since that he has been sanctified and anointed with the Holy Ghost and his wife has been saved.

In the City of Oakland, during the few weeks that the band from Los Angeles were there, Brother and Sister Evans and Sister Florence Crawford, sixty-five souls received the baptism with the Holy Ghost, thirty were sanctified and nineteen converted.

A man who was twice in the insane asylum, an infidel that had been going from place to place denying the name of Jesus Christ, is now saved, sanctified and baptized with the Holy Ghost, and working to win others.

Sometimes, among officers of the law, we find a keen judgment in regard to genuine or spurious religion. In Pasadena, where the Lord was working in power some months ago, the chief of police made the remark: "I would not give much for a meeting that did not have a shout in it."

Sister Lizzie Frazer of Colorado Springs, Colorado, was one of those who received the gift of tongues when the Palestine Missionary band passed through there. She writes that she expects to go to India with a band of missionaries next month. The Lord has given her a wonderful equipment.

Mrs. J. Kring was healed of cancer of the lungs on August 8, after the doctor had given her up. One lung was entirely closed up. When she was prayed for, the Lord immediately touched her body and healed her. She shouted for an hour with strong lungs, and is the happiest woman you ever saw.

A mother brought her son to the Mission to be healed of epileptic fits. He is about twenty-one years old and has been suffering for years, like the boy that was brought to Jesus whom the devil had often caused to fall into the fire and into the water. The boy was so wrecked in mind and body that he was in a semi-conscious condition. Bro. Batman, who is called to Africa, prayed for him, asking the Lord to cast the demon power out of him and give complete healing. The boy raised up from the floor and witnessed that the work was done and went home rejoicing.

A brother living in the east had been down sick for quite a while and sent a handkerchief to be blessed as in Bible times. His sister brought it to the Mission, praying for the Lord to show her to whom she was to give it, and the Lord showed her to give it to Sister Sallie Trainor. She immediately took it upstairs and as she knelt before the Lord, the Spirit came upon her in great power and she prayed in tongues, and kissed the handkerchief three times, as the Spirit seemed to lead her. It was sent with a prayer and the brother was immediately healed.

A PORTUGUESE MINISTER RECEIVES HIS PENTECOST.

Rev. Adolph Rosa, a Portuguese brother from Cape Verde Islands, was baptized with the Holy Ghost in Oakland and is now in Los Angeles preaching the full Gospel. He was a Catholic and his father had expected to have him educated as a Catholic priest; but God had His hand upon him. He came to America, was converted from the power of Romanism and captivity about six years ago in a Portuguese Methodist church in New Bedford, Mass., and entered the ministry of the Methodist church as a missionary to the Portuguese in the state of California. He was sanctified about four years ago, and is now conducting Pentecostal meetings in the People's church in Los Angeles.

Bro. Rosa's Testimony.

When Rev. Evans and his wife and Sister Florence Crawford went to the city of Oakland preaching the full Gospel, I went the first night, not to criticize but to investigate. Many preachers were there to criticize, but when I stepped in, I felt the power of God and could not say that it was the work of the devil, as most of the preachers declared, for I was practically convinced that it was the work of the Holy Ghost. I went home and began to study my Bible, and went to God in prayer to reveal to me if these people were really the people of God. He revealed to me in the attitude of my supplication, that they were preaching exactly what the disciples of old preached. I was convinced that every minister of the Gospel should receive the same baptism with the Holy Ghost and fire that the disciples received on the day of Pentecost, before they are prepared to preach the Gospel. I was teaching that when we receive sanctification, we receive the Holy Ghost, as most of the preachers are teaching. But as I went to my Bible with the spirit of prayer, God revealed to me that the disciples were justified before Christ ascended; but they never were baptized with the Holy Ghost until the day of Pentecost.

The second day that I went to the meeting, the Lord put a real hunger in my soul to go forward, but I was too proud as a minister of the Gospel to humble myself in a lowly mission and let ladies pray over me for the gift of the Holy Ghost, and I had in my mind what people would think of me. But the third day, as I arose to testify in the audience, the only words I could say were: "What does God think of me?" Then I could only weep for some minutes and the power of God came upon me until I dropped to the floor. I was under the power of God for about an hour and a half, and it was there that all pride, and self, and conceit disappeared, and I was really dead to the world, for I had Christ within in His fullness. I was baptized with the Holy Ghost and spoke in a new tongue.

I praise God for the light, and now I am walking in it. The desire of my heart is to see every man and woman that preaches the Gospel of Christ, baptized with the Holy Ghost, for without the Holy Ghost it is almost impossible for us to convince the world of sin, of righteousness, and the judgment.

GET INTO THE CORNFIELD.

"It is an awful hard thing to get a holiness preacher that has been indoctrinated for years to see that he has not received his Pentecost. I have been preaching for twenty years and never preached anything but a full salvation. To get a fellow that has been preaching twenty years to see that he has not received the baptism, when he has been preaching all the time that he had it, and then to get him to turn seeker, is a hard job. I tell you it means for him to get pretty near the end of himself.

"The time has come, in the full blaze of Pentecost, that if you do not walk in the light, you will become a dry chip. I bless God, I humbled myself. On the 10th day of July the Lord gave me the evidence of the Pentecost. It took me three weeks, searching the Word, from Genesis to Revelations to see that these things were so. Any fellow that will get down on his knees and pray through and read through, will find that the Holy Ghost only falls on a clean temple. You must give over and let God have His way.

"So many folks remind me of the hog that was trying to get into a big cornfield. There was a big, hollow, crooked log in the fence, laid in such a way that both ends of the log were on the same side of the fence. The hog would go into one end of the log, expecting that he would get into the cornfield. He would go in and come out, and look all around to see how it was that he was not in the cornfield. There are a lot of folks today just in that place. They crawl through a hollow log of experience and never get anything. Bless God, I would hunt the way. Jesus said: 'I am the way.' Get into the cornfield. Hunt for the wicket gate and you will get in. Hallelujah! I am in the cornfield."

The above is the testimony of Bro. Hill, a Nazarene preacher. He and his wife have both received their personal Pentecost and Bible evidence.

TESTIMONIES OF OUTGOING MISSIONARIES.

A company of three missionaries left Los Angeles September 15, en route for the west coast of Africa. Sister Hutchins has been preaching the Gospel in the power of the Spirit. She has received the baptism with the Holy Ghost and the gift of the Uganda language, the language of the people to whom she is sent. A brother who has been in that country understands and has interpreted the language she speaks. Her husband is with her and her niece, who also has been given the African language.

Sister Hutchins' Testimony.

I was justified on the 4th of July, 1901, and at that time, I felt that the Lord wanted me in Africa, but I was not then at all willing to go. But on the 28th of July, 1903, the Lord sanctified me. Before He sanctified me, He asked me if I would go to Africa. I promised Him I would. From that time on, I have felt the call to Africa, and have been willing to go at any moment, but not knowing just when the Lord would have me leave.

On the sixth of last month, while out in my back yard one afternoon, I heard a voice speaking to me these words: "On the 15th day of September, take your husband and baby and start out for Africa." And I looked around and about me to see if there was not someone speaking to me, but I did not see anyone, and I soon recognized that it was the voice of God. I looked up into the heavens and said: "Lord, I will obey." Since then I have had many tests and temptations from the devil. He has at times told me that I would not even live to see the 15th of September, but I never once doubted God. I knew that He was able to bring everything to pass that He told me to do.

After hearing the voice telling me to leave Los Angeles on the 15th, I went to one of my neighbors and testified to her that the Lord had told me to leave for Africa on the 15th of September. She looked at me with a smile. I asked her what she was smiling about. She said: "Because you have not got street car fare to go to Azusa Street Mission tonight, and talking about going to Africa." But I told her I was trusting in a God that could bring all things to pass that He wanted us to do. He has really supplied all my needs in every way, for the work where He has called me.

I want to testify also about my husband. He was a backslider, and how the devil did test me, saying: "You are going out to cast the devil out of others, and going to take a devil with you." My husband was not saved, but I held on to God and said: "Lord, I will obey."

I continued to testify and to make preparations to leave on the 15th. The Lord reclaimed my husband and sanctified him wholly and put the glory and shout in him. So now it is my time to laugh. The devil has oppressed and mocked me; but praise the Lord, now I can mock him. Glory to God!

It is now ten minutes to four o'clock in the afternoon on the 15th day of September. I am all ready and down to the Mission with my ticket and everything prepared, waiting to have hands laid on and the prayers of the saints, and expect to leave at eight o'clock from the Santa Fe station en route for Africa. We expect to go to Mt. Coffee, Monrovia, Liberia.

Feeling the need of a real companion in the Gospel that was out and out for God, I prayed to God that He might give me one to go with me. I had my eyes upon one that I wanted to go, but in prayer and humility before God, I found out it was not the one the Lord wanted to go. So I said: "Anyone, Lord, that you would have to go will be pleasing to me." And, to my surprise, He gave me my niece—a girl that I had raised from a child. Now she is nineteen years of age, is saved, sanctified and baptized with the Holy Ghost, and is going with me out into the work of the Lord. So instead of giving me one companion, He gave me two—my niece and my husband.

Our first stop will be Chattanooga, Tenn., Harge Row. I want the prayers of the saints that I may stay humble.

Mrs. J. W. Hutchins.

Address Mt. Coffee, Monrovia, Liberia, Africa.

A Girl's Consecration for Africa.

I am saved, sanctified and baptized with the Holy Ghost and have the Bible evidence. The Lord showed me that the language I spoke was the language of Africa. My aunt who has been the same as a mother to me, was going to Africa. I asked the Lord if He wanted me to go, to open up a way for me, and the next morning He opened the way for me. I did not have the means and He gave me the fare and supplied all my needs. I am willing to trust Him through to Africa. I know the Lord wants me to go there. I want to testify to those people and teach the children about the blessed Lord, and to work for the Lord. I am willing to forsake all my loved ones for His sake. I want the saints to pray for me for I am young in the Lord.

Leila McKinney.

THE APOSTOLIC FAITH

"Earnestly contend for the faith which was once delivered unto the saints."—Jude 3.

Vol. 1, No. 3 | Los Angeles, Cal., November, 1906 | Subscription Free

Bible Pentecost

Gracious Pentecostal Showers Continue to Fall.

The news has spread far and wide that Los Angeles is being visited with a "rushing mighty wind from heaven." The how and why of it is to be found in the very opposite of those conditions that are usually thought necessary for a big revival. No instruments of music are used, none are needed. No choir—but bands of angels have been heard by some in the spirit and there is a heavenly singing that is inspired by the Holy Ghost. No collections are taken. No bills have been posted to advertise the meetings. No church or organization is back of it. All who are in touch with God realize as soon as they enter the meetings that the Holy Ghost is the leader. One brother stated that even before his train entered the city, he felt the power of the revival.

Travelers from afar wend their way to the headquarters at Azusa Street. As they enquire their way to the Apostolic Faith Mission, perhaps they are asked, "O, you mean the Holy Rollers," or "It is the Colored Church you mean?" In the vicinity of a tombstone shop ,stables and lumber yard (a fortunate vicinity because no one complains of all-night meetings) you find a two-story, white-washed old building. You would hardly expect heavenly visitations there, unless you remember the stable at Bethlehem.

But here you find a mighty pentecostal revival going on from ten o'clock in the morning till about twelve at night. Yes, Pentecost has come to hundreds of hearts and many homes are made into a sweet paradise below. We remember years ago, when a bright, young missionary was dying in Bombay, India, in his last hours, unconscious with the fever, he kept crying, "Pentecost is coming! Pentecost is coming!" It seemed prophetical. Pentecost has come and is coming in India, and thank God in many other places

A leading Methodist layman of Los Angeles says, "Scenes transpiring here are what Los Angeles churches have been praying for for years. I have been a Methodist for twenty-five years. I was a leader of the praying band of the First Methodist Church. We prayed that the Pentecost might come to the city of Los Angeles. We wanted it to start in the First Methodist Church, but God did not start it there. I bless God that it did not start in any church in this city, but in a barn, so that we might all come and take part in it. If it had started in a fine church, poor colored people and Spanish people would not have got it, but praise God it started here. God Almighty says He will pour out of His Spirit upon all flesh. This is just what is happening here. I want to warn every Methodist in Los Angeles to keep your hands off this work. Tell the people wherever you go that Pentecost has come to Los Angeles."

As soon as it is announced that the altar is open for seekers for pardon, santification, the baptism with the Holy Ghost and healing of the body, the people rise and flock to the altar. There is no urging. What kind of preaching is it that brings them? Why, the simple declaring of the Word of God. There is such power in the preaching of the Word in the Spirit that people are shaken on the benches. Coming to the altar, many fall prostrate under the power of God, and often come out speaking in tongues. Sometimes the power falls on people and they are wrought upon by the Spirit during testimony or preaching and receive Bible experiences.

The testimony meetings which precede the preaching often continue for two hours or more and people are standing waiting to testify all the time. Those who have received the baptism with the Holy Ghost testify that they had a clear evidence of sancification first. Hundreds testify that they received the Bible evidence of speaking in a new tongue that they never knew before. Some have received the "gift of tongues" or "divers tongues" and the interpretation.

The demonstrations are not the shouting, clapping or jumping so often seen in camp meetings. There is a shaking such as the early Quakers had and which the old Methodists called the "jerks." It is while under the power of the Spirit you see the hands raised and hear speaking in tongues. While one sings a song learned from heaven with a shining face, the tears will be trickling down other faces. Many receive the Spirit through the laying on of hands, as they did through Paul at Ephesus.

Little children from eight years to twelve stand up on the altar bench and testify to the baptism with the Holy Ghost and speak in tongues. In the children's meetings little tots get down and seek the Lord.

It is noticeable how free all nationalities feel. If a Mexican or German cannot speak English, he gets up and speaks in his own tongue and feels quite at home for the Spirit interprets through the face and people say amen. No instrument that God can use is rejected on account of color or dress or lack of education. This is why God has so built up the work.

In the testimony meetings, they report from cottage prayer meetings where perhaps a number were baptized with the Holy Ghost or saved or sanctified and those who have been seeking at home report what God has done for them.

The singing is characterized by freedom. "The Comforter has come" is sung every day, also "Heavenly Sunlight" and "Under the Blood." Often one will rise and sing a familiar song in a new tongue.

Seekers for healing are usually taken upstairs and prayed for in the prayer room and many have been healed there. There is a larger room upstairs that is used for Bible study. A brother fittingly describes it in this way, "Upstairs is a long room, furnished with chairs and three California redwod planks, laid end to end on backless chairs. This is the Pentecostal upper room where sanctified souls seek Pentecostal fullness and go out speaking in new tongues."

The sweetest thing of all is the loving harmony. Every church where this has gone is like a part of the family. This description is given for the benefit of the many friends who write in and who would like to be present. So many letters are received in the Apostolic Faith office, which is in the same building as the mission. We cannot but weep as we read these letters and pray for those who are seeking.

The Lord is saving drunkards and taking the appetite for liquor and tobacco completely away.

Reports come from Denver that forty souls have received the Pentecost and are speaking in tongues.

A young man saved from the morphine habit has no more desire for the stuff and gave up his instruments.

Four workers from Texas, Bro. and Sister Oyler and Bro, and Sister Quinton have arrived in Los Angeles lately. God has been using them in Whittier.

Bro. Tom Qualls from Fresno said, "I came 300 miles to this meeting and I feel heaven in my soul. It seems to me I am getting some of the crumbs that fall from Father's table. I feel the presence of God here."

"Cartoons in the newspapers were my first introduction to this meeting," said a brother, "and I said, this is what I have been praying for for years. I was warned by leaders that it was of the devil, but I came and got a touch of heaven in my soul."

Before th's fire broke out [illegible] a brother had a vision of fires springing up and then gathering together and advancing in a solid wall of flame. A preacher was trying to put it out with a wet gunny sack, but it was evident there was no use fighting it. Our God is marching on. Hallelujah. The man with the wet gunny sack is here also, but his efforts only call attention to the fire.

The blind man who was saved and had his sight restored was saved because of hearing a few praying in tongues in a cottage meeting. He was a sinner; a very profane man, and was convicted because of tongues. Praise God for His marvelous works to the children of men.

Sister Lemon of Whittier, who had been a sufferer for eighteen years and could receive no help from physicians, and had been bed-ridden for fourteen years of that time, has been marvelously healed by the Lord through the laying on of hands and the prayer of faith. She has been walking to meetings. The opposers of the work cannot deny that a notable miracle has been performed through the mighty name of Jesus.

Mother Griffith, who has been matron of a rescue home, has received her Pentecost. She testified, "It seemed to me when I got saved, I got into the ocean; and when I got sanctified, it seemed the ocean got into me; and when I was baptized with the Holy Ghost, it seemed I got the life preserver on and began floating on the ocean of salvation. Jesus lives in me, and I live and have my being in Him. Thank God for salvation, sanctification, the baptism with the Holy Ghost and the witness."

Sister Bridget Welch has been powerfully baptized with the Holy Ghost and is working for the Lord both in laboring for souls and in service with her hands ministering to others. She testifies, "I was a dope fiend and in and out of prisons for twenty years. God Almighty has surely healed my body and given me divine strength. He healed me of cancer of the nose and did not leave a scar. I have no time for a drug store any more. The Lord took me out of an awful pit and set my feet on the solid rock and established my goings and put a new song in my mouth. He sanctified me and baptized me with the Holy Ghost and gave me the gift of tongues."

A sister who was very hungry for the Pentecost prayed for the Lord to strip her of everything, but give more of Himself. Then shortly afterwards when her house was in flames, she went out and knelt down in the weeds and prayed, "Lord, you said all things work together for good to them that love you. Give me more of God." And He answered prayer and gave her a mighty baptism with the Holy Ghost and fire and she is shining for God.

PENTECOST IN DENVER.

1934 E. 18th ave., Denver, Colo.

What I received on that memorable Sunday night in Los Angeles has never left me for one moment and last night in particular at the meeting, did the Holy Ghost magnify the simple Gospel of our Lord in demonstration and power, until about twenty-five crowded the altar and got definite experiences of justification, sanctification, baptism with the Holy Ghost, and healing. One dear old man, who because of his back, could not straighten up nor stoop down without severe pain, was instantly healed, got up and showed the people how the dear Lord had healed him. He stood as straight as a young man, stooped down, touched the floor with his hands without a bit of pain. Then he knelt down and said, "I want the baptism with the Holy Ghost," and Glory to God, he got it, and there was great joy.

Dear Bro. Seymour, God surely sent me here. These dear, hungry people, when they learned I came from the meeting at Los Angeles, received me with open arms. They gave me the evening, and during the meeting, they embraced me and our joy in the Lord knew no bounds. One dear brother from Los Angeles picked me up and held me as if I were a child. This is but the beginning of a work here such as we knew in Los Angeles. This people have been praying that God would send someone to teach them and give them light and wisdom, and they believe God has answered their prayers, hence their great joy. I feel the need of your prayers. I never saw in all my travels a people so hungry for the truth.

Dear Bro. G. F. Fink, the brother in charge, was coming to Los Angeles to Azusa street to learn and get a better understanding of the baptism with the Holy Ghost. While I was talking to the people last night, he arose and embraced me crying, I love you, I love you, my brother. Surely God has sent you to us; and the people wept for joy, and shouted praises unto God. These people here were set on fire by the Holy Ghost through Bro. Johnson and the two sisters who passed through here, and it is marvelous how the Holy Ghost has led them. You little know how the people have been praying for you and the meetings in Los Angeles in the midst of their own struggles. Give my love in Jesus to all the saints.

—T. Hezmalhalch.

VICTORY IN OAKLAND.

Bro. Harmon Clifford, the young man who was saved, sanctified, and baptized with the Holy Ghost all in an hour and a half at Azusa Street Mission, and who was also healed of consumption, has been increasing in power, and God has bestowed on him many gifts. He writes from Oakland where the Lord sent him:

"How I praise God for ever sending me to Oakland with Bro. Ross. I was never so happy in all my life as I have been this last week. It did seem as though I would go up at any moment, but of course God has a work for me to do yet. Praise His dear name. There was some trouble about the Bible evidence to the baptism with the Holy Ghost, but as soon as that was straight, God began to work and has been working ever since. O glory to God! Many have been saved, sanctified, and healed. Six have received Pentecost and spoke in a good, clear language up to Thursday night. People were laid out all over the mission. The people have been very quiet and let the Holy Ghost have right of way. and sometimes before the preaching is over people come, to the altar. There are many hungry souls in this city"

336 Ninth st., Oakland, Cal.

VISION AND MESSAGE.

A sister who has been healed and baptized with the Holy Ghost related the following vision, "Two days ago the power of God came over me and He said, 'Whatsoever ye ask in my name believing, ye shall receive.' I said 'Give wisdom to speak to the people.' Immediately I was in a great hall with tables spread all about, and the Lord was the waiter, and I saw His beautiful, smiling face. He spoke to me and said, 'I have called my friends and they did not come, therefore go out and ask everyone you find to come to the wedding.' As I looked around to see something beautiful, the scene changed and I was in a hospital and saw poor creatures dying, looking like skeletons. I thought my call was to the hospital and telephoned to know when it was open for visitors, but the Lord revealed to me that it meant all those who are sick in their souls."

A CORRECTION.

In our last issue, there was a prophecy by Sister Mary Golmond of an earthquake coming to Los Angeles. She stated that the Lord had not showed the time, but that it would NOT come on Sunday. The word "not" was accidentally omitted.

HIS BANQUETING HOUSE.

"He took me into his banqueting house, and his banner over me was love." A brother says the Lord gave him a vision of the banqueting house. He passed under the great arches. Each one had a name upon it. The first was love, then there was joy, peace, and among others he saw, "Independence." He asked what that meant. The answer was, "Is it not wonderful to be free?" Dear saints, this is one of the sweetest arches in the banqueting house. This bondage to love sets me perfectly free.

UNUSUAL NOISE.

There has been some unusual noise in the town of Whittier, the prayers of those who are burdened for the lost, the sound of praises to God and speaking in new tongues. A few days ago, four workers were arrested while praying in the cottage that had been offered free of rent for the use of the workers. The following letter was received at Azusa street.

"Brother Seymour in Jesus: We are charged with using boisterous language, unusual noise, or in other words praising God and speaking in tongues. This happened in the cottage this morning. The defendants are Sister May Mayo, Sister Jacobson, Bro. and Sister McLain. Trial comes off at 4 p. m. We are standing steadfast, seeing the glory of God We believe the judge is under conviction. Sunday night nine souls were at the altar Souls getting saved and sanctified. Power is falling in the audience. People being slain."

When the word came to Azusa street, fifteen workers rallied to take the place of the four and meetings have been going on there with victory and power ever since.

The band that were arrested are rejoicing in the Lord that they were permitted to go through the trial. The judge gave them the choice of leaving town or going to jail. They consulted the Lord about it and He said: "When they persecute you in one city, flee ye to another." So the sisters obeyed but Bro. McLain preferred to stand a few days in jail and working on the chain gang. When the judge gave sentence, Sister Mayo raised her hands to heaven and prayed for him and for Whittier

PENTECOST IN INDIA.

News comes from India that the baptism with the Holy Ghost and gift of tongues is being received there by natives who are simply taught of God. The India Alliance says, "Some of the gifts which have been scarcely heard of in the church for many centuries, are now being given by the Holy Ghost to simple, unlearned members of the body of Christ, and communities are being stirred and transformed by the wonderful grace of God. Healing, the gift of tongues, visions, and dreams, discernment of spirits, the power to prophecy and to pray the prayer of faith, all have a place in the present revival." Hallelujah! God is sending the Pentecost to India. He is no respector of persons.

VERNON MISSION.

Bro. and Sister F. E. Hill are now conducting [illegible] Forty-third and Forty-fourth streets, 4307 Central avenue. Since they received their Pentecost, they have been holding cottage meetings at their home with seekers every night. Then they told the people God had showed them to start a meeting in that section and in about five minutes the rent was paid for the hall in advance. Bro. Hill has dropped his business and is giving all his time to Gospel work. The Nazarene Church forbade speaking in tongues or testifying on the line of the baptism with the Holy Ghost upon the sanctified life, so they with others have walked out with the Bible and the Spirit, and God is giving them souls. There is room for Spirit filled workers everywhere.

SPREADING THE FULL GOSPEL.

A number of Spirit filled workers have been going out of late. Bro. Adolph Ross and Bro. Harmon Clifford went to Oakland and God has been using them there. Then a band of seven left on the steamer for the north, for Oakland, Salem and Seattle. They were, Sister Florence Crawford, Bro. and Sister G. W. Evans, Bro. and Sister Thomas Junk, Sister Ophelia Wiley and Sister Lulu Miller, Bro. Post went to Santa Barbara, Bro. T. Hezmalhalch to Denver, Sister Potter and Violet Price to Fresno, Bro. F. W. Williams to Alabama a Spanish brother, Brigido Perez, to San Diego. Sister Elsie Robinson to Onawa, Michigan. Bro. Seymour has been called for a short time to Oakland, but expects soon to return to headquarters at Los Angeles. We wish to keep track of the workers in the field and be united together in prayer for each other and the work in the different fields..

BAPTIZED ON A FRUIT WAGON.

Bro. G. Zigler, who runs a fruit wagon, driving into Los Angeles early in the morning, says, "I was on my wagon coming down to the market praising God, when the Lord covered me with His power and I began to sing such a sweet song I had never sung anything like before. I was riding along at three o'clock in the morning. All at once I commenced to talk in a new tongue, and it was the most wonderful blessing I have ever received. What He has done for me, He will do for everybody."

The meetings have been going on now for about six months at Azusa Street day and night. How long are they going to continue? We expect them to keep on till Jesus comes, by the grace of God.

The religion of Jesus Christ is no more popular now than it was when Jesus was here. Many are rejecting the truth and are not going to receive it. The word not only says that signs shall follow them that believe, but that "They that live godly in Christ Jesus shall suffer persecution." This also is being fulfilled.

The Apostolic Faith

"Earnestly contend for the faith which was once delivered unto the saints."—Jude 3.

Vol. 1, No. 4. Los Angeles, Cal., December, 1906. Subscription Free

PENTECOST WITH SIGNS FOLLOWING

Seven Months of Pentecostal Showers. Jesus, Our Projector and Great Shepherd.

Many are asking how the work in Azusa Mission started and who is the founder. The Lord was the founder and He is the Projector of this movement. A band of humble people in Los Angeles had been praying for a year or more for more power with God for the salvation of lost and suffering humanity. They did not know just what they needed, but one thing they knew, people were not getting saved and healed as they desired to see. They continued to hold cottage prayer meetings for several months.

Then they felt led of the Lord to call Bro. Seymour from Houston Texas to Los Angeles, the saints in Los Angeles sending his fare. It was as truly a call from God as when He sent His holy angel to tell Cornelius to send for Peter. He came and told them about the baptism with the Spirit, and that every afternoon at three o'clock they would pray for the enduement of power. He told them he did not have the Pentecost but was seeking it and wanted all the saints to pray with him till all received their Pentecost. Some believed they had it, and others believed they did not have it because the signs were not following. Hardly anyone was getting saved.

There was a great deal of opposition, but they continued to fast and pray for the baptism with the Holy Spirit, till on April 9th the fire of God fell in a cottage on Bonnie Brae. Pentecost was poured out upon workers and saints. Three days after that, Bro. Seymour received his Pentecost. Two who had been working with him in Houston came to Los Angeles just before Pentecost fell. They came filled with the Holy Ghost and power. One of them had received her personal Pentecost, Sister Lucy Farrow, and said the Lord had sent her to join us in holding up this precious truth. She came with love and power holding up the blood of Jesus Christ in all His fullness.

And the fire has been falling ever since. Hundreds of souls have received salvation and healing. We can truly say that the revival is still going on. The Lord God is in Los Angeles in different missions and churches in mighty power, in spite of opposition. This revival has spread through towns about Los Angeles and through the state and over the United States in different places and across the ocean. The blood of Jesus prevails against every force and power of the enemy. Glory to God.

Some are asking if Dr. Chas. F. Parham is the leader of this movement. We can answer, no he is not the leader of this movement of Azusa Mission. We thought of having him to be our leader and so stated in our paper, before waiting on the Lord.

We can be rather hasty, especially when we are very young in the power of the Holy Spirit. We are just like a baby—full of love and were willing to accept anyone that had the baptism with the Holy Spirit as our leader. But the Lord commenced settling us down, and we saw that the Lord should be our leader. So we honor Jesus as the great Shepherd of the sheep. He is our model.

The Lord adds here daily such as should be saved, and plants them in the body to suit Himself, and all work together in harmony under the power of the Holy Spirit. There is no pope, Dowieism, or Sanfordism, but we are all little children knowing only Jesus and Him crucified. This work is carried on by the people of Los Angeles that God has united by the precious blood of our Lord Jesus Christ and the power of the Holy Spirit.

Bro. Seymour is simply a humble pastor of the flock over which the Holy Ghost has made him overseer, according to Acts. 20.28, "Take heed therefore, unto yourself and to the flock over which the Holy Ghost hath made you overseer, to feed the church of God which He hath purchased with His own blood." And as missionary workers and teachers go out from this place, they have the same privilege of being pastors over the people the Lord puts them over by the Holy Spirit, and of feeding them with the pure Word of God. Each mission will be united in harmony, having its own pastor simply that the Holy Ghost shall appoint.

We believe in old time repentance, old time conversion, old time sanctification, healing of our bodies and the baptism with the Holy Ghost. We believe that God made Adam in His own image, according to Gen. 5. 1; Ps. 8. 4; and Matt. 19. 4. We do not believe in any eighth day creation, as some have taught, and we do not believe in the annihilation of the wicked.

We stand on Bible truth without compromise. We recognize every man that honors the blood of Jesus Christ to be our brother, regardless of denomination, creed, or doctrine. But we are not willing to accept any errors, it matters not how charming and sweet they may seem to be. If they do not tally with the Word of God, we reject them.

This is the year of jubilee when God is sending the latter rain, and the refreshing times have come. He has raised up a nation in seven months' time that will preach Jesus and Him crucified in all His fullness in spite of what is costs.

"The long, long night is past,
The morning breaks at last."

It seems that God is sweeping things. He is running right over the devil here–not paying any attention to Him–saving, sanctifying, and baptizing souls, bringing them out of darkness into the marvelous light of the Son of God. Hallelujah! Glory to our God.

PENTECOST AMONG THE YOUNG PEOPLE.

A band of Spirit filled boys went down to Anaheim, a town near Los Angeles. They testified what God had done for them and it made the people hungry. The second night the altar was full. In two nights, eight were sanctified, six converted, and five received the baptism. One night at about one o'clock in the morning, the Holy Ghost spoke words in Spanish through one of the young men, and a girl who was seeking her Pentecost understood that language and joyfully interpreted it, "Keep awake, do not sleep, and I will come to thy house." This same girl in about an hour and a-half received the baptism with the Holy Ghost. The work among the children was very touching. The power of God fell the second night as at the house of Cornelius. Little children had their hands up shouting. The first to get the baptism was a little boy of ten years. He began clapping his hands and singing "Jesus Savior, pilot me" in and unknown tongue in clear distinct words, also "Nearer my God to thee." Four in the same family inside of twenty minutes got the baptism with the Holy Ghost. It was heaven there. The work is going on and other little children are being filled with the Spirit.

The band of young men that the Lord is using there and in Whittier are all in one accord and keep in the unity of the Spirit. They do not preach big sermons but simply testify and sing and pray in the Spirit. Their names are Henry Prentiss, Curtis Nichols, Orly Nichols, Tom Anderson, Wm. Millson and Isaac Berg. One night recently, seven were slain under the power of God and several received their Pentecost. Many of the people in Anaheim understand German and the workers were permitted to speak and pray in that language. Some words spoken by the Spirit in German were, "God is in our midst."

PENTECOST IN FORT WORTH.

Workers went to Ft. Worth, Tex., and preached this Gospel and Pentecost has fallen there. Mrs. C. A. Roll, of 1005 Edwards street, Ft. Worth, writes, "Three of us women began to tarry and pray the last of August. About three weeks from that time, Pentecost fell on our street. Since that time, nine have received their Pentecost. The Lord is pouring His Spirit on us. We are feeling the need of a man filled with the Holy Ghost to preach. How my heart burns within me since the Holy Spirit abides. I thank God that Pentecost has come to Ft. Worth. I just marvel at myself, by nature a timid, shrinking woman, but thank God, I am relieved of all that. We praise God for speaking to Sister Hagg and telling her to come over and help us. Then Bro. and Sister Kent came and were such a blessing to us. Two have received their Pentecost in the last few days. Others are seeking.

PENTECOST IN BENTON HARBOR.

Benton Harbor, Mich., Oct. 29th.

Greeting in our Lord to all the dear saints. I reached this place finding a warm welcome from Bro. and Sister York. Had our first meeting that afternoon with a room full. The meeting continued both day and night. About thirty received the mesage gladly and searched the scriptures daily, and began to cry mightily to God for their Pentecost. After six days waiting, the fire began to fall. Now I have been here eight days and three souls have been baptized with the Holy Ghost and fire, speaking in new tongues. One young man spoke in several tongues, six or seven have received the annointing and twenty-five seeking earnestly. Victory through the blood. Hallelujah to my God. The Pentecost has come to Benton Harbor and several ministers and mission workers are among the seekers. Glory to God. He saves me and lets His power fill me. He wonderfully supplies my needs. The battle was hot here for a time, but God gave the victory. I expect to meet you when Jesus calls us up Elsie L. Robinson.

PENTECOST IN SEATTLE.

The Lord has been working in a marvelous way in Seattle, Wash., where Bro. and Sister Junk and Sister Lulu Miller went as workers from Los Angeles. The devil has been opposing but he always misses the mark and advertises the meetings. Five window lights were broken and one shot through, and the papers call them, "holy rollers," but the last reports are that some eight have been saved, ten sanctified and six received the Pentecost and are speaking in tongues. Also in a suburb town of Ballard four have received their Pentecost.

Bro. Junk writes the folowing incident of how God used the writing in an unknown tongue:

"The Lord sent in a young Hebrew and he got soundly converted the other night. He sobbed and cried till you could have heard him a block. His cry was for the blood to cover him. O for old time repentance. When I pulled out my Testament to read him some Scripture, his eyes fell upon some writing I had done while under the power of God in Oakland. When he saw it, he pronounced it Hebrew. The hardest work we had to do was to convince him that I had not studied the language, but when this was clear, he trembled from head to foot and said he truly believed the Messiah was come. O glory. These signs are to them that believe not. He took my writing to a Hebrew scholar., It is Isaiah 55 commencing with the 2nd verse, Ps. 46. 3., the Lord's prayer, and Rom. 3.26. They told him not to believe me, for without studying Hebrew it would be impossible to write it, for it was perfect. Praise God, for He does only perfect work. Thos. Junk, 1617 7th avenue, Seattle, Wash.

PENTECOST IN WOODLAND.

Bro. G. W. Evans, who has just come from Woodland, California, reports a Pentecostal revival in that place. Thirty-two have been baptized with the Holy Ghost, thirty-one sanctified, and twenty saved. Seventeen members out of the Baptist Church are filled with the Holy Ghost including the superintendent of the Sunday School and his wife. The Sunday School superintendent of the Methodist Church is also baptized with the Holy Ghost, and the difficulty now on hand is the need of a larger building to accommodate the crowds. Fourteen were healed at one meeting. God's word is made so clear and plain that the crowds are pressing in spiritual hunger for the living truth. Sisters Sophie and Reece from Oakland, whom God has been using, are at present in charge.

A man that had been possessed with a mad demon and had been in the asylum was delivered. The Lord cast out this demon, clothed him in his right mind and completed the work, baptizing him with the Holy Ghost. Another remarkable case was where a party was under sentence of court, which decision was suspended and the defendant saved, sanctified, and filled with the Holy Ghost and became a good citizen.

PENTECOST IN SAN DIEGO.

San Diego, Cal., Nov. 28th.

We are praising God for victory in San Diego. Bro. Love and I came down here last Thursday to see if the Lord was preparing to take out a people for Himself in this city by the sea. On arriving in the city, we were not long in finding my old friend and brother, Geo. Reilly, who was earnestly tarrying for the Pentecost. We appointed a meeting at his house the same night and he was gloriously baptized with the Holy Ghost and spake with tongues. We met again the next evening and two more received their Pentecost with Bible evidence. Hallelujah! The Lord had already laid it upon Bro. Reilly to open up a mission on this line. He had secured the building and we had it ready for service by Saturday night. The people came out and nearly filled the seating capacity and we had a most wonderful meeting. Some were justified and sanctified and blessedly anointed. Interest is increasing. Some falling under the power of the Holy Ghost and mighty conviction of the people. We believe the Lord wants Azusa Street Mission duplicated in this city. We expect to stay here till the Lord says, "Flee ye to another." He has showed us that He has much people in this city. Hallelujah! Pray for us and San Diego.—F. E. Hill.

PENTECOST IN SAN JOSE

They are having a real old time Pentecostal revival in San Jose, California. The devil is stirred and doing his best to put out the fire, but they just ignore him and shout the victory. The altars are crowded day and night. Twelve have received their Pentecost and are speaking in tongues. Devils are being cast out and the sick healed. All glory to God. Some come to the altars and the Holy Ghost shows them they are backslidden in heart, so they repent and do their first works over. Soon they get to the place where the Holy Ghost falls upon them and they rise to their feet speaking in a clear language as the Spirit gives utterance. Some of the Salvation Army people in that city are receiving the Pentecost. Bro. Harmon Clifford has returned from working in Oakland and San Jose and brings good news of a mighty work of God.

Bro. H. M. Turney, who came from Alaska to get his Pentecost in Los Angeles, is being used of the Lord in San Jose. His last report, dated November 16 is, "Yesterday was a high day in Zion. The meeting opened at 10 a. m. and was still running at one o'clock this morning. Altars are crowded at every service. Many are slain under the mighty power of God. Several received their Pentecost yesterday. One woman was instantly healed of rheumatism. Several have been saved. Many backsliders reclaimed and sanctified."

PENTECOST IN PORTSMOUTH.

God has done a wonderful work in Portsmouth, Va. It is reported that about 150 have received the Pentecost. The whole country about there is stirred by the power of God. The Lord sent Sister Lucy Farrow there from Los Angeles and has been using her to preach this Gospel. She feels a call from God to go to Monrovia, Liberia, Africa, and wants some one to come and help carry on the work. She says, "Give all the saints love from me. Tell them I have many children here too. They do not want me to leave, but you all know when the Lord says go, I must go. I move as the Lord says move. No time to visit only for the Lord. I go night and day in rain and sunshine. There is no time to stop. Jesus is coming soon. Pray for me and the work here."

Another Witness.

It pleased God by His Almighty power to send us Sister Lucy Farrow to bring us the light as we had not seen it. The power of God has fallen upon us. I praise Him for being a witness in Jerusalem, Samaria, Judea, and unto the uttermost parts of the earth. I praise Him for the power in the sign He gave me of speaking in tongues and interpreting the same and singing in tongues. I praise God for the healing power. He has healed me from my head to my feet.—Georgetta Jeffries, Portsmouth, Va.

PENTECOST IN SALEM, ORE.

We are unable to tell of the great glory and power that came upon the meetings, Sunday, November 11. With astonishment and great conviction the people witnessed the great power of another Pentecost in several speaking in tongues, and some singing songs in different languages with an unction and glory that is past human language to describe.

Waves of thrilling glory pass over me as I reflect on what God is doing in this place. A spirit of divine love prevails among the workers, and those who are baptized with the Holy Ghost take hold of the office work ... peals for help are pouring in from every quarter, and it takes about five persons to answer the correspondence. God is raising up the workers.

People are coming and making their confessions and giving up all, to get ready for the coming of Jesus. Never in the history of this work has there been so much confession and restitution.—Apostolic Light.

It is every believer's birthright to be baptized with the Holy Ghost.

Two bands of Apostolic Faith workers have been arrested in Whittier, but it has only increased the interest and deepened the work.

An anointed handkerchief was sent to Elizabeth Smith, Brunswick, Ga., and as soon as she opened the letter, she was instantly healed.

We have heard the funeral of the Gospel preached, the power of nobody unto nothing, now we are preaching the power of God unto salvation.

One came here that had been suffering for years in body, and was healed by the power of God while in the meeting without even asking for prayers.

A young lady was contemplating suicide came to the meeting and was saved, then sanctified and baptized with the Holy Ghost. She is very happy in the Lord.

When the conditions are just right, the Lord is just as responsible for the healing of our body as of our souls. The reason so many are sick, is because they trust in the arm of flesh instead of God.

A brother testified, "Last week I came in a backslider and half drunk and the Lord forgave my backsliding right in my seat, and a few days afterward, He sanctified me and baptized me with the Holy Ghost."

The gift of tongues is the glory of God flooding your soul and the Spirit taking possession. You will never know what it means to be clay in the hands of the Potter until you receive the Pentecostal baptism.

Pentecost has fallen in Long Beach, Cal. Souls are slain under the power of God and meetings cannot close. A number have received the baptism with the Holy Ghost. The Lord is using Bro. E. McCauley to push the work there.

It was God's eternal purpose that Jesus should be born in a humble place. No place is too humble for Jesus to dwell in. He poured out His Spirit in the humblest meeting place in Los Angeles, that no flesh should glory in His presence.

Interpreted message spoken in tongues: "Open your heart and receive the Spirit. I will give good gifts to My children. Blessed are they that trust me. O drink of the living waters. Believe in Me. O believe in Me, and ye shall find everything ye ask for."

This meeting has been a melting time. The people are all melted together by the power of the blood and the Holy Ghost. They are made one lump, one bread, all one body in Christ Jesus. There is no Jew or Gentile, bond or free, in the Azusa street Mission.

Bro. A. Suiger, a Danish young man from Chicago, has received his Pentecost and is filled and saturated with the melting power of God. He expects to be on his way east soon, and, as the Lord opens the way, will go to Denmark where the Lord is calling him to preach the Gospel. His father is a Lutheran preacher.

Bro. Tom Hezmalhalch has returned for a short time to Los Angeles from Chicago, Colorado Springs, Denver, and other places where the Lord has been using him and reports a wonderful work of God in those places and that many souls are being saved, healed, and baptized with the Holy Ghost with signs following.

"Jesus is coming again soon. Do not reject His voice. Don't reject Him, don't reject Him. He was nailed on the cross for you." The above is the interpretation of a message in unknown language given by one who came a sinner and is now filled with the Holy Ghost speaking and preaching in new tongues.

A brother writes that he received the baptism with the Holy Ghost on a Santa Fe train running forty miles an hour, and ten more after him received the same gift. They were all waiting for the promise of the Father. He is no respector of persons or places. To tarry at Jerusalem is to wait at Jesus' feet wherever you are in His will.

Companies of Christians in many places are waiting on God, tarrying for the baptism with the Holy Ghost. The most spiritual people in this land and across the ocean, and missionaries in foreign lands are writing that they are seeking the Pentecost. This is a significant fact. It means that the Lord is preparing His people for His soon coming.

On Thanksgiving day a baptismal service was held at the Pentecostal Mission on Maple and Eighth streets, where there is a baptistry. Twenty-four were baptized by immersion. The Spirit of God was upon the people. The candidates for baptism were filled with the Spirit and shouted and praised God as they came out of the water.

Sister Hagg is now back in Los Angeles from Ft. Worth, Tex., rejoicing in the Holy Ghost and continually witnessing to the Pentecost, which she received last May. She says, "Not a single doubt about this being of God. I know I was sanctified before, and I know this is separate from sanctification. He fills me with His glory. Since I have received the baptism with the Holy Ghost, I have understood God better and His truth has opened up to me as never before. It enables me to stand in every place. I have sweet fellowship with my Lord in all trials and tests. The Lord gave me the interpretation of some words I was speaking in the unknown tongue and the interpretation was, 'My soul cannot tell it.'"

The Lord has been working in Chattanooga, Tenn., where a band of Africa missionaries stopped on their way. Souls have been saved, a numbers have been baptized with the Holy Ghost and received the Bible evidence. Brother and Sister Hutchins and Sister McKinney have now gone on to New York. Their destination is Monrovia, Liberia, Africa.

A little girl who knows the Lord as her healer, was suffering from fever. After different ones had prayed for her, she said, "Now maybe the Lord wants me to pray." so she said, "Dear Jesus, you have heard all these people's prayers, now heal me for Jesus sake." Then she lay down and went to sleep. God heals many times in answer to children's prayers.

The devil says he has no lake of fire, though sinners, skeptics, and ungodly preachers all are trying to find consolation in the doctrines of no hell, annihilation, and universalism. But God says in Rev. 20. 14 that there is a lake of fire. Jesus warned us of hell. Hades in Greek and Gehenna in Hebrew mean "lake of fire." What can we do but believe the Word?

We can truly say that Pentecost has come, for all the signs are following. God is pouring out His Spirit upon His sons and daughters and giving dreams and visions, speaking in tongues. A woman who had been an invalid for 16 years is walking and shouting and praising God. The blind have received their sight. Missionaries are going out without purse or scrip. Everything is pointing toward the coming of the Lord.

The great Shekina glory is still resting upon us as a pillar of fire by night and a pillar of cloud by day, where hundreds and thousands of souls have come and been blest through the mighty power of our blessed Lord. Hungry and thirsty souls are coming from hundreds and thousands of miles to get their personal Pentecost, and receiving and taking the glad tidings back home to hungry and thirsty souls that are waiting their arrival.

People from thousands of miles have been coming to Los Angeles to get into the rivers of salvation. John saw a river proceding out of the throne of God and the Lamb, and on either side of that river was the tree of life. We can get the fruit on either side of the river, but we have to swim to get it. If you want this great blessing, you must launch out by faith into the river. It is a very sweet thing to be where the rivers are flowing.

It is so blessed to be sanctified, cleansed, crucified, nailed to the cross of Christ. Old things have passed away, the old man is crucified, slain, and Jesus Christ is enthroned in the heart and crowned within. He sits upon the throne of our hearts reigning as a king, swaying His scepter of righteousness and true holiness, and keeping the heart clean and pure from sin. Then you are just ready to receive the baptism with the Holy Ghost and fire.

The Lord Jesus said, when He had one foot in the cloud going back to heaven, "Tarry ye in the city of Jerusalem until ye be endued with power." They did not go away from Jerusalem until they received the enduement of power. And on the day of Pentecost, they were all in one accord and all were filled with the Holy Ghost and spoke with new tongues, as the Spirit gave utterance. God taught the church a lesson on that day what the baptism with the Holy Ghost was and what would prepare them to be a witness to the uttermost parts of the earth.

Newspapers in Salem, Oregon, are publishing columns about the Pentecostal meetings. While they deride, they tell enough truth to draw any hungry soul. They say of Sister Wiley that her face "shines like new money," that her face is transfigured, so to speak, and that "she could not put that on." They say that the tongues spoken by the preacher "really sounded like Oriental dialect; it certainly seems impossible for anyone, however adept he may be, to imitate a language in that way." They say that "well authenticated cases of remarkable cures from disease are recorded."

Bro. and Sister Eric Hollingsworth, who have received their Pentecost and are on the way to Sweden to carry the Gospel write from Oakland, "God is working here in Oakland also. As a rule, one and sometimes two souls a day are receiving their Pentecost and the signs following. We are going to continue on our trip east and to Sweden Monday. I hope you will pray for us. We are going to a poor country and at a hard time of the year and we will find strong opposition in preaching this wonderful Gospel. I feel just like stepping into the lion's den, but Daniel's God is my God."

"Jesus has brought me into His banqueting chamber. Oh, I am feasting upon the delicious wine of the kingdom. Hallelujah!"

The above is the interpretation of a testimony given by a sister from Washington, who received the baptism of the Holy Ghost in Los Angeles and speaks several unknown languages. A brother who understands Marathi, a language of India, identified this language and interpreted. Many have spoken in the languages of India, China, Africa, Asia, Europe, and the islands of the sea, as well as the learned languages of Greek, Latin, etc. The Holy Ghost speaks any language He chooses.

In Denver, Colorado, in Bro. Fink's home, a woman was brought in that was hurt in falling from a wagon. She had been a cripple for thirty-two years and unable to walk. Her toes were drawn up under her feet and could not be straightened. She was unsaved. The next morning, as she was sitting in the front room alone, a little six year old girl, who has received the baptism and speaks with tongues, walked in and put her hand on the woman and said, "Jesus wants to heal you, the Spirit has sent me to put my hands on you." Instantly those toes on the woman's feet straightened and she arose and walked

The Apostolic Faith

"Earnestly contend for the faith which was once delivered unto the saints."—Jude 3.

Volume 1, No. 5   **Los Angeles, Cal., January, 1907**   **Subscription Free**

BEGINNING OF WORLD WIDE REVIVAL

We are expecting wonderful things from the Lord for 1907. The closing up of the old year and beginning of the new found us on our knees at Azusa Mission. And as the new year was announced, such a wave of glory, and divine love and unity came over us. The meeting went on till morning and all the next day. It is a jubilee year. May we all spend it at His feet, learning of Him.

The Lord did great things in 1906. Pentecost first fell in Los Angeles on April 9th. Since then the good tidings has spread in two hemispheres. Many are rejoicing in pardon, purity, and the power of the Holy Ghost. Wherever the work goes, souls are saved, and not only saved from hell but through and through, and prepared to meet the Lord at His coming. Hundreds have been baptized with the Holy Ghost. Many of them are now out in the field, and some in foreign lands, and God is working with them, granting signs and wonders to follow the preaching of the full Gospel.

People all over the land have heard that the oil of the Spirit is being poured out in Los Angeles, and they are coming for all-coming thousands of miles. And they are being filled with the holy oil, the baptism with the Holy Ghost, and wherever they go, it is being poured out.

From the little mustard seed faith that was given to a little company of people waiting on God in a cottage prayer meeting, a great tree has grown, so that people from all parts of the country are coming like birds to lodge in the branches thereof. (Matt. 13:31-32.) The faith is still growing, and we are still just in the beginning, earnestly contending for the faith once delivered unto the saints.

It is a continual organ room tarrying at Azusa Street. It is like a continual campmeeting or convention. All classes and nationalities meet on a common level. One who came for the first time said, "The thing that impressed me most was the humility of the people, and I went to my room and got down on my knees and asked God to give me humility."

The altars are filled with seekers. Sometimes the meetings go on all night. People are alike under the power of God and assembled or rise up speaking in new tongues. In the meetings, you see the holy joy of the Lord in the countenances, and people

are melted in the presence of the Lord, filled with His praises.

The Lord is graciously healing many sick bodies. People are healed at the Mission almost every day. Requests come in for prayer from all over. They are presented in the meeting and the Spirit witnesses in many cases that prayer is answered, and when we hear from them they get healed. Handkerchiefs are sent in to be blest, and are returned in the sick and they are healed in many cases. One day nine handkerchiefs were blest, another day sixteen. A man came with a broken arm and was healed. The mission people never take medicine. They do not want it. They have taken Jesus for their healer and He always heals.

There is a very sweet spirit of unity among Pentecostal missions in Los Angeles and workers in suburban towns. Every Monday morning, the ministers and workers from these different points meet together for prayer and counsel. The missions in Los Angeles are at 327½ S. Spring, of which Bro. Fisher is pastor; 8th and Maple Ave., of which Bro. Pendleton is pastor; and 1231 E. 51st St., where Bro. and Sister Kent have charge. Workers from Long Beach, Pasadena, Clearwater, Anaheim, and other nearby places also come in. All are in one accord. In our first greeting several messages were given to numbers through our Bro. Post, and interpreted as follows:

We acknowledge Christ only, His truth, His Word. We must tarry much before Him. We must acknowledge that He is in our midst, walking among the golden candlesticks, pruning, purging. He who moved among the golden candlesticks, is moving in our midst now. We must recognize Him alone as Head over all, and know no man after the flesh. The Spirit of God will teach us, if we keep low in love and humility before Him. Our Lord says, "I unite upon you, whom you are seeking My will, My glory only. There must be no glorying in names or orders or systems, only in My-self alone. All fullness is in me, all power is in My Gospel."

We must give God all the glory in this work. We must keep very humble at His feet. He recognizes no flesh, no color, no names. We must not glory in Azusa Mission, nor in anything but the Lord Jesus Christ by whom the world is crucified unto us and we unto the world.

We stand as assemblies and missions all in perfect harmony. Azusa Mission stands for the unity of God's people everywhere. God is uniting His people, baptizing them by one Spirit into one body.

—Florence Crawford,
216 2nd Ave.

PENTECOST RESTORED.

Write . after My Pentecostal anointing, on the train, by J. W. Elliott, Des Moines, Iowa.

O glorious promise of heaven!
Fulfilled to His people at last;
The languages of fire have descended,
And sealed us as those in the past.

The Pentecost power is now spreading,
The Bible rings clear as a bell;
The finished work of the Saviour,
We now are commissioned to tell.

The touch of the hand brings conviction,
The look of the eye startles sin,
The flood gates of heaven are opened,
And souls are now entering in.

The altar is banished forever,
And sickness and pain flee away,
The touch of Jesus is so powerful,
As it was in that wonderful day.

The vision of heaven is like magic,
And bodies are molded like clay;
Souls that are sealed by His Spirit
Have entered the heavenlies to stay.

Sinners who once have been careless
Have wakened to a sense of their need;
Pentecost surely is spreading,
Regardless of doctrine or creed.

Then glory to Jesus who loved me,
And glory to Jesus who came,
And glory to Jesus who fills me,
And seals with His own precious name.

PENTECOSTAL POWER IN SAN DIEGO.

San Diego, Cal., Jan. 5.

Dear Saints, Greeting!

Grace and peace be multiplied unto you all, through our Lord Jesus Christ, who always causeth us to triumph in every place, and maketh manifest through us the savor of His knowledge.

The dear Lord has blessed us with continuous victory, reclaimed, sanctified, and some baptized with the Holy Ghost every week. The interest is increasing, notwithstanding the continuous wet weather. The altar is filled with seekers at most every service.

We have had some marvelous cases where those possessed by the devil have been wonderfully and completely delivered and clothed in their right minds. We wish to note one case in particular for the glory of God and the power of our Lord Jesus Christ. A man of German birth came to the meetings, a master in Theosophy and Spiritualism, who claimed he was Christ incarnate—that he was immortal, and had all wisdom and knowledge. The blessed Holy Ghost gave the saints the discerning of spirits, and they rebuked the devils in him. And the man fell to the floor, trembling from head to foot. The devils were commanded to come out of him in Jesus' name. And immediately he began to confess his sins and crimes, too awful to mention. He continued to pray and call upon God for mercy, and in a few days he found peace. He was taken down on to the cleansing Blood, and has received his Pentecost, and in humility is owning Jesus as his perfect Savior, clothed in his right mind, joyful and happy.

About twelve have received their Pentecost and a number are still seeking. We are praying that the Lord will establish this work in in Los Angeles. This is an open field with virgin soil, and the work is taking deep and firm hold upon the people. Our hearts are burdened for salvation of the people of San Diego.

F. B. Hill.

PORTLAND IS STIRRED.

Portland, Ore., Dec. 21st.

Peace from God the Father be upon you and all the saints.

Well, God has stirred up this North till every devil in hell is stirred also.

I finished my work in Salem; was there two weeks. Seven received Pentecost. The saints are in perfect harmony. Students, city officials and the first people of the place heard the Gospel, but as far as we can see now, they have rejected the Gospel. Most of the ones that received their Pentecost are from the little places around, and they have gone home to spread the glad tidings of this precious Gospel. O my heart is so full this morning. Glory! Glory! Glory!

Well, Sister Glasco and three of God's dear, got their Pentecost in Salem. And before they got home, on Christmas day, while Bro. Glasco was preaching Pentecost fell on the meeting and two spoke with tongues. We had planned to come on Saturday and this was Tuesday. When we got here, three more had received the baptism. We arrived here at noon and went into the

meeting at three. The power fell before the meeting was half through and two received Pentecost; at night, two more. Last night Mildred received her Pentecost. The chin of the Lord lay so you can't move about the altar. The altar is full before the meeting is half over. The house is just packed. O if we only had a larger hall. I cannot tell how God is working here.

Now I must tell you about Mildred. She spoke in four tongues and sang so sweetly and interpreted every word. The interpretation of the song was:

"Jesus is calling you
Jesus is calling, O sinner, come home.
Glory to His name, O sinner, come home."

Then she arose and the crowd was silenced like death. She began to wave her arms and preach in tongues and interpret. Will give you a part of it. "He that comes unto me, I will in no wise cast out." (Tongues.) "The Lord has prepared me to preach His Gospel." (Tongues.) "Jesus is coming soon." (Tongues.) "He will take away His pride, one will be taken and the other left."

Jan. 8.—The crowd through the hall. We have to have a policeman to keep the altar clear. They tell us crowds of people come and are turned away. The Zion people held a mass meeting Sunday and decided to come in a body for their Pentecost.

O I am so glad He has chosen me. The Lord has healed souls bad cases. One woman had epileptic fits. When the devil went out of her, she was so weak she could not stand. A man's hand that was broken was healed. A woman with her hip and good gone was healed in the hall last night before the sinners' eyes.

Pentecost falls on people when they come the second time to the meeting, sitting in their seats.

I stay in the mission. It's humble quarters, but Jesus is here. Every minute of my time is given to God. I get tired sometimes. Was sent for to pray for a man with a black fever. I prayed before I went; was so tired. Jesus said, "I do the healing." When I got there, Jesus healed him before I laid hands on him. He put me and came to meeting. Oh, I am learning the wondrous secret; it is letting Jesus do the work and carry all the load. Oh I so happy in His love and service.

People from all over are coming. A young lady came from Albany. She was a sinner and got sick ... even by her Pentecost; yesterday, in one day. There are 32 now that have received the baptism, right since Saturday, and this is Tuesday morning.

I hear the word: "San Francisco is fine. Souls saved, sanc. ed and baptized and the church people coming in. O, God is spreading this Gospel in spite of the devil. Now glad I am I, ev'r found my way into the dear old mission on Azusa St. Love to all the saints.

—Florence Crawford,
216 2nd Ave.

BLESSED DEALINGS IN SEATTLE.

1617 7th Ave., Seattle, Wash., Dec. 11.

May the peace of our Lord Jesus Christ be with you.

We are having some good times, and so far there are about forty-five baptized souls. We had a wonderful service out on Puget Sound and I baptized about thirty, young and old. It was raining and somewhat cold, but the Lord was with us. A little girl about twelve years of age, who had been seeking her Pentecost, got it right there when she put her feet touched the water. The Lord cut her tongue loose, and she spoke all the while going out and coming in. The Lord was with us in wonderful power. O, He is a wonderful Savior. We have been praying for power for two weeks now.

The weather is very rainy here. It rains about six days of every week, but our Father's smile is upon us, and that is better than anything else.

Jan. 7.—In the last few days, the Lord has poured out His Spirit here, and there must be in the neighborhood of about seventy souls that are baptized now.

Yours in Him,
—Thos. Junk and wife.

APOSTOLIC FAITH MISSION IN SAN JOSE.

San Jose, Cal., Jan. 24.

Dear Apostolic Faith:

God our Father has been doing great things for us since we last wrote. We are now worshiping in our own hall. We have a very nicely furnished mission, for which we praise the Lord.

The fire is still falling. Last Sunday we had a wonderful all-day meeting. The saving power was manifest in a remarkable manner. One by her hours under the power. A young girl took God at His Word, opened her mouth wide, and the Lord filled it with praises in new tongues.

A Mrs. Williamson brought her daughter to the meetings for healing for her eyes, which were very bad. The power was present to heal and the child went home completely recovered. Many others have been healed since the meeting opened. Sister Williamson has received her Pentecost and God has put her in His heavenly choir, in the heavenly songs for His glory. She also writes in many languages. She interprets most of the songs that she sings, and when she speaks in tongues, she also interprets.

Several of those who have received their Pentecost have been called to the foreign field to labor for Him. One young woman is making preparations to leave for Hawaii very soon.

I am just holding the fort till my Father sends someone to take charge of the work here, when I expect to leave for a trip around the world, sounding the golden trumpet, heralding the year of jubilee. For the coming of the Lord is near, even at the door. And he wants the heathen nations to hear the glad tidings and be ready for His coming.

I believe this movement is the last call that the world will receive before He comes for His bride. Rev. 18. 7, 8. These are the days of preparation. Nahum 2, 3, 4. The chariots that Nahum saw are the automobiles which we see running in our streets today.

I am anxious to be on the go, for I feel that the time is short. What we do, we must do while it is day.

—H. M. Turney.

PENTECOST IN NORTH CAROLINA.

Dunn, N. C., Jan. 2.

To the Saints in Azusa Mission, and through all California, greeting in Jesus' Name:

O praise Him! It is wonderful! Last week I held a few services in the country in one of the Holiness churches and two received their Pentecost and spoke in tongues. The languages were as perfect as I ever heard. One was a Sunday school superintendent and the other an elder of the church. I had to leave that meeting to fill my appointment here, but the meeting is still going on there.

This is only the third day here and already about ten have received their Pentecost. Five preachers received the baptism and some of them have two or three tongues already and can preach sermons and pray in the tongues. The church is filled to overflow and people come from all over the country. Sinners are being convicted and others repenting. This town of about 2,000 has never seen Pentecost before but praise God, it has come and the town is stirred from center to circumference. People have laid aside eating and business to a great extent and are going down before God in earnest. How I praise God for this wonderful salvation. All the signs follow sending me to Los Angeles and from all it won't be long to miss. I never praise God for He does it all. O how I praise God for sending me to Los Angeles.

Jan. 11.—Our God is raining His promises and His Spirit is being poured out here in Dunn as never before. Many have come from South Carolina and Georgia and have received their Pentecost and gone back and there some have received the baptism. The fire is spreading. The moving continues here in broadest interest. Nearly every service someone receives their Pentecost and speaks in tongues. Some of our preachers have preached, sung and prayed in unknown tongues, and without speaking a word of English, have awakened sinners.

Several colored people have received their real Pentecost and spoke in tongues. God has wonderfully been some of the people with the gift of song. One colored man, a school teacher, received the Pentecost the other night and spoke in tongues for some time. She has manifested a call to foreign fields. All the people of God will give her as an interpreter. The witnesses to the blessed truths that God would give me access to my brethren, and then I shall remember but also that God woul give the foreign work, but our Pathset's smile is upon us, and that is better than anything else.

I praised much that God would give me access to my brethren, and then I shall remember him and be a member of the body of Christ through the foreign fields now. How I praise God for giving food and getting ready for the foreign fields now. O how I praise God!

Brothers, pray, and spread the tidings broadcast. The devil is mad. I may never see you in the flesh any more, but I am coming up, coming up, the morning.

Many are getting their Pentecost at home and abroad. I go from here to High Point, N. C. I have more calls than I can fill in six months.

Your brother and servant of God.
—G. B. Caldwell.

PENTECOST IN LAMONT, OKLA.

Jan. 17th

Dear Saints, Greeting!

Left Los Angeles Dec. 4, and arrived in Oklahoma just one week later, making a nice stop on the way. Quite a number were tarrying and waiting for Pentecost when I arrived, but much had to be done before God could pour out His Spirit. The people had been to much bondage. Eating pork, wearing neckties, drinking coffee, and wearing a moustache were taught to be very sinful, and except you were circumcised in these you were lost.

After about ten days of prayer and holding up the Blood, God began to break them up and they began to lay the pardon of one another and their neighbors. And in a short time, in a cottage prayer meeting, God poured out His Spirit in saving power and nearly all went down, one woman through speaking in tongues. God now began to work and souls were saved, backsliders reclaimed, and believers sanctified at nearly every service. The country was stirred for miles around. Some came 100 miles to get Pentecost and healing.

One lady who had been a Free Methodist was reclaimed and sanctified and baptized with the Holy Ghost. She speaks and sings in tongues. Her husband was under much conviction he could scarcely do His work, and in a few days came to the altar and was beautifully saved. The power is trust in Jesus.

The Lord told me to move on, last Sunday morning. Before leaving Sunday night with many seekers at the altar. The saints will go right on and push the battle.

Jan. 21.—Arrived here Friday morning after spending two days in Chicago. Quite a number here are seeking the baptism. We expect great things here. Pray much for me. I can feel it when they pray for me in public. Some time ago to be a prayer service, the Lord showed me Bro. Seymour praying for me, and I seemed to be carried away in the Spirit. Under the Blood.

—G. Cook.
412 Terrace Ave., Indianapolis, Ind.

Several have already received the baptism with the Holy Ghost in Des Moines, Ia. It is not through anyone sent there, but they were carrying before God and Pentecost fell.

In Toronto, a number have received the baptism. Bro. G. Adams went there from Los Angeles. He had not yet received his Pentecost, yet told those about what God had done in Azusa Mission and in those places. They went right to tarrying before God. A company started after meeting to pray through and the Spirit fell and three were filled with the Holy Ghost.

We are receiving hundreds of names and addresses for the paper. Please write very plainly. Those that do not regularly are enrolled on the books. We are sending out thousands of sample copies to friends whose names are kept in by others. If we do not hear from them, we send only two or three numbers. Please notify us of any mistakes.

If you want to keep hot and filled with the power of the Holy Ghost, live off of the Word.

The Lord is sending us to publish anaidy ... number of 30,000 papers for the 5th number of the Apostolic Faith. He has already blest in getting it out. Though it is somewhat late, we trust it will be the greatest blessing.

When you were poor and ugly in your own sight, then was the time God raised and used you, but when you get to be some great Nebuchadnezzar, then God turns you out to eat grass like an ox. Keep little and God will use you.

A boy that accidentally took poison that if found in a bottle in a closet, was healed in answer to prayer. The mother laid on to G-d in agonizing prayer. "Lord, save my boy." The little thing was cold, but the Lord healed it completely.

The Holy Ghost is blessing us daily, but we must wear a great outpouring of the Holy Spirit for there are people in our midst that are staying night and day for a great awakening among the people.—Mrs. C. A. McL..., Edwards St., Fort Worth, Tex. Jan 7

Sickness is all the work of satan. Sometimes we bring it upon ourselves by over-exerting. Sometimes it is permitted of the Lord because of sins of omission or commission. Satan cannot afflict us unless God permits. He has no power over us unless we get on his territory.

I am getting the baptism in Clearwater, Cal. Mother Winston went down to tarry with them and was baptized with the Holy Ghost and spoke in two languages. She is very happy and filled with the Holy Ghost and God is using her. Bro McLain writes that there are lots of hungry souls there and the dev'l is stirred.

Several have written and asked if we received the offerings sent. We can answer that they all came safely, even to letters that came through the fire in a train wreck and were scorched on the edges and stained by water, but they came safely and money in them. So we see how the Lord takes care of consecrated offerings.

"I received my Pentecost last Saturday morning, 11 a.m. Praise God! I am wholly given up to His will. Words cannot express the blessed peace I have in my soul. My soul is filled with His glory. Hallelujah! Praise God for His wonderful Gift to men. We are praying for and expecting His glad baptism soon to take this sheep for God."—B. A. M..., I. ... (2)

The Scandinavian people here are receiving their Pentecost. I was with them last week in their watch night meeting. O how God poured out His Spirit on all flesh. Many spoke in new tongues and every sign of heaven-send fall. Some are falling under the power of God. My soul doth magnify the Lord. He thrills my spirit, soul and body.—Mrs. Ic... C. Magle, 210 Times St., Ballard, Wash.

A sanctified body is one in perfect harmony through faith in God. It does not mean we could not get sick, but we are maintained in health by faith. We do not want to teach people they could never get sick, because they would think they were inhibited creatures. "As the branch cannot bear fruit except it abide in the vine, no more can ye except ye abide in Me." So we must abide in Christ for health.

In Akron, Ohio, a young man went to the Pentecostal meetings and got under conviction through the preaching. And went to the pastor of the First Congregational Church and returned to him $10 that he had stolen about fourteen years before, and promised to pay the rest. The pastor was very much surprised, for the man had been under his preaching for years and never got under conviction. He said, "That kind of religion is loaded with power. There are no blank cartridges in it."

Bro. Tom Hezmalhalch has been home to Los Angeles on a visit and we have been hearing together on the good things of Father's table. On his way back to Colorado, the Spirit directed him to stop off at the Needles. Taking the train on Tuesday morning to resume his journey, to our surprise the train to which he was coupled jumped the track and was taken at Los Angeles for Denver, every car laid in the ditch. By some means they had left the coach off, and the dear engineer and the Blood was badly injured. The would have been in the ditch and precious souls would have suffered. It pays to know the Lord and obey Him.

How will you time keep hot if you stumble over this precious Gospel, if you ignore this Gospel when God has granted signs and wonders to follow? If you grieve the Holy Spirit, and trample upon the Blood of Jesus Christ, how will you miss hell? There is no way for you to escape hell if you reject the Gospel of Jesus Christ. God so loved the world that He gave His only begotten Son, that whosoever believeth on Him, should not perish but have everlasting life. O my friends, the precious Blood is flowing for you. If you come to Him, He will wash away your sin, and cleanse you from all unrighteousness and iniquity, and set up His throne in your heart.

One who received the Holy Ghost baptism in Clearwater testified: "It was in morning worship. We read a chapter and I wanted to pray but the Lord did my mouth. The power began to operate in me. The Lord took full possession. I fell over like a dead man. I was dead to the world. I tried to pray while lying on the floor but my tongue was loosened, it was in a different language. Came little into my soul as God came into my house and wrecked all that was old; I talked about an hour. This is some of the whole world and the precious Blood worked a different cause Jesus had come to set me free, never was His praise or I felt His praises while eternity rolls."

The Apostolic Faith

"Earnestly contend for the faith which was once delivered unto the saints."—Jude 3.

Volume 1, No. 6 | **Los Angeles, Cal., February-March, 1907** | **Subscription Free**

PENTECOST BOTH SIDES THE OCEAN

God is still manifesting His power in Los Angeles.

* * *

The Pentecost has crossed the water on both sides to the Hawaiian Islands on the west, and England, Norway, Sweden, and India on the east.

* * *

A brother in Honolulu received the Pentecost, by hearing of God's work through the paper. He said when he got down to seeking in earnest, the Lord baptized him with the Holy Ghost and he spoke in two languages.

* * *

We rejoice to hear that Pentecost has fallen in Calcutta, India, over ten thousand miles away on the other side of the world: Praise God. We have letters from China, Germany, Switzerland, Norway, Sweden, England, Ireland, Australia, and other countries from hungry souls that want their Pentecost. Some of these letters are in foreign languages. Missionaries write that they are hungry for this outpouring of the Spirit which they believe to be the real Pentecost. The world seems ripe for the Pentecost in all lands and God is sending it. Amen.

* * *

One of the missionaries from Los Angeles in Liberia, Africa, has been able to speak to the people in the Cru tongue. Another sister there wrote in an unknown language under the power of the Spirit, and it was understood and read by one of the native kings there.

* * *

Requests for prayer from hungry souls are coming in from all over. They want salvation from sin, and santification, and the baptism with the Holy Ghost, and healing of their bodies. So the requests are presented and handkerchiefs are blest and the power of God comes upon us in praying for them; and we receive letters saying that they are receiving their Pentecost and being healed. Praise God.

* * *

March 19th was a wonderful day at the Mission on Azusa St. Three ministers from Tennessee received the enduement of power from on high and the glory of God filled the upper room. Others received the anointing of the Spirit and some were slain under the power of God.

* * *

Bro. Stewart from Phoenix, Arizona, came to Azusa Mission and sought the baptism with the Holy Ghost, and God laid him out under the power of the Spirit and took complete control of him, speaking through him in tongues. He was filled and overflowing with the Holy Ghost when he returned to Arizona. And Mother Griffith, also from Phoenix, has come and received her baptism.

* * *

The work at Azusa Mission is growing deeper and more powerful than ever. Praise God. Meetings continue every day with seekers at every service, and the three meetings run very near together. All day meetings on Sunday. Three other Apostolic Faith Missions continue in the city and God's blessing is upon them. The workers from these missions and from suburban towns meet together for conference on Mondays to study the Scriptures and get deeper into the things of God and for conference in the work of the Lord. The spirit of unity, love and power is manifest. Other like missions are being established in a number of towns.

* * *

Bro. Andrews and wife, Gospel workers from Tennessee, came to Azusa Mission for the express purpose of receiving their Pentecost and Bro. Andrews has been baptized with the Holy Ghost and is filled and overflowing with the Spirit. He and his wife were so hungry and had such faith that the Lord wanted them to come, that, not having the means, they started and walked quite a distance, till the Lord gave them the fare, and He is abundantly rewarding them.

* * *

Bro. W. H. Durham of 943 North Ave., Chicago, Ill., and Bro. H. L. Blake of Ruthton, Minn., who are both preachers of the Gospel, came to Los Angeles to see and investigate what God was doing. They both were baptized with the Holy Ghost and went back filled and saturated with the power of God, speaking in tongues and magnifying God. It was a great blessing to us to have them with us and see what great things the Lord did for them and the blessing overflowed upon all God's children. They are members of the World's Faith Missionary Association.

* * *

Sister Rees from Oakland visited Azusa Mission recently. She brought a report from the saints in Oakland that a leader was needed there in the work, one called and prepared of the Lord. We prayed for God to call someone. Bro. Irwin received the call and went with his wife. His report comes just as the paper is going to press: Oakland, Cal., Mar. 21.—"God is undertaking for us here. Two received their Pentecost last night with Bible evidence. Others are seeking pardon, sanctification, the promise of the Father."—B. H. Irwin.

A number from Winnipeg, Canada, have come to Los Angeles and are now rejoicing in the baptism with the Holy Ghost. Others have come from the Atlantic coast and from Colorado and different states and they have received a Bible Pentecost, evidenced by speaking in tongues, and from other centers workers are going out to the ends of the earth, till we cannot keep track of them. The Lord is speedily preparing His people for His coming.

* * *

We cannot give a report of all that have gone out into the work since the last paper, for they are going almost every day. Bro. and Sister H. McLain have gone to San Jose, Cal., to take charge of the work there and Sister Agnes Jacobson and Bro. Harmon Clifford are also in the work in San Jose. See report from there of how God is working. Bro. Turney and wife who were at San Jose are now in Honolulu. Bro. and Sister E. W. Vinton from near Boston, Mass., who received their Pentecost in Los Angeles, have returned to tell the glad tidings. Their address is 12 Leyden St., Medford, Mass. Bro. C. E. Marsh expects to join them there in preaching this Gospel Bands of workers have gone out to other places and started the work.

* * *

Since the last paper, Bro. Seymour visited San Francisco and San Jose and reported that God had some of the most precious saints there filled with the Holy Ghost and shining for God that he had ever seen and that the power of God was wonderfully manifest.

* * *

There are a number of papers on the Apostolic line that are springing up. We cannot tell how many there are, because we hear of new ones we have not seen. But there are three clean cut papers besides Apostolic Faith, out and out for a Bible Pentecost according to Acts. 2. 4 and with subscription free. They are the **Apostolic Light**, Portland, Ore., **The New Acts**, Alliance, Ohio (which now includes Pentecostal Wonders) and **The Apostolic Evangel**, Royston, Ga. (formerly Live Coals.) These papers are all about the size of the January number of this paper and they are filled with the wonderful works of God, and are spreading the glad tidings of another Pentecost all over the world. They are all supported entirely by free will offerings.

PENTECOST IN OTHER LANDS.

In London.

23 Gairloch Road, Camberwell, S. E., London, Jan. 20.—A little band of Christians have been waiting here about nine months for their Pentecost and am glad to say that one sister has received her Pentecost with tongues. Praise Him! Will you continue to pray that all may receive, the writer included. I feel very hungry. Yours in Jesus Christ, C. H. Hook.

In Stockholm.

Stockholm, Sweden, March 3.—Please, dear ones, help us to praise the Lord. The first soul came through tonight receiving the baptism with the Holy Ghost and Bible evidence. Bless God!—Eric Hollingsworth and wife.

This message was just received from our brother and sister who have gone to Sweden with this precious Gospel. They wrote of the salvation and sanctification of souls and now we rejoice with them that Pentecost has fallen in Sweden's capitol.

In Sweden.

We are having a wonderful time in Sweden. Hundreds have been saved and sanctified. Over a hundred baptized with the Holy Ghost. Praise God! Glory! Glory! Glory! Many have been healed by the dear Lord. Signs as on the day of Pentecost are following, talking and singing in tongues. I cannot tell you all now that God has been doing. The work is spreading fast. Many are seeking for a clean heart and there is oneness among God's people. God shall have all the glory.

I am still talking and writing in tongues. A missionary interpreted what I have been writing in Syriac and Armenian. I was singing Chinese one night, a missionary said. I am busy every day and going from place to place. Strong opposition from many, but God gives the victory. Glory! Andrew G. Johnson, Address, 48 Skofde, Sweden.

In Honolulu.

Honolulu, Hawaii, March 11.—Immediately upon our arrival here, we found two wholly consecrated souls, hungering for more of God. Bro. Mayfield threw his mission open to us and told us to go to work. So we opened fire upon the enemy the first night of our arrival here. God owned and blest the truth. Nine have received their Pentecost, and in every case they have spoken in new tongues. Sister Mayfield has received her Pentecost and healing for lung trouble. Myself and wife have both spoken in the Corean language, Coreans present testifying to the same. We believe that will be our next field of labor.—H. M. Turney and wife.

IN CALCUTTA, INDIA.

Feb. 21.—The Lord has led Sister Nelson and myself here to Calcutta to behold the wonderful works of God. He has sent three of His witnesses from America, filled with the Holy Ghost, to show forth His power and proclaim this wonderful Gospel which we and many others have been hungering for so long. Praise His dear name! It is Mr. and Mrs. A. G. Garr and Miss Gammon. God is working in mighty power in our midst. Several have received the baptism with the Holy Ghost and speak with tongues, and many have been saved. We have meetings every day beginning about four p. m. and go on as long as the Lord leads. We are so hungry and do believe that God will soon satisfy our longing souls.

Mary Johnson.

Home address: Dehiwala, Court Lodge, Ceylon, India.

In Norway.

Solfies, Pl. 2, Christiania, Norway, Jan. 29.—God is wonderfully demonstrating His power here in the Norwegian capital. It is about ten days since I held the first meeting in the large gymnasium that will take when crowded from 1,500 to 2,000 people. People from all denominations are rushing to the meetings. Over twenty have received their Pentecost and are speaking in tongues. Several have been in trances and had heavenly visions. Some have seen Jesus at our meetings, and the tongues of fire have been seen again over my head by a freethinker, convincing him of the power of God. Many are seeking salvation and souls are being gloriously saved. Hundreds are seeking a clean heart, and the fire is falling on the purified sacrifice. The fire is spreading very rapidly. Glory to God! I received word from the country districts that the fire is falling there. People who have attended the meetings are taking the fire with them to the towns around about. The account of God's work for my soul has been inserted in many religious papers, and has caused a stir. All can see it is the work of God's Holy Spirit. Hallelujah! Some of the languages spoken are European. One man was thrown on his back, a preacher, last Sunday morning in the Students' Hall, and when he rose, he spoke in four languages, one of these was English. He could speak none of them before. After that, he prophesied and invited sinners to come to Christ. Numbers threw themselves down and cried for salvation, cleansing, and the fiery baptism with the Spirit. Praised be God! Several preachers are seeking their Pentecost. Go on praying for the advancement of the Kingdom of our Lord and King this grand old country. Fraternal greetings from those baptized with the power and fire from on high. Yours in Christ Jesus, T. B. Barratt.

If you get the light on your soul, you will go forward or else backslide.

The more of the Holy Ghost you have, the more love, the more humility, the more praises.

This is not a "do, do" religion, but it is the religion of the Lord Jesus Christ. Man has got to be born again. You cannot get it through moral culture, refinement, or giving up, but you must be born into it. It is through God's beloved Son who washes you, cleanses you, and makes you a fit subject for heaven.

Every sanctified person has the abiding anointing in their soul, and they know His Blood cleanses every moment, but you need the baptism with the Holy Ghost which is the enduement of power, that will make you a witness to the uttermost parts of the earth.

This Gospel cost us too much to run off into fanaticism and be led by visions and dreams. When we get spiritual, there is greater temptation to get puffed up. We must put all visions and dreams on the square of God's Word and try them. The Word must prove all things. When we throw down God's truth, the plummet of His Word, is shows up the counterfeit.

People receive the baptism with the Holy Ghost while about their work. One sister in Whittier received hers while she was baking a cake.

The Holy Ghost is a real living Person that comes down upon you in great and mighty power. Dear loved ones, when He comes upon you, you know it. When He comes in, He comes talking. Your jaws will be unloosed, and He will commence speaking through you.

We are Christ's spiritual birde now, but there is to be a real wedding take place and a real marriage supper. Those that sit down to this supper will be His queen, the ones that have made their robes white and have the seal of God in their foreheads. O let us not miss this supper. We are listening now for the sound of His chariot wheels.

The Lord has taken Spiritualism and Christian Science out of people in this mission, and filled them with the Spirit, and they are sitting at the feet of Jesus. We teach against Theosophy, Christian Science, Magnetic Healing, Spiritualism, Hypnotism and all works of the devil.

NEW SCANDINAVIAN REVIVAL.

The Witness of "Tongues" Manifested in Christiania.

The following report of the Pentecostal revival in Norway is published in the North Mail, Edinburg, England. It is a letter from the Vicar of All Saints, Sunderland, England, Bro. A. A. Body. He had been to Christiania, Norway, visiting Bro. Barratt's meeting.

My four days in Christiania cannot easily be forgotten. I remember well the scenes two years ago, when I stood with Evan Roberts in the pulpit at Ton-y-Pandy, but, wonderful as such scenes in Wales were, the scenes in the Torvegadon Mission Room and other places were more supernatural. I believe that very soon we shall witness the same in England.

Warmly welcomed by the pastor and his co-workers, I sat, of necessity, on the low, large platform, with its table and four forms. The room was an upper chamber, down a court out of a busy street. It was very bare, with forms without any backs. But the enthusiastic congregation did not think of comfort.

Boys and girls around me, from seven to twelve years of age, were seeing visions and speaking in tongues—as well as older folk.

A bright-faced lad cried out with intense vehemence (eyes closed, right hand on heart, left hand stretched out)—"Oh . . . I see the house of Satan thrust down and down . . . . and now the host are entering Heaven. Oh! . . . . they are going to shut the door: and some will be too late. Oh! Jesus, Jesus." Then he commenced to shout in a rapid unknown tongue, and a few minutes later he was just a simple, lovable Norwegian boy again.

Then a university student (under the power of the Spirit) cries with great vehemence (to the "Djarvlen"), "Go- . . . Will you go: . . . Will you go!" All this time perhaps a dozen are speaking or praying in Tongues, or prophesying, and prayer and praise "in the Spirit" is going on all over. Then suddenly a high-pitched musical voice is heard cutting into everything—prolonged, and then dying away. It is a woman praising Christ in the Spirit.

A brother on my left breaks out into Tongues; three times in that meeting he did the same. First it seems to be in English, very rapidly spoken: "Come, come, come, come now to the Savior," etc. Then it seems to be like Chinese: "Chung, chew, chow" etc., or [illegible]. Then he changes into a chattering sort of Tongue. I am assured that all there are Holy Ghost people. "The flesh may get in a little," says the good pastor, "but not much."

"Tongues" at Keswick.

People of course, ridicule; but those meetings go on every day, and twice a day, and not in one place of meeting only nor in one single town. At Christiansand and Frederickshaldt and many other places the same is going on, and it spreads quickly from each person who receives the Gift!

A Christian merchant in a high position in Denmark came with others to see and hear, and he told me that he was convinced it is of God. The working people chiefly fill the meetings, and the difficulty is to get them to leave when the time comes to close.

And, it must be added, practical results follow these strange meetings.

Pastor Barratt (of whom more below) said that till recently it was difficult to attract to religious meetings. A Salvation Army officer advertised that a man would rise from his coffin and preach the Gospel, but even this did not effectively draw. But now twice a day and every day and week after week these meetings are thronged by enthusiastic crowds, who go out to spread the strange flame, which they are convinced is Pentecostal and Heavenly and Scriptural.

The meetings are liable at any moment to be swept by a wave of spiritual power sweeping through all human arrangements. At times the noise is strangely awesome, almost appalling to an "outsider."

Some of us ask ourselves the question, how will this affect the Keswick Convention meetings and other gatherings this year? Those who have "Tongues" will be present, and unable and unwilling to control them when moved by the Spirit.

The Rev. Thomas Ball Barratt, the leader of this movement, is almost a Norwegian. He was fours years old when his Cornish parents brought him to Hardanger. Eventually he becamd a missioner of the Methodist Episcopal Church, but he has practically detached himself from any church ties, and the world he feels is his parish.

He was in New York last autumn when influences from the Los Angeles movement began to reach him, and he received a mighty "Pentecost," witnessed to by "Tongues." A letter he wrote home stirred up the spirit of expectancy, and on his arrival the work immediately began, and on New Year's Day in Norway the revival commenced, and has continued ever since, and is spreading all the time.

Of my own inner experiences whilst in these meetings I must refrain from writing at this point, but I reverently thank God for the privilege of being present.

"He will guide you into all truth." We ought to take the Holy Ghost before any other teacher. We should have no teacher between us and the Holy Ghost.

The Apostolic Faith

"Earnestly contend for the faith which was once delivered unto the saints."—Jude 3.

Volume 1, No. 7 | Los Angeles, Cal., April, 1907 | Subscription Free

Many Witnesses to the Power of the Blood and of the Holy Ghost.

In Africa.

Monrovia, Liberia, Mar. 26.—We opened a ten days' meeting in a school house, and on the tenth night, the Lord came in mighty power. Two were baptized with the Holy Ghost and spoke in tongues. Ten here have received sanctification, and five are filled with the Holy Ghost and speaking in tongues. A brother and his household have been baptized with the Holy Ghost. God has called him to the ministry and he will be baptized Sunday the 30th of March. Have been holding meetings going on three months. The Lord is sending a crowd of the African natives to the meeting and He is working wonderfully with them. The house is filled with the natives every service and they are being saved and sanctified and filled with the Holy Ghost and healed of all manner of diseases. The Lord surely is working with the native Africans of this land. All the saints send love.

In London.

Allerman Road, Brixton, London, S.W., March 18.—Words fail to express our gratitude to God for pouring out so wonderfully Hish blessed Spirit. We can read nothing else now but our Bible and the accounts of His glorious doings in your midst and elsewhere. The reading of it has intensified the deep hunger of soul in the few waiting upon God and seeking our Personal Pentecost here. A dear sister here, a mother of three little ones yielded herself fully to God and sought the baptism with the Holy Ghost. One night she waited upon God and at midnight the Holy Ghost came down upon her and gave her the witness of tongues. The next day while at prayer, I being with her, she had a mighty anointing and has spoken in two or three tongues. This was on January 9. She could not give utterance to the raptures of her soul in praising the "Bleeding Lamb," and talked to God sometimes in a loud voice praising and adoring Him in a new tongue. Glory to His holy name.—J. Hinmers.

In Calcutta, India.

55 Creek Row— God is spreading Pentecost here in Calcutta, and thirteen or fourteen missionaries and other workers have received it. The Spirit is giving the interpretation, song and writing in tongues, and other wonderful manifestations of His presence among us. O we do praise Him that the way ever opened for us to come to India. I cannot tell you how the Word is opening. Have never seen a meeting in my life where God has given more wonderful power on his blessed Word. We are among Bible teachers, and they have the Word so stored away; but now the Spirit is putting life and power into it, which is wonderful to behold. Praise our precious Christ.

God has put quite a burden on my heart for India's hungry souls. The Spirit has groaned through my soul for hungry ones until the pain was like travail. Oh how grateful we are for His working with us in this needy field.

We enjoy the paper very much, in fact, much of it is read in the meetings, and all rejoice. The little paper was a forerunner for us. We came to find that its contents had made God's children hungry for the light to come to India, and when we arrived we found some waiting for their Pentecost. We found India ripe for this light, in fact the revival had already broken out among the natives, and some were speaking in tongues.

Miss Easton, the head of the American Women's Board of Missions, the oldest womans' missionary board in India, has been baptized and is a power for God.

We learn that the power has broken out in Russia, also in London.—Sister A. G. Garr.

In Sweden.

Viby, April 2.—Peace be unto you! Glory to God and praise His Holy name for evermore. Glory to God for victory through the Blood of Christ! I am happy in Jesus Christ and glad for what He has been doing in Sweden. The Lord has wonderfully kept me every day. Praise the Lord! Glory! There are now about twelve preachers who have received the Holy Ghost with signs following, and a few hundred have been saved, many getting a clean heart. Some have been healed, and many of God's children have received the Holy Ghost. I am called to many places and the cry for help comes from all over Sweden. I am very busy every day going from place to place. There is strong opposition and talking about me, and writing in the papers even. Glory to God, my King, for that. Glory! Glory!

Tell the saints to love one another and keep united in love, and under the Blood every day, and humble. I am with you every day in the Spirit and praying for you all. Glory to my King for victory! God's people are going to be one soon. Glory!

Apr. 15th 43 Skofde, Sweden.—The Lord Jesus Christ has done wonderful things in the last days, saving hundreds, sanctifying many, and hundreds have received their Pentecost with signs following. Praise the the Lord. Many have been healed. Here is much to do every day. Many seekers after God. Over a hundred at the altar some meetings. A few interpret what they speak in tongues, and even myself. One day I interpreted these words, "Be ye separate from the world, that ye may be one," and "Abide in My love." and "For Thy greatness and might does the earth tremble," and Matt. 28. 19,20. The Lord has supplied all my needs. Glory to God.

Many churches have been stirred up here. I expect greater things yet. A few who can read the paper are very glad to read it and are getting blest by it. My love to all the saints.—Andrew G. Johnson.

In Bellvernon, Pa.

April 19th.—The Lord is working here in Bellvernon. People are being healed, devils are being cast out in Jesus' name. People are being baptized with the Holy Ghost and speaking with other tongues.—J. F. Mitchell.

In Bellingham, Washington.

In Bellingham, Wash, the Pentecost has fallen, quite a number have received the baptism and they have a mission of their own. Fourteen converts have been baptized in the bay.

In Mobile, Ala.

Davis and Anne street, April 28.—The Lord has been working wonderfully here the past two weeks. Souls have been justified, sanctified, and are receiving the baptism with the Holy Ghost. One who was a sinner was healed in our meeting and the next night got saved. Her mother got healed and received the Holy Ghost all at the same time. Praise the Lord for victory.—F. W. Williams.

In South Carolina.

Alvin, S. C., April 19.—My wife and I have been in six wonderful meetings of late in which quite a number of saints have received the baptism with the Holy Ghost, and all spoke with other tongues. Backsliders are being reclaimed and some honest souls being converted, quite a lot of sick ones being healed, and also many demon possessed persons are being delivered in Jesus's name from the power of Satan. Glory to God!—F. M. Britton.

In Lincoln, Pa.

April 10.—God is having His way with many of His children in this part of the country. A great many, in the midst of much opposition, are being baptized with the Holy Spirit and speaking in tongues, among them a number of young people and children. The work is spreading in and about Pittsburg and Allegheny, in Homestead, Braddock, McKeesport, and other places in this vicinity.—J. T. Boddy, pastor Pentecost church.

In San Antonio, Tex.

425 N. Pine street, April 13.—We are in the midst of a glorious meeting in this city. Ten have received Pentecost with the Bible evidence of speaking in tongues, and a number have been saved and sanctified. God has enabled us to create a widespread interest throughout the city, and the opposition is forming in a very formidable way, we know that our God is able to deliver. We are going forward in simple faith in Him.—Daniel C. O. Opperman.

In Allegheny, Pa.

216 E. Stockton Ave., April 16.—Join with us in praising Him for the outpouring of Gods' Spirit in Pentecostal power in the district of Pittsburg, Pa. We had heard of God's outpouring all over the world, so we began to seek for God's best for ourselves. I saw that power came only through heart purity, so I yielded myself up to God's searching power and get a glimpse of "Calvary;" and then, praise God, the power fell with the signs following. Pentecost first fell in the third week of January and is still going on. Hallelujah. Almost every meeting there are some prostrated under the power and coming through. Almost every one that speaks in tongues gets the message that Jesus, is coming soon. He is just the same yesterday today and forever.—M. R. C.

In Honolulu, Hawaii.

March 18.— We are just holding up Jesus before this people, and God is doing the rest. We had quite a scene at the altar last night, when a demon possessed man who was kneeling at the altar was picked up by demon power, thrown over the altar rail on his head, and when we commanded them to come out of him they barked at us and said that they would not come out of him, but they were cast out in the Name of Jesus and the man was set free. A Salvation Army captain has received his Pentecost. He is noble young man, and desires to labor with the Apostolic Faith Movement. We are believing for a great work in the Islands. Jesus is coming very soon. Hallelujah!—H. M. and A. E. Turney

In Durham, N. C.

March 28.—"Some of the Lord's people here have received their Pentecost and spoken in tongues. Glory! A red hot meeting is now going on. Bro. Fulford, who has the gift of tongues, is leading it under the direction of the Holy Ghost. The saints are being baptized with the Spirit. I too have received Him and have spoken in some kind of a language, I know not what. It is glory here now. What we are now praying for is to have the nine gifts of the Spirit here in full operation. This city has been mightily stirred on account of the tongues. Nearly the whole of North Carolina is being stirred among the Holiness people, white and colored.—W. L. Fisher, Box 208.

In Springboro, P.

April 26.—"God is meeting us here in some very marked ways. Many have gotten clear in their experience of sanctification, a backslider came back last evening, others are just on the eve of Pentecost, five have gotten through. The town is stirred. They say it is a work of the devil, and fight me, but, oh, what victory God gives in the midst. The preachers turn out well to these meetings. I don't know them until someone points them out to me afterward, so they get hit very often. The Free Methodist preacher confessed yesterday he was not sanctified. I think he will soon get somewhere. He said he was afraid to say anything about this movement. He knows God is in it.—Ivey Campbell.

In Dayton, O.

April 6.—"Oh, I praise God for the gift of the Spirit. There were some seeking it on the west side here, and when it came, some of them refused it and said it was of the devil, but I was simple enough to take God at His Word, and two of us received our Pentecost. I received it February 22. Bless the dear Lord. There was a little preacher that went to Akron, O., and received his Pentecost, returning to Dayton. There are about 25 have received Pentecost through God using him. God picked him up a drunken gambler and saved and sanctified him, and sent him out to preach, and when he got his Pentecost most of the church people rejected him. We are going through hard persecution and we are having a time to get a place to worship; but we are holding on to God. We need your prayers. we are only babies, but our God is able and we are trusting Him."—Delia Powell, 302 Spitler Ave.

In San Diego, Cal.

Praise God! The fire still burns, sinners coming home to God, believers being sanctified and baptized with the Holy Ghost, speaking with other tongues as the Spirit gives them utterance. We joined with you all of like precious faith on April 9th, and commemorated the anniversary of the Pentecostal outpouring in California. We had a most blessed and victorious day. Hallelujah! The streams of living water and salvation flowed, and glorious deliverance came to some precious souls. The tide is rising higher and higher, the conviction going deeper and deeper, and the way growing brighter day by day. Oh, Glory! Hallelujah! This little army is marching on to sure and glorious victory through the precious blood of the Lamb.—F. E. Hill.

726 14th street, April 6.—The dear Lord is wonderfully blessing the work here in San Diego. Last night we had a powerful meeting; two were slain under the power of God, three received their Pentecost with the Bible evidence. Sinners were crying to God for mercy, and the saints were wonderfully blessed.—G. H. Reilly.

In Homestead, Pa.

The Pentecost has fallen in Homestead, Pa. The meeting began in the Christian and Missionary Alliance Hall, Jan. 11. The power of the Holy Ghost was felt from the first service and a deep digging up begun among the people who were willing to go with God at any cost. Restitution, apologies and repentance was the business of the meeting for the first six days and nights. In fact the state to which some were led seemed perilous at times, but with confidence in the leading of God and with hearts desirous of going all the way, there was scarcely a halt, till everything in the past life had been fully reviewed from a Pentecostal standpoint, and every crooked or questionable act adjusted. On the seventh day the walls began to fall, and people fell under the power of God. The baptism was first received by Sister Robinson, who laid under the power for some time, then came through speaking in tongues. The next night the husband received his Pentecost at his home, and spoke and sang in new tongues. From this on the work has been going forward with uninterrupted sway.

The hall soon became too small when we were compelled to secure a larger one in order to accommodate the increasing crowds.

Many have received their personal Pentecost and speak and sing in new tongues, and have power over demons to cast them out and to pray the prayer of faith for the healing of the sick.

For miles around people are coming in to investigate this work and to receive their Pentecost.—"The Latter Rain."

In Fort Worth, Tex.

1.005 Edward St., April 12.—We have a small band here. Have been meeting in private houses asking the Lord to open a door for us that no man could shut. We are praising the Lord this morning that we have a tent paid for and lights and seats secured. O, how happy I am at the prospect. Just as soon as the weather clears away, we want to begin meetings. We are expecting our God to do great things, for when I read of the wonderful work at Azusa, my heart rejoices so that I fall to my knees to thank God. We want the heavenly showers to fall on us too. We have four now waiting for the promise of the Father. A young man, a preacher, came to see me last Tuesday. He said that a little more than four months ago he was down waiting on God for an infilling of the Holy Spirit, when after waiting on God he began to pray in language unknown to him. This came on him in a few days. He told his presiding elder, who said that was foolishness. He said that once after that he felt like letting the Lord have His way with him, but on account of discouragements he did not do so. When he came here he hunted us up, and the power all came back to him. He never had anyone to help or tell him about this great movement.—Mrs. C. A. Roll.

In Toronto, Canada.

The Lord is wonderfully blessing the work in 651 Queen street, E. Toronto. For five months it has gone on without a break. Nearly 80 have received the Baptism with the Holy Ghost, speaking in tongues. Four workers have gone out from here to preach the full Gospel. Many are being healed. Last Sunday we had a glorious time all day, especially in the afternoon service, when the power of God prostrated two brothers and came upon many at the altar. The whole meeting place was used as an altar, everyone turning their seats and getting down before the Lord. One brother who began speaking in tongues staggered to his feet exclaiming: "This is glory, glory, glory!" and before he had got through a sister rose under the power of God and commenced saying: "This is glory, glory." A spirit of great rejoicing seized everyone. It was a time of magnifying God. Truly He has done great things. A band of workers from this mission went to a place just outside the city limits and held services, and the power of God came down upon the people. We are believing for a mighty outpouring upon the people in that district.—Sister Hebden.

In Indianapolis, Ind.

2341 Fletcher Ave., April 20.—Praise God for ever and ever. It is wonderful how God is manifesting His power here in bringing dear souls through and healing the sick. This is stirring up the ministers and people, and the newspaper are lying and trying to put the people against us, but God is overruling, and people who never dreamt of coming under the influence of God's power have been stricken down and are getting salvation, their baptism and speaking in tongues.

Yesterday afternoon God took a young colored brother and a young sister, and in a most marvelous manner the Holy Spirit spoke through them in tongues, giving the interpretation, and with such power and force that the whole audience was stricken with awe. Weeping was seen all over the place, and they acknowledge it was God and the power of the Holy Ghost. There must have been a dozen ministers or more present, and one of them the leading or one of the leading ministers of this city. He was advertised to preach against us next Sunday, April 21; but, thank God, he and his wife wept with the rest. When I asked: Is there a man or woman who dare stand up and say these children were hypocrites? this same minister said: "No, it is God."

One man who did not know anything about the meetings, but saw the sign as he was passing, came in out of curiosity. He is a doctor and medical nurse, has spent some time in India, and can talk in many of the Indian languages. He said he was surprised soon after he had taken his seat, then God struck him and he was brought under deep conviction. It kept increasing. He got desperate. God kept telling him to go to the penitent form. He did not want to for fear he would be laid out upon the floor. He got more desperate, until he bought some poison, and if he did not get through last Thursday afternoon he intended taking the poison. He had not slept any since last Sunday night. Praise God, he came and went through and got the whole thing. When he received his baptism he threw up his hands, gave a shout of Glory, and over he went backwards upon the floor. While there, Jesus came to him and told him He wanted him to return to India and preach the Gospel. He promised he would and take others with him, if it is His will. Glory to our Christ for ever and ever. He identified one of the tongues spoken by a young sister and told us it was the Marathi language. He also identified other languages in others. He had to give up all his business before God would receive him, and go to the medical staff and tell them what for. Our only desire and heart's cry is: Precious souls for Jesus and heaven.—T. Hezmalhalch.

The Apostolic Faith

"Earnestly contend for the faith which was once delivered unto the saints."—Jude 3.

Volume 1, No. 8 | Los Angeles, Cal., May, 1907 | Subscription Free

Los Angeles Campmeeting of the Apostolic Faith Missions.

We expect to have a grand campmeeting in Los Angeles, beginning June 1, and continuing about four months.

* * *

The spot selected for it is adjoining the city limits, several miles from the center of town in a grove of sycamore and live oak trees near Hermon. The fare is only five cents on the electric cars which run every seven minutes. It is only three blocks from where the cars stop to the Campmeeting.

* * *

We expect to have a tabernacle with seating capacity of about 1000 people. There will be room in the grove for many tents. Free camping grounds. The air is fresh with the sea breeze which comes in from the distant ocean, and there is plenty of good water. You can pray there as loud as you like. There are wooded hills all about which we expect will ring with the songs and prayers of the saints and shouts of new born souls.

* * *

There will be a separate tabernacle for meetings for the children with services daily, so it will be a children's campmeeting as well as a grown up people's meeting. There will be competent workers to teach and help them spiritually. We expect it to be a time of salvation among the children. Mother's meetings are also planned for.

* * *

Workers from all missions in and about Los Angeles who are one with us, by virtue of having been baptized by one Spirit into one body, are uniting in this campmeeting. Services will be continued in Azusa Mission every night just the same as ever, a band going from the campmeeting to carry on the work. Other missions will also carry on their work.

* * *

A large band of Holy Ghost workers, men and women whom God has equipped for His service will be present to carry on the meeting, under the guidance of our blessed Redeemer whom we honor as the great Leader and Manager. Much prayer is going up to God that He will make this a time of visiting His people with salvation and an outpouring of Pentecost such as we have never witnessed before. The business part of the work is being arranged in orderly and systematic shape. Proper officers will have charge of the grounds, putting up tents, etc.

* * *

The workers from the different missions first met to counsel together about the campmeeting. We got down to ask the Lord for the money, and the witness came that prayer was heard; the Spirit was poured out upon us. We arose and decided to lease the ground for four months. Before the meeting was over, the power of God so filled the room that one fell under the power and the meeting turned into a Pentecostal service.

* * *

A number are willingly giving their services in clearing and preparing the grounds. No collections have been taken, but several hundred dollars have already been offered for the campmeeting. God hears prayer and is putting His seal on it.

* * *

Viewing the Campground.

Last summer during the hot days when the crowds would fill Azusa Mission all day, people would often get up and say they praised God for what he was doing for them "this morning;" not realizing that the sun was going down in the evening. They had not eaten all day and yet they were so taken up with sitting at the feet of Jesus that they lost track of the time and would sit there in the heat, wiping the perspiration from their faces. I thought how God was pleased with it, and how He would be pleased to give them a nice shady place in which to worship.

A few weeks ago, as our sister was reading the letters on Sunday morning in Azusa Mission from the foreign lands and the home land, as she was reading about a campmeeting in the east, she said she believed the Lord would give us a campmeeting here. The Lord began to talk to me about the campmeeting. He talked to me during the night and the next morning the burden of the campmeeting was so on my heart, that I laid aside my work and went over to the Mission and asked our sister if the Lord had laid it on her heart where He was going to have the campmeeting. It seemed to me that morning I could see in a vision the grove and the little white tents all through it. And God was showing us both the same spot. While we were talking, a brother came in with the burden of the camp-meeting on his heart. He had not been able to sleep for thinking of it and where to have it. We said we would all go and view the grounds, so a company of us started.

As we landed there, every step we took seemed to praise God. The very trees seemed to clap their hands and say "Praise God." As we walked down the Arroyo, heaven came down our souls to greet, and we said, "Surely God is in it." We began to get thirsty and went to a sister's house to get a drink from the well in her yard. She came out rejoicing, seeking her Pentecost. As we began to drink, we thought of how God will water thirsty souls there, and we sang, "By Samaria's wayside well, once a blessed message fell, On a woman's thirsty soul long ago." And the power of God came upon us all. We went back and viewed the ground again. Surely it looks like the hand of Beaulah around there. We went on and visited a dear old brother in Hermon and he rejoiced at the prospect of the camp-meeting. All welcomed us and praised God.—One of the Committee.

* * *

Arrangements are being made for reduced rates on all lines of railroad for those coming to the camp-meeting.

* * *

On arriving in Los Angeles, take the South Pasadena or Church of Angels car, and get off at Sixtieth Ave.

* * *

Tents can be purchased or rented at reasonable prices on the camp ground. Bring with you necessary provision for living in tents.

* * *

For full information in regard to the camp-meeting, address APOSTOLIC FAITH CAMP-MEETING, 312 AZUSA ST., LOS ANGELES, CAL.

PENTECOSTAL MEETINGS.

In Little Rock, Ark.

May 7.—I thank God that I am able to report victory through Jesus Christ our Lord. We are now in the midst of a [illegible]. The fire is falling and the people are getting the baptism right along. The Holy Ghost is working in our midst as never before. The Lord has made known to us that the speaking in tongues is the Bible evidence of the baptism with the Holy Ghost. Bro. Jeter and I are holding the meeting here with some others of the brethren. The Holy Ghost has charge. Pray much that we may get out of the way of the Holy Ghost, so that He can run things to suit Himself.—D. J. Young, 212 N. Hickory St., Pine Bluff, Ark.

In Topeka, Kansas.

Mission, 926 N. Kans. Ave., May 9.—It is surely wonderful how the Lord is working all over the world, and I am glad I have a part in this great work. Praise His name. The work here is moving ahead and several are tarrying and seeking Pentecost. A half dozen or more have received the baptism and have spoken in tongues. Sister Culp has returned to us from Los Angeles, where she received her Pentecost. God is using her here to His glory in speaking in tongues and telling of His wonderful works. We had a blessed day Sunday. The afternoon service ran on into the night. The power of God came on one sister. She got up from the altar and shouted all over the house and praised God. Her husband went down on his back under the power. He said he was nearer the Lord than he had ever been. Others are earnestly seeking. The devil is fighting hard, but we are determined to stay on the field and let God have His way with us.—C. E. Foster.

In Chicago, Ill.

943 W. North Ave., April 11.—Our meetings are wonderful, indeed, since I received my Pentecost. From the first day I arrived home, the mission will not hold the people, and I have moved out of the rooms in the rear of the Mission and we use them for overflow and prayer rooms, and still we cannot accommodate the crowds on Sunday. Best of all, the Spirit works in mighty power, and people fall under it, and many have come through and spoken in tongues. My dear wife received her Pentecost soon after I reached home, and yesterday one of our elders, who has been seeking for months, came through. Hallelujah! People are coming from all directions, and the interest and power is increasing daily, until I never saw more of the power of God anywhere than we see here from time to time. Best of all it is all of God,—no one can claim any credit,—God just comes with power and takes possession.

We never forget to pray for Azusa St. Mission, and hope you remember us. Beloved, let us walk in meekness before the Lord, and give Him all the glory for what He is doing, and He will be with us. I feel like staying at His feet all the time.

April 18.—It is wonderful how He is working in our midst. One after another are coming through and speaking in tongues. Last night the meeting lasted all night.

In Memphis, Tenn.

May 2.—The Lord our God is with us at this place, and the saints are receiving their Pentecost. I have never met with such power of the devil as here. One man came to the service and dragged his wife from the altar by force and threatened to kill me and others. But, glory to God, he was overpowered by our God. His wife got the baptism and spoke in tongues, and last night he was back to the service and says he must have his Pentecost. Praise God. I heard from Bro. Mason's church. The power is falling and many souls being filled and speaking in tongues. I met Bro. Mason last week and found him filled with the blessed Holy Ghost. He is a precious brother. Here is a battle but our God is fighting it for us. We are only here to stand still and see the salvation of the Lord. The saints are gathering here from Mississippi, Missouri and points in Tennessee. This work at Memphis is now on footing to continue till summer. I long to see you all in life, but if not I will meet you at the marriage supper of the Lamb.—G. B. Cashwell.

In Alliance, O.

We are in the midst of a gracious outpouring of God's Spirit in our ten days consecration; people are coming up as they did to Jerusalem, anxious to know the way of God more perfectly. Thirteen were laid out under the power at once, some who had had their Pentecost receiving prophecy, many sweet heavenly messages. A young Irish boy, 20 years an orphan, was saved on the vessel two years ago as Rev. Lupton was on his way to Africa. He came to the Home here two weeks ago and received Pentecost in a few days. God has been so mervelously using him and making him such a blessing to all. He prophesied under the power more than six hours. He was telling of the countries of Africa, and spoke of many of the places Rev. Lupton had visited. The boy himself was never in Africa, but was on his way to England when converted.

A doctor from Oberlin College arose in the meeting while Rev. McKenney was giving the message and said: "I believe it, I have been sekptical, but I do know it is true." The altar filled at once with men some women knelt at the front seats.

Oh, how we love to honor the precious Blood. It is so blessed to stand and see the salvation of God. We count the Holy Ghost faithful.

A very large company of us are enjoying Pentecost now in Ohio. It is spreading rapidly. We are getting many urgent calls. Pray much for the laborers. The devil is hard after us."—I. C.

In Minneapolis.

320 S. Cedar St., April 15.—Yesterday, our first Sunday, was a day of great victory for the Lord. At the afternoon and evening services, the altar was crowded with earnest, anxious seekers,—between fifty and sixty last night. I feel that God is going to sweep Minneapolis as she was never swept before. Glory! We are giving the strong meat of the Word, preaching repentance and restitution as the only foundation upon which the Holy Ghost will build; and it is taking. The Dowieites are closing up their missions and coming with us. We have a large hall, and it was filled all day yesterday. Hallelujah.

May 3. This is a blessed day after our great victory of last night. One sister received her Pentecost and talked for some time in tongues. Some understood her when she spoke the Polish and others recognized several sentences spoken in the Bohemian. I recognized the Chinese when she spoke that and another recognized the Italian. She sang beautifully in the Norwegian tongue. Of course the devil was stirred and there were threats of throwing me in jail because someone suggested hypnotism. We are having wonderful meetings. Bro. Pendleton felt the presence of the Holy Ghost fire as I did at the beginning of the meeting last night. He had no sermon we went to the altar after singing a couple of songs. The Swedish sisters are with us. Their ship sails May 17. They are blessed women of God.—J. R. Conlee.

In Denver, Colo.

1312 Welton St., March 18.—Sinners are being saved, believers are being sanctified and baptized with the Holy Ghost and fire and speaking in tongues. The altar is full of seekers every afternoon and evening and people are being healed of scrofula, salt rheum, curvature of the spine, locomotive ataxia, diseases of the eyes, ears, etc.

One lady had a legion of demons cast out of her, was saved, sanctified and baptized with the Holy Ghost inside an hour, and spoke in tongues at the night meeting. One Swedish young man here had a demon cast out and received the baptism with the Holy Ghost, speaking in tongues, inside of two and a half hours.

People of all ages with all manner of diseases are coming for healing, and the deaf, lame, and blind. The Acts of the Apostles are being repeated here now. Handkerchiefs are being blessed and sent to sick people in other places, and children of God are getting handkerchiefs blessed for unbelieveing husbands and children and for sick folks here in and around Denver. This gives an outline of the work going on here the past two or three weeks. I want to tell you also that God sends in an interpreter from time to time. One night here a young cowboy from the Creek Indians dropped in and heard one of the sisters speak the Creek Indian language, and another night a doctor dropped in who understood three languages she spoke.—Mrs. Nora Wilcox.

PENTECOST IN ENGLAND.

The brother who went from England to investigate the work in Norway, Bro. A. A. Boddy, All Saints' Vicarage, Monkwearmouth, Sunderland, England, sent out the following in tract form.

Speaking in Tongues. Is this of God?

In the spring and summer of 1906, God began to answer the very prolonged cry of some of His hungry children, a cry for a Pentecost with scripture evidences.

One after another became at last conscious, as the mighty power of God came upon them, that they were speaking in divine ecstacy with a voice that was not their own, and in a language whether of men and angels they knew not, for until some received the gift of interpretation it was not known what they said. They were speaking mysteries to God for their own strengthening. (1 Cor., xiv., 2-4.)

The work which the writer believes was of God then came nearer to us. He, himself, has heard (this year, 1907) numbers of Spirit-filled men and women and even children magnifying God in tongues. They were all trusting in the Work of the Cross, adoring the Crucified; and sinners were being converted. He was in eight meetings, and he praises God with full heart for that fellowship. He can witness that all are strengthened by the knowledge that the Holy Ghost has come into fuller possession, they are filled with joy unspeakable and full of glory. But God is now graciously working in our midst with the signs and gifts. gifts.

The writer can testify as a rejoicing witness. He could write of very strange things. Earnest prayer which has ascended for months has been gloriously answered and greater things are yet to happen. Glory to the Lamb with Seven Horns and Seven Eyes! May we ever keep true to Him and hidden in him. (Rev. v. 6; Col. iii. 3).

God is girding the whole world with this sign of His outpouring of the Spirit.

A letter from another part of our own land says:—

"Our sister and two or three others have been seeking for months. She got so hungry that it came to a point of real travail of soul, after which came a rest of faith, joy and peace. Not long after this (about three weeks) while about her domestic work, the Holy Ghost came upon her, and she spoke a few utterances in tongues, and as time went on it became more fluent. Our brother who has recently received was praising the Lamb of God (under the power of the Spirit) when he began a song without words for a time (worshipping in the Spirit) then a few utterances in tongues, and so on till he spoke most fluently. I can say from experience that we have a terrible battle with the powers of Hell, but we are learning to claim the victory through the Blood and the Lord is teaching us to let all go into His Hands."

The wonderful sign in 1906 is the restoration of tongues, which foretells the preaching of the pure gospel to all nations, which must be done before the Gentile Times end. (Matt. 24:14.)—The Prophetic Age.

You do not have to strain your mind in order to receive the Holy Ghost, but just believe the Word of Jesus and the Lord pours the Holy Ghost into your heart just as freely as the air you breathe.

What the people need today is an experimental salvation wrought out in their hearts, we have something that will stand against all the forces and powers of hell. God is our life. He is our all in all, it is Christ the Son of the living God.

The "Vanguard" people in St. Louis are waiting on God for the outpouring of the Spirit, and one brother has received the baptism of the Holy Ghost and is speaking in tongues. Their paper is now called "The Banner of Truth."

A Norwegian brother in Brooklyn, New York was reading about the Pentecost in Christiana when he was baptized with the Holy Ghost and began to speak in different languages. It was about midnight on January 26. His name is Oscar Halvorsen of 293 13th street. Three others in Brooklyn are speaking in tongues.

THE APOSTOLIC FAITH

"Earnestly contend for the faith which was once delivered unto the saints."—Jude 3.

VOLUME 1. NO. 9. LOS ANGELES, CAL., JUNE TO SEPTEMBER, 1907 SUBSCRIPTION FREE

IN THE LAST DAYS

"And it shall come to pass in the last days, saith the Lord, I will pour out of My Spirit upon all flesh."—Acts 2. 17.

The Revival in Portland.

One of the mightiest revivals that Portland ever knew has taken place in that city The devil raged, shots were fired, some were arrested and brought up before the judges, but the Lord worked on and healed all manner of diseases that were brought baptized and saved many precious souls.

In June a campmeeting was opened up there, where 100 souls were baptized with the Holy Ghost. Ministers were brought into the work. The Christian and Missionary Alliance in Portland came into the work in a body. God is working there in mighty power today.

One poor soul that had spent five years strapped to her bed in an insane asylum was healed. Her brother, hearing of the wonderful work wrought through this people went and got her and brought her to the Mission, and God wonderfully healed and saved and sanctified her. Her brother testified that he did not believe in God and was an infidel. Now he is saved and has gone back to live with his wife he had left This Gospel surely is building up homes.

A lady was instantly healed of lesion of the muscles which the doctors have been working on for eleven years. The saints are leaving off their glasses and their eyes are being instantly healed. An old lady well on to seventy years old had her eyes completely restored while listening to a brother preaching.

When the plague in Portland was taking the children off at a fearful rate, the Lord healed all the Pentecostal flock as soon as it put in its appearance. Not one of them lost one of their family. The people were told to read the 91st Psalm, stand on the Word, and keep under the Blood, and fear nothing.

The Portland campmeeting opened at Twelfth and Division streets with 1000 people in attendance, sometimes hundreds could not get in. They had all things common at the camp, and such love and unity exists. The poor saint could have a tent as well as the rich one and all were free to eat at the tables. No collections taken, and yet the needs were abundantly supplied.

The work is spreading. Some came from Dallas and received their baptism and went back and set that town on fire and started a campmeeting there.

Sixty-seven were baptized in water one day. People brought their dear ones from the asylum and God healed them. Three from the asylum testified daily of the healing power of God.

A sanctified Nazarene preacher came to the meeting and got her baptism. Three preachers got through one day. The altars are packed.

A sister writing from there said, "O I wish you could hear these Holy Ghost people testify. No straps on anyone. The Holy Ghost works here. Saints filled so they can hardly talk jump up quickly, say a few words and sit down. Such a humble people, such love and unity I never saw. —Address, Pentecostal Meeting, Twelfth and Division streets, Portland, Ore.

The "Latter Rain" in Zion City, Ill.

God is doing a mighty work in Zion City among those heart-broken and crushed people. First they started meetings in the Edina Hospice, now a faith home called "The Haven," then they had the large auditorium in the college, and now have the large tabernacle.

One morning in the upper room of "The Haven," the Holy Ghost fell, as they were praying for Him to come and manifest Himself. First one began to drop and then another until the floor was covered. The first to speak in unknown tongues was a young men who spoke in Chinese, Italian and Zulu, which were identified. Then it was not long till the flood of joy began and all over the room they were praising and glorifying God in different tongues. Some were justified and sanctified. About twenty came through speaking in tongues.

God is using the children, young men and young women, in a marvelous manner. It is the most wonderful demonstration of the power of God upon human hearts. Denounce it as they will, when they see these little children under the power of the Holy Spirit, preaching, singing and speaking in different languages (which are many times identified by foreigners) they will in our meetings confess that their fighting has come to an end, and say that they have never seen anything after this manner.

Brother Seymour when he was in Zion City wrote, "People here receive the baptism in their pews while the service is going on and sometimes scores of them receive it. It is the sweetest thing you want to see. It reminds me of old Azusa ten months ago. The people that receive the baptism seem so happy, they remind me of our people at home. There are little children from six years and on up who have the baptism with the Holy Ghost, just as we have it in Los Angeles. Praise our God. This is another Azusa. It would do you good to hear these people speak under the power of the Holy Ghost. Some of them converse in tongues. Brother Tom has never lost the spirit of the Azusa. He is still fired up the same as ever. Everywhere I have traveled among our baptized souls they seem to have such joy and freedom in the Holy Ghost."—Address "The Haven," Zion City, Ills.

In Minneapolis, Minn.

One Sunday the power of God came upon us in the morning meeting and in the evening the Pentecost began to fall, and by 11:30 the next morning six had received Pentecost, "For they heard them speak with tongues and magnify God." It was like some scenes in Azusa, all around lay the slain, Methodists, Baptists, and Lutherans. Young people arose with shining faces speaking in the power of the Holy Ghost in unknown tongues. Two elderly sisters also spoke in tongues, magnifying God. We have the happiest band of baptized people you ever saw. Young ladies that were so timid, now clap their hands and shout Glory, all the time.

Another night when the meeting lasted till five o'clock in the morning, one young man, a Methodist, came through about one a. m. and spoke in tongues for two hours, giving some of the most blessed messages and interpreting: the burden was, "Jesus is coming soon, get ready to meet Him."

One little girl received her baptism and spoke beautifully in tongues, and then spoke to some unconverted young men in tongues and interpreted, which was a plea for them to give their hearts to Jesus now as He was soon coming and they would be lost. The men were visably affected by the message.

Three baptismal services were held (up to June 19th) at a suburban lake, and 44 were buried in the likeness of His death.

Most of those who received the baptism in the Spirit are prostrated on the floor. Some received it while sitting in a chair or standing on their feet. Some have received it at home. Those who are prostrated, many of them tell of having a vision of heaven or of Jesus the Lord or otherwise of having come into a full and far deeper sense of God than ever thought of before. A brother coming out from under the power where he had received revelations said, "The hand of God is certainly on this work, and those who scoff and oppose it are likely to have the Lord's hand put on them in a terrible way."

The papers published many false reports, and they were threatened with arrest and to have the meetings stopped on the charge of disturbing the peace; but Bro. Pendleton announced that the meetings would continue for they must obey God. If they went to jail, they would have meetings there.

Some get to God in every meeting. They obtained a large hall that will set four or five hundred, where a permanent mission will be established.

Pentecost in Winnipeg, Manitoba

For more than a year here some of the saints tarried before God for an outpouring of His Spirit upon all flesh, and especially for a revival of the Bible standard in Winnipeg. God has heard prayers and is repeating Pentecost. Praise His name.

The Holy Ghost first fell in a cottage meeting and three received their Pentecost with Bible evidence. An aged saint came in from Poplar Point, a small town about 40 miles distant, and the second afternoon he got his Pentecost and says he feels a lot younger. He and others went back and had tarrying meetings, and since then about twenty have received Pentecost at that place.

At the Pentecost Mission, while a brother was speaking from Acts 10:40-46, "While Peter yet spake these words, the Holy Ghost fell on all them which heard the Word," as he was speaking, the Holy Ghost fell on two sisters. One started speaking right off in tongues, and another who had come about 100 miles to attend the meeting, fell under the power for a time and began to sing in tongues. It was heavenly. Souls are being saved, believers sanctified and baptized with the Holy Ghost while sitting in their seats.

Baptismal services took place on the banks of the River Assiniboine at this place 23 persons receiving baptism by immersion. It was a sacred occasion. The Holy Ghost witnessed through the speaking in tongues of those who were baptized.

Some wonderful cases of healing have occurred the past few weeks. A lady of some 60 years of age who had been a cripple from inflammatory rheumatism for ten years or more, was brought in an invalid chair accompanied by her two daughters. She was prayed for, and during the service was noticed to stretch forth her ailing limbs, which up to this time had been of little use to her. She then rose from her chair under the power of the Holy Ghost. O that men would praise the Lord for His goodness and His wonderful works to the children of men.

Home & Foreign Mission, 159 Alexander St., Winnipeg, Man., Can.

FROM DISTANT LANDS

How wonderful it is that today in different parts of India, Russia, Norway, Sweden, England, Canada, Africa and America, God's saints are enjoying the latter rain and are being satisfied. Persecution is arising everywhere, but this is only a mark of the Lord's work, and makes us more sure we shall reign with Him whose sufferings we are privileged to share. Bless His name! The Lord is coming—our precious King is coming soon. "Even so come Lord Jesus." Hallelujah.

Salvation in Sweden

In Stockholm, Sweden, many souls are filled with the Holy Ghost and have the Bible evidence. The tidal wave is sweeping on, on to victory. Hundreds of souls are at the feet of Jesus.

"The work of the Lord is spreading. In Gottenberg, the second city of Sweden, the Lord has set many of His people free, filling them with the Spirit of Christ. Some are speaking with new tongues I have Bro. Eric Hollingsworth and his wife here with me now in this city, and hope we shall have a house like Azusa Mission.

"The church in Skofde is growing I think there are about 40 now who are baptized with the Holy Ghost and speaking and singing in new tongues there. Hallelujah! In a meeting at Skofde there were seven young folks who were singing in tongues together. It was a heavenly song, as Bro. Eric told me.

"In many other cities and towns God is working mightily. One place is on an island between Sweden and Russia, and God is pouring out His Spirit. To God be all the praise."—Andrew G. Johnson, Bramaregarden, Hisingstad, Gottenberg, Sweden.

[Since the last report, two Spirit-filled sisters, Sister Anderson and Sister Jacobson, have gone to help in the work in Sweden.]

Reports from England

"Three have received the baptism with Bible evidence here. When we hear the Holy Ghost speaking and singing through these dear ones, it is so solemn and yet so heavenly and deepens one's hunger."—J. H. 13 Akerman Road, Brixton, London, S. W.

From another part of London where there has been a tarrying meeting, word comes that two have received the Pentecost, and other hungry souls seeking.

A sister in England who has received the Holy Ghost, testifies:

"When all had retired that night, past twelve o'clock, and I was left alone, praise and adoration filled my soul (for the words kept ringing in my ear that had been spoken from, "Faithful is He that calleth you, who also will do it.") The joy was flowing—after months of inexpressible yearnings, and waiting upon God. That night I seemed to lie down in His almighty arms like a weary little child. The last cord that bound me to earth was broken and that was a little anxiety concerning my home and dear ones. I gave them up to Him, and just rested absolutely in Him.

"While praising Him I had a vision of Jesus upon the cross. It was dark, He extended His arms to me and said, "Come to Me." Oh! the unutterable love and compassion in His voice. I obeyed, and groaned in the spirit, seeming to suffer with Him. Then the darkness fled, and I was raised with Him in glory. I involuntarily threw up my arms to praise Him and suddenly they seemed to be charged with electricity, and a power came upon me and I praised Him in another tongue. He immediately gave the interpretation which was "Glory to Jesus—the bleeding Lamb." The next morning the Holy Ghost came in mighty power, causing me to laugh as I had never done in my life (being very matter of fact and unemotional), and speaking in four or five languages sometimes giving the interpretation. For one and a half hours this continued. I was quite powerless. The glory of God filled my soul, and sometimes the deepest anguish of heart at the cross. What I felt and realized of the sorrow and love of Jesus was beyond all expression, finding vent only in another "tongue." Glory to His Name!

"The same evening I went to another meeting in connection with the foregoing special services, and the Spirit came upon me again causing me to speak in three or four languages with the interpretation."—From a tract published in England by Bro. A. A. Body, All Saints' Vicarage, Monkwearmouth, Sunderland, England.

The Work in India

There are at least five or six hundred witnesses in India today, "earnestly contending for the faith once delivered unto the saints."

Some of the choicest spirits of India have been baptized with the Holy Ghost. It is wonderful to hear one of these tell how for nine years she had hunted meetings where she could receive the Holy Ghost, and how she has found Him whom her soul so long has craved. She and her friend are missionaries from Colombo, Ceylon. One of them has been clearly healed of a disease of several years standing.

Four witnesses have gone to Darjeeling India.

A prominent missionary who has been baptized with the Holy Ghost and has received wonderful power has thrown open the dooors of her beautiful mission home and today is preaching the word with power.

The missionaries are searching the Word. They find this movement is prophesied as the forerunner of Jesus, and the precious souls are so glad to receive the power; but in India Bible teachers who know the Word are not jumping at every new doctrine but are weighing everything by the Word and are being convinced of the truth.

The Lord gave one missionary a vision of the Holy Ghost as a chest of jewels, and she saw the Savior open the chest, and with a look of great love and satisfaction, unroll gift after gift from the chest. It has not occurred to many the joy that must fill the heart of the dear Lord, when He sees that His gifts are being appreciated

The Lord also gave Sister Garr a vision of Himself one night, while in Calcutta and His hands were filled with golden crowns ready to place on heads. And the same evening, He gave her the message "Let no man take thy crown." A missionary arose and said that on that day God had spoken those words to her, and she did not know what it meant.

Reaching the missionaries is laying the axe at the root of the tree, for they know all the customs of India and also the languages. The only way the nations can be reached is by getting the missionaries baptized with the Holy Ghost. Missionaries are receiving and praising God for letting them hear this Gospel and receive this great outpouring of the Spirit.

In a school of 1,500 native girls and 200 boys, besides European and native teachers the head of the school has been tarrying and the Comforter has come to her and also to her daughter, a number of her teachers, and 300 native girls. Hallelujah! At Dhond, a school of boys, numbers have been saved, some are speaking in tongues.

In Calcutta, one Missionary who was baptized in the meeting, went back to her high school and in a short time forty-five precious native girls were baptized in the Spirit. Then the matron of a Rescue Home received her Pentecost and shortly the dear girls who had been redeemed from such lives of sin, were learning how to glorify Jesus and the Holy Ghost was given. Missionaries who have gone down to their stations, write of the abiding Comforter and rivers of living water are flowing.

False reports have been circulated of the work in India. Do not believe them.—Address Bro. and Sister A. G. Garr, Bethany, Slave Island, Colombo, Ceylon, India.

When Jesus comes, He is going to reveal to us, all the hidden love that He had for us all through the ages.

If your testimony is backed up by the Blood of Christ in your heart, there is power in it.

God stands today to save every sinner, to sanctify every believer, and to baptize every sanctified believer with the Holy Ghost.

We are measuring everything by the Word, every experience must measure up with the Bible. Some say that is going too far, but if we have lived too close to the Word, we will settle that with the Lord when we meet Him in the air.

Some people build their houses on the sand, not on the experience of the Blood in their hearts. They say they have not got the witness, but are just going by faith. Well, everyone that is born of God has the witness in himself. I John 5:10.

When we preach a sinless life, some people say we are too strict. They say we will not get many to heaven that way. But beloved, God cannot save contrary to His Word. All salvation contrary to the Word is not saving salvation.

The baptism with the Holy Ghost is the seal of the living God in your forehead. God wants you to wear this seal, and not the badges of men and devils. He does not want you to be unequally yoked together with unbelievers, but come out from among the creeds and doctrines of men and devils. Our ignorance in the past God winked at, but that time is past. He is seeking for a clean people, a people that have not defiled their garments. The priests that bore the holy vessels had to be clean, so now those that bear the messages of the Lord must be clean and holy.

John the Baptist lost his head because he preached against divorces. There are a few people today that are willing to lose their heads for preaching against divorces. This Apostolic Faith stands for one wife and one husband. Our God is going to have a clean people, a people that will stand for the whole counsel of God. Praise God for a people that are willing to stand for the Gospel and die for it if need be.

THE APOSTOLIC FAITH

"Earnestly contend for the faith which was once delivered unto the saints."—Jude 3.

VOLUME 1. NO. 10. LOS ANGELES, CAL., SEPTEMBER, 1907 SUBSCRIPTION FREE

"EVERYWHERE PREACHING THE WORD"

This is a time as never before when the baptized saints are scattering abroad everywhere preaching the Word. They have gone out from Los Angeles far and near, carrying the sweet message that the Comforter has come. Some have gone to Canada, some east, some south, and some are on the way to foreign fields.

Many of the campmeeting saints are gathering back to the old "manger home" at Azusa. The pillar of fire still rests there. Meetings went on here all summer souls seeking and finding the Lord.

The Lord taught His people at the Campground and gave them some practical experiences that will stand them in good stead on the field. The enemy came in as an angel of light, and we had a battle with the powers of darkness; but it was turned into victory after all. The Spirit was poured out and many souls baptized. God only knows the number. They were slain about the altars and in the "upper room tent," and came through speaking and singing in tongnes and rejoicing in God.

Many were saved and sanctified. Over 100 were baptized in the stream near by. The baptizmal services were sweet and heavenly. Numbers of children followed Jesus in baptism, and came out of the water praising God. Many testified to healing The Lord performed some real miracles. Praise God!

There were over 200 living tents in the camp, besides a number of large tents; the big tabernacle where God met with us gaciously; the "upper room tent" where many sought and obtained the Pentacost; the children's tabernacle where they were taught the Word and many of them found the Lord, and we shall never forget that spot for it was so sweet to hear the children praying and praising the Lord; then there was the dining tent, where hundreds sat down to the tables and no charge made except as the Lord laid it on them to put into the box. We enjoyed some blessed times in the Spirit there, and also in the workers' dining tent, before we got the big tabernacle on the "all things common" line. One morning while at prayer after breakfast, the power of God so came on us that ten of the workers were slain and we did not get away till noon. We had a foretaste of heaven.

The hills around would sometimes ring with prayer and praise. Some sought and found the Lord on the hills, and came down with faces shining.

The early morning meetings before breakfast when the saints met will never be forgotten. The Lord met with us. There were three other services in the big tabernacle during the day, which often ran into the night, if not till morning. The altar workers were very faithful. They would stay and pray with seekers all night.

People came from hundreds and thousands of miles seeking Pentecost, and went back with the rivers of salvation. The songs from the camp could be heard distinctly up in Hermon. One sister who had been told it was all the power of the devil was up in Hermon listening, and she said to herself, "So that is the devil: well, the devil has some sweet singers." She came down and the result was she went to the altar and received the baptism with the Holy Ghost.

From Hermon, one sister saw fire issuing out of the tabernacle, as it were a tongue of fire. Her daughter also saw it. And a little boy who was in the power of the Spirit in the tabernacle, saw a ball of fire in the top of the tabernacle which broke and filled the whole place with light. God surely did send the fire. Many were the heavenly anthems the Spirit sang through His people. And He gave many beautiful messages in unknown tongues, speaking of His soon coming, invitations to come to the Lord, and exhortations from the Word.

We had some precious saints' meetings feasting on the Word. One blessed thing was the unity of the ministers and workers in the doctrines of the Bible, so plainly taught by our Lord. The Lord put His seal upon it. Those who were not present will find the doctrines in this paper as they were taught there. Our power in this Gospel is in standing in the Word. O how precious it is when we are in the Apostles' doctrine and fellowship. Some, it is sad to say, will not pay the price.

In Washington, D. C.

In the capital city, the Pentecost has fallen in a colored Holiness Mission. Bro and Sister S. S. Crawford were preaching the Pentecost at another mission, and they sent for them, as Cornelius sent for Peter to preach this Gospel. Twenty-two came to the altar the first service and four received Pentecost with the Bible evidence The meeting went on for five weeks with 16 receiving the Pentecost, four of them preachers.

Minnesota Campmeetings

He is pouring out His Spirit on him that is thirsty and floods upon the dry ground Our annual campmeeting at Fairmont Minn., June 14-24 was a season of precious waiting before the Lord. Heretofore it has been a tarrying place where the full Gospel was preached. But this year in the added light of Pentecostal blessings and power which a number present had received during the past few months, it swung out into a Pentecostal meeting. God was pleased to work graciously in our midst saving, sanctifying, and healing persons and several were baptized with the Holy Ghost, while the blessings flowed out upon others as the Holy Spirit fell upon the people.

At the Maxwell Campmeeting, on Thursday, July 5th, the Lord poured out His Spirit in power: and while numbers were prostrate under the power, He was pleased to use two young women under the power of the Spirit, in speaking through them so that the hearts of the people were melted like wax in His presence, and realized they were in the very presence of God. The afternoon meeting merged into the evening meeting with no time to prepare supper. O it was most blessed indeed.—H. L. Blake Ruthton, Minn.

In North Carolina

The Holy Ghost is being poured out in Rowan Free Will Baptist Church and many are speaking and singing in new tongues, and some interpreting and receiving other manifestations of the Spirit. On the 17th of May Bro. Harrell received his Pentecost, and from that time to this the Holy Ghost has been sought by others and about 28 have received their Pentecost, while several have been converted and some sanctified. In nearly every service someone gets their Pentecost. People are coming from other sections of the country to see for themselves the wonderful works of God in our midst.

The fire is falling at the F. W. Baptist Church at Frenches Creek, and also at the F. W. Baptist Church in Wilmington, N. C. and several have received their Pentecost at each of these places. At Wilmington three little girls from 10 to 12 years old have received their Pentecost and are gloriously happy."—A. J. Bordeau, Colly N. C.

At High Point, N. C., the Pentecost mission is growing, souls are getting saved and the sick healed. At Durham, there is a happy band of baptized believers. At Winston-Salem, some are being baptized with the Holy Ghost and speaking in tongues.

In New Orleans, La.

As soon as we received those Apostolic Faith papers, we began praying, and fasted and prayed, and Glory to His name, He made Himself known in our midst, and came and baptized four with the Holy Ghost and fire. O what a grand time we did have, and the Lord has been continuing to baptize different ones. The fire is falling down here, and the Lord is bringing His saints together as Jesus prayed in the 17th of John. He is giving the gift of speaking with tongues and other gifts. —Alice Taylor, 2323 Washington Avenue.

Other Points

In Oakland just as the paper goes to press, word comes from Sister Crawford who is on her way east that the power of God is falling. In San Francisco the work is going forward with two young brothers from the campmeeting in charge.

In Atlanta, Ga., reports come of many baptized with the Holy Ghost. Signs and wonders have been given by the Lord.

At Dayton, Ohio, the Holy Ghost first fell in February on those that were earnestly seeking the fulness. Thirty-six souls were reported to have received the Pentecost and the altar full of seekers. Bro. W. W. Bailey, a baptized preacher there opened up a Pentecost Gospel Union Mission at 707 S. Brown St.

At Chambersburg, Pa., about 25 got baptized and some spoke in tongues, some saved, sanctified and healed.

At Youngstown, Ohio, a number have received the baptism. One night they were in prayer all the evening praising God and the Lord gave the heavenly song which sounded to them like angelic strains. One sister saw into glory and saw the heavenly city. Such a sight to behold!" It seemed the celestial city was so near, the veil was almost worn through.

At Memphis, Tenn., many hungry souls have been baptized.

At Durant, Fla., there has been a gracious meeting in which about 50 have received the Holy Ghost. Some have been healed, unclean spirits crying with loud voices have come out of some that were possessed with them, souls are saved and sanctified.

Pentecost has fallen at Council Bluffs Ia., at Caldwell, Kans., at Mankato, Minn. at New Castle, Pa., at Watertown, N. Y. and the work has been increasing at many other points.

Truly this is a refreshing time, according to Acts 3. 18-21. "Repent ye therefore and be converted, that your sins may be blotted out, when the time of refeshing shall come from the presence of the Lord. And He shall send Jesus Christ." We can see the refreshing times are now flowing.

In Portland, Oregon, there has been a Holy Ghost campmeeting going on all summer. Hundreds have been baptized with the Holy Ghost, many saved, sanctified and healed. They have such love and harmony among the saints that they have all things on Pentecostal lines. The saints there are mostly poor, yet making many rich. Tents and eating tabernacle free and no collections. God abundantly supplied Portland has become an example of this Pentecostal faith. Glory to God for what He has done.

This great movement is like a little mustard seed planted in Los Angeles. It took root in a humble place which proved to be good soil and, watered with rivers from heaven, it soon put forth its branches to nearby towns as Long Beach and out to Oakland. Soon the limbs spread north and far over the eastern states, and then clear over into Sweden and India. Now it is spreading all over the world, and how beautiful and green it is, and how the birds are coming to lodge in its branches.

Christ is making up His jewels quickly O how the "latter rain" is falling. We hear from Canada, from the east and south the sound of abundance of rain. Praise God. It is falling in Sweden, in Norway and refreshing showers in India. Also we hear of gracious drops falling in other distant lands. We hear the rumbling of the chariots of heaven. Some are trying to stop it but you might as well try to stop a cloud burst in the mountains. This thing is in God's hands.

Men and women have prayed for years to see this precious light, prayed to see Los Angeles revived. Now we can see the fruits of Pentecost here. God healing people, saving, sanctifying, baptizing with the Holy Ghost, speaking through the power of the Spirit and singing in unknown tongues, giving sweet anthems from heaven. God has graciously answered the prayers of His people, though many are blinded and cannot see it; but praise God, our eyes have seen this great salvation and we ought to be encouraged to go forward as never before.

In Minneapolis there is a precious Holy Ghost mission band of about 200 Holy Ghost people who are united in love and harmony, filled with the glory of God. Though they have been persecuted and maligned by the secular papers, yet God has only used it as a free advertisement to draw honest souls. One woman heard of it 250 miles away and came all the way to receive her Pentecost, and in a short time she received a mighty baptism with the Holy Ghost, speaking in tongues and interpreting, and went back with the precious oil of the Holy Ghost.

Hungry souls rejoice to hear of the Pentecost. Sister Mary Yaegge of Baltimore was one who rejoiced to hear of the Pentecost at Los Angeles. She prized the little paper for it seemed to be just what her soul longed for. She had been raised a Catholic and had received the Gospel gladly and was sanctified and hungering for the Holy Ghost. She came to the Campmeeting. Received her Pentecost on the way, while at Oakland and is truly anointed with power and divine love. She is on her way back to Switzerland, her native home, to give this Gospel to her people.

Missionaries in China have been seeking the baptism with the Holy Ghost ever since they received the first Apostolic Faith papers from Los Angeles. One dear missionary, Brother B. Berntsen from South Chih-li, Tai-Ming-Fu, North China came all the way to Los Angeles to receive his Pentecost. And, bless God, he went to the altar at Azusa Mission, and soon fell under the power, and arose drunk on the new wine of the kingdom, magnifying God in a new tongue. As soon as he could speak English, he said, "This means much for China." Then he told how he had felt the need of the fulness of the Pentecost in China, and we fell on our knees and prayed that the dear missionaries might be anointed and China might receive the Gospel.

The manager of the Union Rescue Mission in Los Angeles, Bro. Will Trotter, received the baptism with the Holy Ghost and as a result he lost his position under men, but God has marvelously anointed him and is using him in the evangelistic work.

In Chicago there are a number of Pentecostal meetings. Many are magnifying God for the baptism with the Holy Ghost. The Lord is using Bro. Durham as a river that overflows its banks and waters the thirsty ground. Many hungry ones are seeking and obtaining their baptism. Some of the Moody Institute people have received their Pentecost, but the theologians are not accepting it.

The Scandinavian Apostolic Faith Mission at 775 Wall street, Los Angeles, is one of the sweetest places you ever were in. The people there are filled with the Spirit praising God. They seem so sincere and full of divine love. There are a number of precious young men and women there that God has cleansed and filled with the Spirit. It is blessed to see them.

THE LOVE OF JESUS

"Surely He hath borne our griefs and carried our sorrows." The Son of God went into the garden when He was bearing this world of sin. The blood gushed out from His skin and fell in great drops to the ground. He prayed, "Father, if it be thy will remove this cup from Me, nevertheless not my will but Thine be done." He suffered until His heart swelled in His body and forced the blood through the flesh. His soul burned in Him with the weight of sin of this old world on our conquering King. Then He did not stop but went through Pilate's judgement hall and was whipped and the blood ran down in that judgment hall, and was shed all the way to Calvary. O those stripes reach our sicknesses and our infirmities and heal us. He bled and died and went down into the grave and rose again. O beloved, He atoned for you. He hung and bled for you, and if you will accept Him today He will fill your heart.

At the annual Christian and Missionary Alliance Convention in Nyack, New York some were present who had received their Pentecost, and a great interest was awakened. In a tarrying meeting one young lady who was called to Africa fell under the power, received the baptism with the Holy Ghost and began to speak in an African tongue, which was recognized by missionaries from Africa as being the very language of the part of Africa to which the sister was expecting to go. Others sought and obtained the baptism.

A minister who had been opposing this work went to one of the Pentecostal meetings and got under conviction. He confessed to all that he was in the wrong and stated to his congregation that he must have this Pentecostal power, that he would not preach until he had it; he would work on the rock pile first. Then he called all his people to the altar that wanted it and they came in crowds. O the hungry souls. If the ministers would only go in themselves and let their hungry flocks go in what a wave of salvation there would be This minister we hear has been mightily baptized and many of his people.

In Santa Barbara in a Pentecostal meeting, as they were kneeling about the altar, some whiskey bottles were thrown which came from a saloon near by. Two of the saints were struck with them. Sister Crawford was cut on the temple by one of these ugly weapons, but the saints prayed for her and the meeting went on. She writes that she is rejoicing to be counted worthy to bear about in her body the marks of the Lord Jesus.

In Zion City, Ills., a little girl of about six years came to her mother and said she was going to get saved. She went upstairs and commenced to pray, and the Lord heard her. She called down to her mother "Mamma, if something in me says I am saved, is that Jesus?" Her mother said "Yes." Again she prayed and called to her mother again, "Mamma, if something in me says I am sanctified, is that Jesus speaking?" Her mother said, "Yes." Then she said, "Mamma, I am sanctified." She got down and prayed again and was baptized with the Holy Ghost, and the Lord has had her preaching, and gave her a message to one of Dowie's elders that had fought this work. So God spoke through this little child unable to read. He could preach through the ass of Balaam and He can take a little child and preach through it

We must keep where God can use us, and the secret is humility, the Word and the Blood.

This Gospel, the full Gospel of Jesus must be preached in all the earth for a witness then shall the end come.

Jesus Christ tasted death for every man but He did not taste death for the devil or fallen angels. We do not believe the devil or fallen angels are going to be saved. The Lord Jesus did not die for the devil or demons. Everyone that will repent of their sins can find rest in the Blood of Calvary.

When Christ is in you, He is married to you in spirit. He calls you, "My love and My dove." Everyone that has Christ is married to Him in spirit. "Ye are become dead to the law by the body of Christ; that ye should be married to another, even to Him who is raised from the dead." Rom. 7. 4. We are under the law of the Spirit of Christ. O how sweet it is You would not depart from this husband of your soul for anything.

THE APOSTOLIC FAITH

"Earnestly contend for the faith which was once delivered unto the saints."—Jude 3.

VOLUME I. NO. 11. LOS ANGELES, CAL., OCTOBER TO JANUARY, 1908. SUBSCRIPTION FREE.

GOOD TIDINGS OF GREAT JOY

Pentecost In Many Lands—News of Salvation—Jesus Soon Coming

PENTECOST SPREADS TO OTHER LANDS.

Denmark.

"Kirkeklokken," a Danish gospel paper, reports that through the Pentecostal outburst in Copenhagen recently, many sinners have come to the Savior, many backsliders have been restored to the joy of salvation, many believers have been filled with the Spirit and have received supernatural gifts.

In Wales

"Praise God for another brother here who has also now received the Pentecost with tongues. He went home from here speaking in tongues all along the street. There are others to follow. Glory to Jesus. Tonight five or six brothers are coming here for their Pentecost. O, I do praise God that He sent me to Sunderland to get such a wonderful blessing. Praise His holy name."—W. J. Tomlinson, Lynton House, Grove Place, Port Talbot.

Honolulu

Brother and Sister Turney, who have returned from Honolulu, now on their way to Africa report the work in Honolulu: "We had a glorious meeting Honolulu. The power came down and one young man a captain of the Salvation Army, who received his Pentecost, has now opened up an Apostolic Faith Mission in Santa Cruz, Cal. A lieutenant also received his Pentecost and went to carry the news to London, England. Charley Puck, who had a most wonderful experience, is preaching the Gospel on the Island of Hawaii in the city of Kanucla. They are having good meetings and good attendance. People are hungry for the truth.

London, England

I do thank God that there are a few whose eyes God has opened to see their lack and who have waited upon His in prayer for quite a year and a half at 14 Ackerman Rd., Brixon S. W., London. God has manifested His almighty power there in the baptism of dear Sister Price and one brother and myself, and I am so glad to send in my testimony to the glory of God and the encouragement of all His children. People are coming from far and near, and no one has been even invited. They just hear how God is working and come. This power was mightily present last Thursday, two sisters being shaken and nearly spoke in tongues. One night the very room was shaken as we read in the Word: "And when they had prayed the place was shaken." Several have had blessed anointings, outpourings of the Spirit and revelations of Jesus Christ. Praise His Holy name.—Mary A. Martin, 119 Southampton St., Camberwell, London, England.

China.

Brother and Sister Garr are in Hong Kong, China, last report. God is using them blessedly. A glorious revival is breaking out. Several souls in Hong Kong have received their Pentecost.

In Macao and Canton, China, numbers have received the baptism with the Spirit. They are hungry for the Holy Ghost. Brother McIntosh wrote, "They come to our house at all times of the day and rap at our door at 11 and 12 o'clock at night, coming to seek for the Holy Ghost, and we stay up till one and two o'clock praying with them, and glory to God, the Pentecost falls and they speak in tongues." Two sisters who received their Pentecost in Brother Cashwell's work in the South have gone over to help Brother and Sister McIntosh. They are Sister A. E. Kirby and Sister Mabel Evans. Address Macao, China, care S. C. Todd.

Sweden.

Bramaregarden, Hisingstad, Goteborg, Nov. 19.—"I am very glad to hear from the old Azusa Mission, my home. I have victory through the dear, cleansing Blood of Christ. Glory to His great name! It is one year today since I came over to Sweden and this city Goteborg. God is still saving, sanctifying, and baptizing with the Holy Ghost, and people are getting healed of God. Last Sunday two got their Pentecostal blessing. We had a wonderful day, the Holy Ghost running the meetings, God's children testifying, praising God, talking in unknown tongues. The fire has begun to fall on small islands near the city. Bless God! The work is still going on in many places in Sweden and God's people are getting more hungry than ever. We trust God to send out more workers into the field. The fire is falling in 'Norrland.' Yet many, many have not heard this Gospel yet. This work will go on till Jesus our Lord comes back. All the saints in Goteborg salute you."—Andrew G. Johnson.

Germany.

"Auf der Warte," a German paper, says: At Cassel many children of God received the fullness of the Spirit after God had cleansesd their hearts by faith. Many children of God have put right old debts. Through the speaking in tongues and the preaching, sins and bonds were revealed, and it was clearly taught that deliverance from the power of sin and the experience of heart cleansing are the conditions for receiving the Pentecostal baptism.

The manifestations of the Spirit when the souls were touched were different according to I Cor. 12. Some were knocked down to the floor, some were overflowed gently while sitting in their chairs. Some cried with loud voice, others shouted Hallelujah! clapped their hands, jumped or laughed with joy. Some saw the Lord not only in the meetings, but when silent in the houses, or in bed, or when walking on the road. God touched their souls.

All that was uttered in tongues as far as it concerned salvation was in perfect accord with Scripture. What the Lord gave to utter about His Cross, His Glory, and the Second Coming was refreshment and comfort for every believing soul. Through the speaking of tongues and prophesy those in the audience received conviction of their sins; which statement is proven by confessions made afterwards to the minister.

The fire is already burning at Grossalmerode. The Lord is doing great things. Many have received the Pentecostal baptism; and the Lord bestowed gifts upon many, especially the gift of tongues and interpretation.

WITNESSES IN ENGLAND

(From reports printed at Sunderland, Eng.)

Children Receive Pentecost

I was present when the two girls, who were the first children to speak in tongues in England, Janie and May Boddy (the two daughters of the Rev. Alex. A. Boddy, All Saints' Vicarage, Sunderland), received their Pentecost. It was at the Vicarage.

The nine or ten persons present will never forget the scene. Janie received the interpretation for each sentence, and her childlike simplicity and joy, her beaming face, that I shall never forget, she turned message she received was: "Jesus is coming!" With a surprised look of joy on her fact, that I shall never forget, she turned to her mother and kissed her, repeating the words: "Jesus is coming, mother!"

Then her fact became serious. She bowed her head a little and lifted her left hand to her cheek (she was kneeling all the time at the end of the table). Again a foreign language was heard. Then came the interpretation: "The Heavens are opened!" followed by the same jubilant glee.

One message was very solemn, spoken, too, with emphasis: "The first shall be last, and the last first." Coming from such childlike lips, it made a great impression on us all.

Oh, what joy when she said: "Oh! mummie, Jesus has come, and come to stay; oh, good Jesus, good Jesus!" then peals of joybells of laughter.

As she related her experience the next day to a large *crowd of children* at the Parish Hall, she said, whilst inviting them to seek their Pentecost, "Oh, it is so wonderful, so *wonderful!*" It was wonderful, it was the Holy Spirit come to dwell within them.

May Boddy had a great revelation of God's power. She prayed so earnestly that she might not "be left out." It was touching, too, to see Janie, who had just received her Pentecost, as she laid her hand on her sister's head and encouraged her: "It's all through the Blood, May, all through the Blood! Jesus is come, He said, May too, May too."

May spoke a long time. Some words were very clear. It seemed as if she was constantly claiming Jesus. His name was repeated time upon time. The words, "Aa, Ja, Jesus! Ja, ja, ja, Jesus!" were distinctly Norwegian, with the correct pronunciation (Oh, yes, Jesus! yes, yes, yes, Jesus!)

These two dear children have been kind and good girls before and loved Jesus dearly but now they love Him much more and are bold to tell others of His wonderful power to save—T. B. Barratt.

Testimony of a Vicar's Wife

After a long time of silent waiting upon Him, God gave me a wonderful vision of Christ in the glory at the right hand of the Father, and from Him came a wonderful light on to me, causing me to laugh as I had never done before. I thought this was the Baptism, for this gave me more power in speaking for Christ, and more realization of His indwelling. But yet God had a more excellent way for me. After waiting with others for months at home, in eager and earnest expectation of His Baptism of Fire, God chose that when the fire did begin to fall here, I should be in the South of England, not able to return until Pastor Barratt had been here for nearly a fortnight, and several had received their Pentecost. God was working in me more than I realized, literally drying up all experience, all spiritual life of the flesh. When I returned home on the evening of the 10th of September, I felt utterly callous, and even, to my surprise, uninterested. I could not pray, nor read, nor even think of God, but just rested by naked faith on the Word of God that "I was dead," and only Christ was my all-in-all.

I went to the meeting the next evening, but could not sing nor pray. I just rested in God and asked Him to lead the Pastor to lay hands on me when He wished. Soon the Pastor was "filled with the Holy Ghost" and came to me. When he laid hands on me, I expected a great rush of feeling, such as I have often experienced, as the Life of Jesus thrilled through my body, but I felt nothing. The Spirit then flashed light on to the Word, "They laid hands on them and they received the Holy Ghost." I should like to emphasize that it was at this point of really believing in my heart God's Word, that I had received (Acts viii., 17), that He began to manifest His presence (the empty cleansed vessel receiving the out-poured gift), and I just rested again in the fact that God the Holy Ghost had come and would do His own work. Suddenly the Lord filled His Temple and I was in the glory. What followed I cannot describe, and it is too sacred to do so, but I knew God had come. Though never unconscious, I was quite oblivious to everyone around, just worshipping. Then my mouth began to quiver, my tongue began to move, and a few simple words were uttered, as I just yielded to the Holy Ghost. Much to my astonishment, I began to speak fluently in a foreign language—Chinese I think. The Spirit sang through me. The joy and rapture of this purely spiritual worship can never be described. If for no other purpose, I felt at last satisfied that "there was no difference between me and them as at the bginning." Acts xi., 15. Then came a vision of the Blood. As the Spirit spoke that word I was conscious that ALL heaven oh glory! (myself included) was "worshipping the Lamb, as it had been slain." Oh, the efficacy, the power of the Blood. In one moment, what I had believed in for years was illuminated as a reality. Nothing else can take its place, it is the Blood that cleanseth. Then came more words in 'tongues' with the interpretation. "Worthy is thre Lamb; Jesus is coming."

People say, "What is the difference now?" Just this, and this is all the difference. What one has held on to by faith in the Word, is a reality. I know, as never before, that Christ liveth in me. The Power to love and believe and witness is there, as never before; and last, though not least, after longing with a hungry heart for years to satisfy my God and Saviour, that "He might see the travail of His soul and be satisfied," I thank Him with all my heart that at last He has received from me pure spirit-worship—"mysteries,"—I Cor. 14. 2; John 3. 23. I recognize, as never before, that it is still a walk of faith and obedience, that I am nothing, and Christ is my all in all. I am launched out into the fathomless ocean of God's love, joy and peace. It is "joy unspeakable and full of glory." I thank God for the Pentecostal sign of 'tongues.' I did not ask for 'tongues' but for the Holy Ghost, and He "gave me utterance," and the joy of praising God in the Spirit is truly wonderful.—Mrs. A. A. Body, Sunderland, Eng.

Testimony of a Sunday School Teacher

On Sunday, September 8th, I surrendered my whole being fully to Jesus and accepted cleansing through His most precious Blood, and on Monday, September 9th, while reading a little booklet, I got a great blesing from these two verses:—

Nothing to settle? all has been paid,
Nothing of anger? peace has been made;
Jesus alone is the sinner's resource,
Peace He has made by the Blood of His cross,
Nothing of guilt? no, not a stain,
How could the Blood let any remain,

My conscience is purged, my spirit is free,
Precious that Blood is to God and to me.

And then I claimed my Pentecost through that precious Blood, and stood firm on the blessed promises in Luke xi., 13, and Luke xxiv., 49, and I praised Him for it until Friday, September 13th. Oh, that glorious night when Christ came into my heart in all His fulness. It was about twenty minutes to nine when I went into the meeting and they were singing "Rest in the Lord," the message He gave me on Thursday. Psalm xxxvii., 7. A dear sister gave me the card with "Now I give up all to Jesus" on, and told me to let all go and just yield to Him, and oh, the unspeakable joy that flooded my soul when I, in simple faith, let my whole heart go. It was Jesus Himself who came in, glory to His Name. I could have shouted Glory, Hallelujah! all the way home. On Sunday, September 15th, we had a prayer meeting at a friend's house and the Spirit fell mightily upon me and I spoke in a strange language. Oh, it's all Glory, Glory, Glory, I cannot explain the joy and peace I now have, but I know it is all through the precious Blood of Jesus. Praise Him, praise Him.

Testimony of a Yorkshire Farmer

The Holy Spirit came upon me on Sunday night, showing me the mighty power in the blood of Jesus. The following night it was Jesus himself and the Holy Spirit entering in like a flood. I do thank the Lord that He enabled me to take Him in, or rather, He so melted me that I allowed Him to come in. I took Him in all His fulness, that the life of the head might be the life of the member of the body. How unnatural it would seem to see a person going about with life in the head and not the same life running through the body and the head no control over the body. I feel that I want to be like the bed of a river, perfectly still, but wide enough to admit a flood. When I got home on Tuesday night, I was sitting by myself occupied with the Lord, when I got the sign of tongues. Glory to the name of Jesus.

PENTECOSTAL MISSIONARY REPORTS

Since the last paper, Spirit-filled missionaries have gone out from Los Angeles to Monrovia, Liberia, Africa, two sisters to South China and a band of nine missionaries to North China. Also a band of fourteen missionaries went from Spokane, Wash., to Japan and China. They were able to talk to the Chinese and Japanese at the dock and on the ship in their native language. The "Apostolic Light" is now published by Brothey Ryan in Tokyo, Japan.

Our dear Brother A. H. Post who is on his way to South Africa from Los Angeles, writes from London, England, "Praise our God, the 'latter rain' is falling in England. Glory to our God forever. I do greatly rejoice in Him for this blessed privilege of carrying this wonderful salvation to other nations. My heart leaps with joy and burns with His love for so great a privilege." Address him at 14 Ackeranm Road, Brixton, London, S. W., care Mrs. Price.

We never saw a more humble and Spirit-filled band of missionaries than the dear ones that left Los Angeles for North China, going by the way of Seattle where they were joined by others, making twelve in all, besides children. Brother Bernsten, Brother and Sister Hess and six workers from the Swedish Mission, made up the company from here. They went out trusting God alone for their support. Brother Bernsten says, "God has laid it on my heart to go to a new field and open up the work there. It is on the railroad line south of Peking, a big field, and to open our home for any independent worker filled with the Holy Ghost and fire, to come and stay with us until they are sure where God wants them. Pray for a dwelling-place and a home convenient for Chinese orphans." We are expecting God to wonderfully bless these consecrated and anointed ones. They are going into the famine district. Address B. Bernsten, Tai-ming fu, Chih-li, North China.

Our dear Sister Farrow, who was one of the first to bring Pentecost to Los Angeles, went to Africa and spent seven months at Johnsonville, 25 miles from Monrovia, Liberia, in that most deadly climate. She has now returned and has a wonderful story to tell. Twenty souls received their Pentecost, numbers were saved sanctified and healed. The Lord had given her the gift of the Kru language and she was permitted to preach two sermons to the people in their own tongue. The heathen some of them after receiving the Pentecost, spoke in English and some in other tongues. Praise God. The Lord showed her when she went, the time she was to return and sent her the fare in time, brought her home safely, and used her in Virginia and in the South along the way.

There is no man at the head of this movement. God Himself is speaking in the earth. We are on the verge of the greatest miracle the world has ever seen, when the sons of God shall be manifested, the saints shall come singing from the dust (Isa. 26: 19) and the full overcomers shall be caught up to meet the Lord in the air. The political world realizes that some great crisis is at hand, the scientific world, the religious world all feel it. The coming of the Lord draweth nigh, it is near, even at the doors.

THE APOSTOLIC FAITH

"Earnestly contend for the faith which was once delivered unto the saints."—Jude 3

VOLUME I. NO. 12. LOS ANGELES, CAL., JANUARY, 1908. SUBSCRIPTION FREE.

The Lord Is Speaking in the Earth Today

Indianapolis, Ind.—Many souls have been baptized in Indianapolis, saved and sanctified.

Norwood, Ohio.—Our people are growing, fourteen baptized and interest increasing.—W. H. Cossum, 3952 Hazel avenue.

Colly, N. C.—The fire is still burning here in our midst and souls are being converted and sanctified and baptized with the Holy Ghost.—A. J. Bordeau.

Atlanta, Ga.—The meetings in the hall here have been blessed seasons of refreshing. For six months, every afternoon and night and all day on Sundays, the meetings have continued. Before this "latter rain" such revivals were unheard of. Souls are being saved, sanctified, and healed, and filled with the Holy Ghost. All glory to Jesus' name! Let us follow on to know Him better. This is the beginning of great things.—"The Bridegroom's Messenger," 53½ Auburn avenue.

Hill River, Minn.—I am thankful to God for what He has done for a small group of Christians here in the town of Hill River, where I live. Quite a few have received their Pentecost and others seeking it, and we are continuing to pray to God for His blessing in a greater degree.—Andrew Hausan, Fosston, Minn.

Utica, N. Y.—Blessed be the name of the Lord. Truly these days of the "latter rain" are days of Heaven upon the earth. We are a little band here but full of faith and pressing on. One by one, God is bringing our number into their Pentecost, and is opening other places where there are a few hungry believers longing for their inheritance.—Birdsell & Mason, 61 State street.

Concord Junction, Mass.—God is working in this place. Five of us have the baptism, speaking in tongues and others getting hungry. He came in to abide with me on Oct. 16th and spoke for Himself.—Everett E. Munroe, 397 Main street.

Strole, Va.—Pentecost has come here. Eight of us are speaking in tongues. My gamblers and drunkards have been saved. Praise the dear Lord. We are looking for dear Jesus every day and can hardly wait to see Him.—W. S. Woodworth, Caanan Faith Home and Full Gospel Mission.

Portsmouth and Richmond, Va.—Brother Seymour wrote from these places while he was visiting the missions in the East: "God is working in Portsmouth. Souls were baptized in Richmond and God is working in mighty power. The saints are just as sweet as can be. Glory to God for this Gospel. The saints are so simple here, that is the reason they receive the Pentecost so quickly. They are ready for the power."

Philadelphia, Pa.—I have been helping in the Pentecostal work in one little meeting here. There were a number at the altar last Sunday and a number were slain under the mighthy power of God. I had a letter from a sistter in Danville, Va., a few days ago, and she says that God is blessing them there and that souls are being saved, sanctified, and baptized with the Holy Ghost. Hallelujah! hallelulah!—W. M. Scott, 996 Filbert street, Dec. 4.

Swanton, Ohio.—Praise the Lord. A few have been baptized near home here and a few have been wonderfully healed and a great many more are hungry for more of God. We have had a few wonderful conventions here in Ohio the past summer. One of the most wonderful meetings was at the Annual Christian Alliance Convention at Cleveland. Some evenings there were perhaps from three to four hundred down at the altar, some remaining all night; and a great many received their baptism, and many were saved. Praise the Lord. Jesus is certainly soon coming!—Gideon Ziegler.

Baltimore, Ohio.—There is a little mission here where the leader and about ten people had been seeking for thir baptism for seven months, but none of them came through until last night, when the leader came through gloriously and others have been under the power and some sanctified. Praise God!—Mary A. Yaegge, 1023 N. Eutaw street. (This sister is on her way to Switzerland, where the Lord is calling her to preach the Gospel.)

Denver, Colo.—Our meetings are being blessed of God. Souls are being saved, sanctified, baptized with the Holy Ghost and healed, and the interest is still increasing. All glory be to God for His wonderful works that He is bestowing upon His children, as He is pouring out His Spirit upon all flesh in these latter days; for the coming of the Lord draweth nigh. The Lord has held us here and He has opened up an Apostolic Faith Mission on the corner of Lawrence and Twenty-fourth streets. The altar is filled with seekers.—E. S. Lee, 2305 Lawrence street.

Lynn, Mass.—We are now holding meetings in the mission at 260 Maple street. We commenced this work in a hall last February. One of our number, a girl born blind and blind for twenty-two years, healed and sanctified about eight years ago, received her personal Pentecost last March. She speaks, sings and preaches in different languages, has visions and prophecy. The Lord showed her this mission about two months before we had it. The Lord gave us the name of the mission, Apostolic Faith Mission. A number have been saved and sanctified, speak in new tongues and a number have been healed.—A. J. Rawson, Oct. 26th.

Dallas, Ore.—In the campmeeting here last summer about thirty were baptized with the Holy Spirit, with the evidence of speaking in tongues as the Spirit gave utterance. Many were saved and sanctified. Brother Earnest G. Hansen writes on Jan. 6th: "Since I last wrote, about eight backsliders have got back to the Lord, some have been sanctified, two have been baptized with the Holy Ghost. Meetings are grand." They have a precious little paper there, clean and straight in doctrines, called "The Apostolic Witness."

Portland, Ore.—At 234 Madison street, they have a blessed Apostolic Faith Mission. The saints are filled and overflowing with the Spirit and with love for souls, talking and singing in tongues. The hall is not nearly large enough. Altars are filled with seekers. We shall never forget the precious visit we had there. One secret of the power here is the prayer room where the workers drop in for silent prayer before the services—not to talk or visit. Souls were being saved, sanctified, and baptized. A bartender got wonderfully saved of God, and when he rose and tried to tell it, he broke down and fell on his knees and began to thank Jesus, and it filled everyone with joy. We have lately received some precious letters from Portland telling of God's work there.

with the dear saints in New York. God is working there. Many are coming through. In one church,—a Baptist colored church of two thousand members,—God used us to give out these "latter rain" truths. The pastor who invited us became very hungry. He said he could not preach again till he was filled. Seven from his church received the promise of the Father, Acts 2: 4. Hallelujah to Jesus! Went down to Norfolk, Va., and found quite a few baptized souls. God sent us up here to Baltimore and we found a little assembly here of baptized souls. We are out for God and wherever the Lamb goeth, we intend to follow.—Brother and Sister E. W. Vinton, 12 Leyden street, Medford, Mass.

Chicago, Ill.—God is wonderfully working here. Both the interest and power are increasing. We have stood by the simple Gospel from the very first, preaching only Jesus Christ and Him crucified. And as we have done this, the Holy Ghost has fallen on them that heard the Word, so that tongue can never tell what we have experienced. Praise the Lord!—Wm. H. Durham, 943 W. North avenue.

Sister Jennie E. Moore, who with two other precious sisters from Azusa Mission, Los Angeles, have been working in Chicago and other places, writes: "Truly, beloved, the mission at 943 W. North avenue is a blessed place—many Spirit-filled men and women and children. They have more children than at Azusa and they are filled. Beloved, I would you could see them."

Winnipeg, Can.—There was a great Pentecostal Convention in Winnepeg beginning November 15th. Preachers and workers from all parts of Canada were present. A band of workers who were in Portland at the time received a call from God to go to Winnipeg, and they were present at the convention: Sister Crawford and Mildred, Sister Neal, Brother Conlee and Brother Trotter. About twenty were baptized with the Holy Ghost and many were healed. The people brought handkerchiefs and aprons to be blessed as in Acts 19: 12, and the Lord did wonderful signs through the simple faith of the dear ones that brought them. The Lord healed one young man of the tobacco habit, taking all the desire for the stuff away from him, through an anointed handkerchief, and he was saved in his own room. Demons were cast out of those bound by them. Our last published report from Winnipeg should have been signed, "The Apostolic Faith Mission, 501 Alexander Ave."

Arcadia, Fla., and through the South.—Brother G. B. Cashwell and I are in the midst of a gracious revival in this town. The power is falling and saints are shouting. Bless God! Some have been saved, sanctified, and quite a number have received the Holy Ghost and speaking with other tongues as the Spirit gives utterance as in Acts 2: 4. The altar is filled with seekers. God has kept me in Florida most all this year. Many saints have received the Holy Ghost in Florida with Bible evidence and many saved. A number of them have been baptized in water, buried in baptism, that is the Bible way.—F. M. Britton, Dec. 11.

Brother Cashwell writes from the South: "This truth in the South is spreading as never before and will keep spreading as Praise our God! Pray much and be true to Jesus. Many of us are now suffering much persecution, but our God is fighting our battles. Praise His dear name! Brother McIntosh writes me that seventy have received the Holy Ghost in thirty days after he arrived in Macao, China. O praise God for Pentecost. Salute all the saints for me in the love of Jesus!"—G. B. Cashwell, 53½ Auburn avenue, Atlanta, Ga.

Stockton, Cal.—Five or six have been baptized with the Holy Ghost and several saved and several cases of healing.

Shenandoah, Iowa.—"Salvation has come. Hallelujah! God has come our way at last. Amen. Last Friday afternoon at Francis Jones' a few of us were gathered pleading for the baptism of the Holy Spirit and He gave us the desire of our hearts at last. Glory, O glory. Two of us received our baptism, Sister Leyden and I. The rest are hard after Him. They were here at our house until after three this morning. There is quite a company of us Sister Leyden lay under the power for several hours and talked and sang in the Spirit and the Lord let me join in the song and sing too. Glory, glory, hallelujah! Blessed be the name of Jesus. The song was "Worthy is the Lamb", and nearly the whole chapter. She interpreted it afterwards."—Sister J. S. Jellison.

Minneapolis and St. Paul, Minn.—Wonderful outpouring of the Spirit here and at St. Paul. In five nights just passed in St. Paul alone, nine have received old time baptisms of the Holy Ghost and fire, speaking in many dialects and receiving wonderful visions from the Lord. Amen! Nine have been blessedly sanctified, some being for [illegible] woman dying with cancer—given up to die by three specialists, next morning after being prayed for arose and did her work, and has been doing it ever since—healed. I was in St. Paul last week and Brother Trotter was here, and in both places, the power was wonderful—yesterday especially, many being instantly healed and many saved. People were prostrated under the power of God at 11:30 last night. Many were heavily anointed for their baptism, and we expect a shower in the next few days. Glory is abiding in our hearts.—Florence Crawford, 1315 East 19th street, Minneapolis, Minn., Jan. 6.

A later report written Jan 13th, says: "I wish to report victory in both St. Paul and Minneapolis. Yesterday was a great day. We had the ordinances of the Lord's Supper and Foot-Washing Saturday night, and saints from St. Paul all came over and participated with us. Some fell under the power and lay for several hours. We had a blessed time. We then invited St. Paul saints to worship with us on Sunday afternoon. Sister Crawford gave the message in the afternoon. I gave it in the morning; and Brother Trotter in the evening. People fell under the power all day. And when I left the hall at 5 p. m., they were lying all over the hall under the power. The hall was an altar from the stand to the door. So many are getting saved, and many that have been claiming to be sanctified are finding that they were just saved, and are now getting really sanctified. Greetings to the church at Azusa street." J. R. Conlee, 1003 25th avenue, N. E., Minneapolis.

FROM AZUSA MISSION.

Many souls have been saved, sanctified, baptized with the Holy Ghost and sick bodies healed all over the land and in many lands since our last paper. Souls have been sanctified, baptized and saved at the old mission home at 312 Azusa street, Los Angeles.

When Christ was born, it was in a barn at Bethlehem; and when He began sending the "latter rain" about two years ago, the outpouring of the Spirit, it was in a barn in Los Angeles; for the old Mission is like a barn in its humility and plainness. Its old beams and whitewashed walls have been ringing with the praises and songs of the children of God ever since. Many from here have gone out into the foreign fields and the home fields, and they write back that they remember the blessed old times; and the Lord has been pouring out the same Spirit wherever He has sent them. The Spirit falls on humble hearts and in humble missions and churches.

Azusa Mission is still giving forth the same truth, and the Lord is pouring out His Spirit upon His sons and daughteters, and they are witnessing in burning testimonies that Jesus' Blood does cleanse from all sin and He does sanctify and baptize with the Holy Ghost and speak in tongues.

The holidays are special feast days at the Mission. The saints all gather—not to hear a program, for the Holy Ghost makes the program and the Father spreads the table with "the fatted calf" which represents Jesus, and we feed on Christ. Hallelujah! The Spirit sings the songs, some new and some old. Christmas was a blessed day at the Mission, also Watch Night and New Year's Day. The meetings have been going on every day since the work started and God's word and the Holy Spirit are just as fresh and new as ever. The Lord provides for all the expenses. He has supplied all the needs of the workers, and when they come back they report that they have lacked nothing.

The devil is doing all he can to keep the saints from entering into the greater fullness of Christ; but we know God is raising up armies that will stand for the living God. Some went away from Azusa Mission becauses they thought the teaching on divorce was too straight; but God will not let us lower the standard. He wants a clean people and pure doctrine as a channel for this Pentecostal power. People everywhere are looking after this wonderful salvation that today is turning the world upside down as it did in Paul's time.

We look for a great outpouring of God's Spirit in saving and healing power and power that fills with the Holy Ghost and fire in this year 1908. May all Christ's people be stirred up over this salvation and sink down in deeper humility at the feet of Jesus.

"If we walk in the light as He is in the light, the Blood of Jesus Christ, His Son, cleanseth us from all sin." (I John 1, 7.) Bless His name forever and ever! It is the Blood that cleanseth, the precious Blood of Jesus. May we honor the Blood and keep under the Blood, and God will do mighty things for us. If the devil can get us on something outside of God, He will break our power. May we be watchful and [illegible] on [illegible] the Blood, and God [illegible] break our power. May we be watchful and keep under the Blood. The Lord wants the Blood preached as never before, and people will not have to wait so long to get the baptism. The Spirit follows the Blood. It is the Blood that saves us. We overcome by the Blood. Amen!

FROM THE BIBLE SCHOOL IN MUKTI, INDIA.

It was noisesd one day, that some of the girls in the praying band were praying in different tongues. I had heard of the gift of tongues having been given to God's children in other parts of the country, so was not surprised to hear our girls praying in new tongues. I did not go very near these girls, lest I should stumble them by taking too much notice of them, but quietly sat down and praised God.

One Sunday, as I was coming out of the church, after the morning service, I saw some girls standing near the door of a workers' room. They seemed greatly excited and wondering. I soon found out the cause. A girl was praying aloud, and praising God in the English language. She did not know the language. Some of us gathered around her in the room, and joined her mentally in prayer. She was unconscious of what was going on, and was speaking to the Lord Jesus fluently in English. Before, I had heard her and some other girls uttering only a few syllables. Some repeated certain words over and over again. Some spoke one or more sentences, and some were simply groaning as if under a great agony of heart and mind, and carrying a great burden for souls.

"For with stammering lips and another tongue will He speak to this people."

The gift of prophecy was also given to many of the praying girls, so that they could give God's message in very clear language, taught by the Holy Spirit. The believers and unbelievers were moved alike by these messages, and a deep spiritual work began in our midst.

They who have received the gift of tongues are not using them for delivering messages from the Scriptures, except those who have received the gift of interpretation. They pray and praise God, and sometimes sing hymns in unknown tongues.—Mukti Prayer Bell.

Multitudes in India and China are starving on account of the failure of crops. Any who want to help the famine sufferers can do so by sending money to the "Apostolic Faith", and it will be sent direct to the missionaries in those countries to feed and care for the starving people, especially the orphans.

THE APOSTOLIC FAITH

"Earnestly contend for the faith which was once delivered unto the saints."—Jude 3.,

VOLUME II. NO. 13. LOS ANGELES, CAL., MAY, 1908 SUBSCRIPTION FREE

Fires Are Being Kindled

By The Holy Ghost Throughout The World

Ireland

Both Belfast and Bangor have been visited with Pentecost.

England

In the past year, news comes that probably 500 people have received the Pentecost in England.

China

We hear from South China that about 100 have received the baptism of the Holy Ghost and they now have a paper in the Chinese called "Pentecostal Truths," which is being scattered in China and Japan. It is a blessed paper and one can feel the power in it even though unable to read it.

West Africa

Brother E. McCauley from Long Beach, California, opened a mission in Monrovia, Liberia. God has been blessing the work. Other missionaries are helping. Sister Harmon writes: "It is marvelous at times to see the manifestations of the Spirit and to feel the power. They shake like a person with a hard chill; they are in such earnestness when they pray and God does so bless them, until you can hear them a block away."

Jerusalem

One native minister of Beyroute, Syria, came to Jerusalem to spend the winter. God has baptized him with the Holy Ghost and he speaks with tongues. Praise God! God started this movement in A. D. 33 in this dear old city, and the "latter rain" is falling in 1908. Glory to God! Miss Elizabeth Brown of the Christian and Missionary Alliance, received her baptism more than two weeks ago. She had the real old-fashioned manifestations like many had at Azusa street. The secret of the matter was she was so given up to God. Praise His name! She came to my room and requested me to lay hands on her for her baptism. She felt waves of fire passing through her head and face and then began to speak in tongues. She sings the heavenly chant. It is precious to hear her.—Lucy M. Leatherman, Jerusalem, Palestine, care of American Consulate.

Sweden

The Holy Ghost is falling on the humble in Gottenberg. In one prayer meeting, they saw fire, and four persons were filled with the Holy Ghost and spoke with tongues. They praised God until 5 o'clock in the morning. In a few days, more than twelve persons were baptized with the Holy Ghost and speaking in tongues.

Eight little children have been filled with the Spirit, speaking in tongues. Some of them stand on a chair testifying for Christ.

Many sick have been healed, sinners saved and backsliders coming to the Lord. One day in February, twenty-three were baptized in water in the name of Jesus Christ. Nearly all of them had their Pentecostal experience. Many are seeking the power of God day and night.

One night the Lord sent a fisherman from an island near the city, using this dear brother in the healing of four sick people and two sisters got their baptism of the Holy Ghost at the same time.

Many sinners have come to God in different parts of Sweden. There are Pentecostal companies here and there where the Lord is taking out a people for His name. A number of workers who received their baptism in Los Angeles are there being used of God. Address Brother Andrew G. Johnson, Backevick, 3 Hisingstad, Sweden.

India

In Panditta Ramabai's School at Mukti, edagon, India, God is working in power among the girls again. God is pouring out upon them such a spirit of prayer again. It is like the mighty roaring of the sea when they begin. The workers are looking for a great outpouring of His Spirit again upon Mukti. He has also been blessedly working among the Christian and Missionary Alliance people in Bombay.

Brother Max Wood Moorhead of Bombay, India, writes: "God is working mightily through the Bombay Presidency and there are witnesses now at Bombay, Khamgaon, Akola, Amraoki, Dholka, Dharangaon, Rhes-on, Nasrapur, Pandharpur and Dhond. Praise God! Many natives are entering in, and how blessedly God uses these ignorant, lowly Indians as channels of blessing to their own people. A native boy of 19 was filled with the Holy Ghost in January and has been wonderfully healed of consumption and instrumental in winning souls to Jesus, his heathen mother and a heathen lad, an old friend. He has also been a messenger of power to missionaries from the home land. At Dolka, a station of the Christian and Missionary Alliance, where five missionaries have received Pentecost, six orphan lads are magnifying God in new tongues."

PENTECOSTAL OUTPOURING IN SCOTLAND

From "Confidence," a free Pentecostal paper, to be obtained from the editors, 11 Park Lea Road, Sunderland, England.

Pentecost has fallen in Scotland at Edinburgh, Glasgow, Dumfermline, Sterling, Clydebank, Falkirk, Tarbert, Toll Cross, Banton by Kilsyth, Kirkintilloch, Coatbridge and other places.

Some incidents are reported from Kilsyth, a small Scottish town twelve miles from Glasgow, and other points.

* * *

A fireman at the colliery, as he was leaning on his shovel at work, began to speak in tongues.

* * *

A pitman at Motherwell broke out in the face of the coal—that is, while filling his wagon or tub. He was singing, "How I love that sweet story of old." He said he felt something go down and then come up. Then for two hours he sat on his coal pile speaking in tongues as the Holy Spirit gave him utterance. The men near by working soon heard him, and one cried: "There's Jock through in tongues and me no saved yet."

* * *

A number have been converted just through hearing others speak in tongues. It was so with young H. He loved cycle racing, etc., and kept away from the meetings; but when he heard his sister in the house "speaking mysteries" praising God in an unknown tongue, he was broken down. In the Mission Hall, from 3 one afternoon till 2 the next morning, he dealt with God and was saved, sanctified, and baptized with the Holy Ghost with the Scriptural evidences.

* * *

In a village in this part of Scotland, the little chapel got on fire and about twenty received their Pentecost with signs following and thirteen have been soundly converted. They were holding a "fellowship meeting" for those who had been fully anointed. Outsiders hearing the vehement cries of praise and the speaking in tongues, gathered around. A sympathetic policeman kept the door (his wife and daughter, who had received the blessing were inside). At last he cried, "Lads, I can stand it no longer, here goes." And he flung open the door, and putting down his helmet, was soon pleading with God for the full baptism of the Holy Ghost. And he received it then and there and came through speaking in tongues.

* * *

It is touching to see the boys at Kilsyth (quite a number have got their Pentecost) all with their Bibles in the meeting, and little girls too, speaking in tongues and giving out solemn messages.

* * *

In other places children have had to suffer. We have heard of one whose father in the drink, kicked his little girl because she went to the meetings, and she looking up at him, and through her tears, said, "Glory to Jesus!"

* * *

An engine driver at Kilsyth was making his way to the house, and his legs gave way. The power of God fell on him, and they supported him to Brother Murdoch's kitchen where many have received the baptism, and he was soon "through," singing as the Spirit gave him utterance, and has been singing ever since.

Many have already traveled to Kilsyth from the east and west, the north and south. Some critical investigators arrived one day by train. They agreed to test this thing by putting questions to the first Kilsyth man they met. It was the porter who opened the carriage door.

"Any meetings being held here?"

"Aye, sir, there are."

"Have you been to any of them?"

"Yes, I've been."

"Is it true that some folks are speaking in tongues?"

"It's true enough."

"Do you know anyone?"

"Yes, I'm one myself."

* * *

Scottish people know their Bibles. They are no fools, not carried away easily. But they know that God has appeared in their midst, and they praise Him and exalt the ever precious **Blood** by which victory is assured.

PENTECOST IN AUSTRALIA

The Lord has visited Australia in great power and souls have been baptized with the Holy Ghost and signs following.

In a cottage meeting, in February, 1907, in Melbourne, a young brother received the baptism of the Holy Ghost and began to speak in tongues. Some fell under the power of God, and a great awe came over the meeting. The brother spoke and sang, giving messages in the unknown tongue and also interpreting.

* * *

A few Christians stopped at the house on the way to church one Saturday night, but said they would have a little time of prayer first. The Lord came down in such power that they could not go, and some spoke in tongues and sang heavenly music.

* * *

A sister was washing up the breakfast things, when the Lord called her to prayer, she immediately obeyed Him, and the Spirit soon led her off in praise to Him in an unknown tongue. She says, "I was simply lost in His love."

* * *

A few were waiting upon God one Friday night when the Holy Spirit fell upon a lad of 19. He sang beautifully for over an hour about Jesus' coming. Next morning while at work he sang praises to God in an unknown tongue.

* * *

These great blessings have come upon the lowly and humble. Many have seen visions of Jesus and of heavenly fire, and the interpretations speak of the soon coming of Jesus.

A Policeman Receives Pentecost

A policeman, John Barclay, 161 Elgin street, Carlton, Melbourne, received his Pentecost. The following is a part of his testimony:

On Easter evening, 1907, at a Holiness camp about twenty-seven miles from Melbourne, we all gathered for our usual praise and prayer meeting. A brother read 1 Cor., 12th chapter. Then we all knelt down but no one seemed able to pray aloud. The only words I could utter were these: "Lord, reveal Thyself tonight."

Presently some mighty, marvelous unseen power took hold of me, and I was thrown downward on the floor. Everything around me disappeared. The other friends were as if they never existed. I saw the heavens opened and my precious Jesus sitting on the throne. On the joy and beauty and glory! It is unspeakable. Then Jesus came right down into the room and I saw Him smile all around. But He looked so sadly at me, and His look condemned me for refusing before to yield myself fully up to Him. His loving but sad look broke my heart, and I burst into tears, and cried:

"Lord, I yield my all to You to do with me as Thou wilt!" I just cried from my heart that verse, "I'll go where you want me to go, dear Lord." Then the Lord smiled again. During all this time I saw an innumerable host of angels in glory, and oh, such dazzling light and beauty. Whenever I cried, "I'll go where you want me to go, dear Lord," the dear Lord smiled on me and the angels waved pennons of white. It was simply celestial; no beauty on earth like it! No words on earth can describe what it was like. In visions He showed me that there is as much rejoicing in heaven over a fully surrendered soul as over a lost sinner returning from the wilds.

To come back to Easter Monday evening, I was for about an hour and a half conscious only of the Lord's presence. When I returned to earth again and looked around, some were kneeling in silent prayer, others were lying prostrate on the floor. Presently a sister broke out in prayer entreating God to bless His children and save lost souls. Then she prayed in a strange tongue which sounded like Chinese. Then she started singing in the same tongue. What heavenly music! It sounded very much like an angel's voice coming rolling over the balconies of heaven. Of all the grand singers I have heard, I never heard anything so sweet. She gave messages from God to several. Our meeting lasted till 4 o'clock in the morning.

On return to my work at home, I got so hungry to know more of the dear Lord, that I began seeking in real deep earnest for the baptism of the Holy Ghost and fire. Satan had been giving me a very bad time by telling me that it was all false doctrine. I went into my bedroom and told the Lord to drive Satan away, that his assaults were more than I could bear. Then all at once a beautiful calm and peace filled my soul. I was so happy that I could not even praise Him, but sat at His feet with my eyes closed looking into His dear face, when I saw a light shine from heaven far brighter than the noonday sun; it shone on my face brighter and brighter, until I had to cover my eyes with my hands.

That night I went to a meeting in a private house, and in this meeting Satan came to me with greater power and I was of all men most miserable. About 10:30 p. m., Satan did his best to get me to go home; but my Jesus kept me waiting on the Lord with others, some of whom were under the Spirit and speaking in tongues. About 1 o'clock a. m., a brother laid hands on me, and I received my baptism. My hands, arms, and whole body trembled greatly and I was thrown on the floor. All the others were praising the Lord. He is the same, yesterday, today, and forever. He baptizes with the Holy Ghost the same today as nineteen centuries ago. On that night week the Lord gave me the tongues and since then I have spoken in four or five different languages. All glory to His Name!

People have told me that it is all of the devil; but the Jesus I serve and trust will not allow Satan to deceive me. It is now over six months since I received this baptism, and I know that Satan does not give the peace, joy, and happiness that I have got.

A burglar came to the altar at Azusa Mission, threw his skeleton keys under the bench (he had been plotting to rob a house). He got gloriously saved, soon he was sanctified. He was baptized down at the ocean and shouted and jumped in the water and out of the water, he was so filled with the power of God. That afternoon he was baptized with the Holy Ghost and spake in tongues. He praises God and weeps as he tells of His wonderful love and mercy.

A sister finding there were some things hindering her from getting her baptism, shut herself in her room and prayed practically all day and all night. She prayed through and got all her idols out of her heart and the power fell on her "like hail," she says. She talked in tongues for a long time, though she said when she came to the mission that she did not want tongues. But God baptized her like all the rest.

A brother came from China to Los Angeles and received the baptism of the Holy Ghost and went on his way to England, and writes that it was the most wonderful experience of his life and he is rejoicing in the fullness of the Spirit.

The leading man among the colored Free-masons in Indianapolis and who was also cartoonist for two newspapers, was sanctified and baptized with the Holy Ghost speaking in divers new tongues. He resigned and had prayer with his members in the lodge room, and they were much touched. Some of his brethren have since received their Pentecost also.

What Hath God Wrought. In two precious years since the Lord poured out the Pentecost in Los Angeles in a little cottage on Bonnie Brae street, He has spread it around the world. Hallelujah. Many are rejoicing with joy unspeakable for the great blessings that God is pouring out in this latter rain. Many saved, sanctified, healed of disease and baptized with the Holy Ghost and fire. Many happy families filled with the Spirit and working for Jesus. Soon after the Pentecost fell, the saints rented the lower room in the old building on Azusa street, which has been much blest of God. To Him be all the glory and praise. When the place was about to be sold so that the Mission would have to move, the saints agreed to purchase it with three years' time to pay the $15,000, expecting the Lord to send the money all in before that time, and He has done it and answered our prayers in a wonderful way. We humbly thank God. We love to think of the blessed old "Manger Home" where so many of us have received the baptism of the Holy Ghost. Many saints love the spot and will rejoice that God has given it to us.

Christ's character is our pattern and His word is our discipline. We want to be just like Jesus in His suffering, His passion, His death. He is our ideal. Glory to God!

AUTHOR
CONTACT INFORMATION

ROBERTS LIARDON MINISTRIES

P.O. Box 30710

Laguna Hills, CA 92654

Phone: 949-833-3555

Fax: 949-833-9555

Web: www.robertsliardon.org

WEBSITE

Visit the following Web site if you would like to see rare film footage, photographs, voice recordings, some Smith Wigglesworth, Aimee Semple McPherson, A.A. Allen, Kathryn Kuhlman and many more.

www.godsgenerals.org

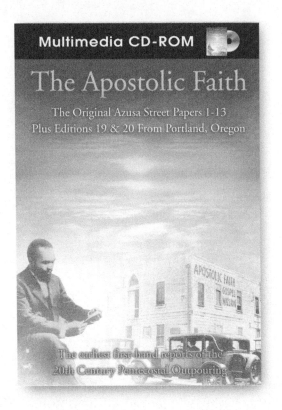

Multimedia CD-ROM

The Apostolic Faith

The Original Azusa Street Papers 1-13
Plus Editions 19 & 20 From Portland, Oregon

The earliest first-hand reports of the
20th Century Pentecostal Outpouring

THE APOSTOLIC FAITH
The Original Azusa Street Papers

The great Azusa Street Pentecostal Revival occurred between 1906 and 1913 and centered on the Apostolic Faith Mission of 312 Azusa Street in Los Angeles, California.

In September 1906 William J. Seymour began a publication, *The Apostolic Faith* [commonly referred to as The Azusa Street Papers]. This publication quickly became the main means of communicating the Pentecostal message to the wider world. These vibrant, first-hand accounts capture the excitement, passion, and vision of the early Pentecostal leaders William J. Seymour, Charles Partham, and Frank Bartleman.

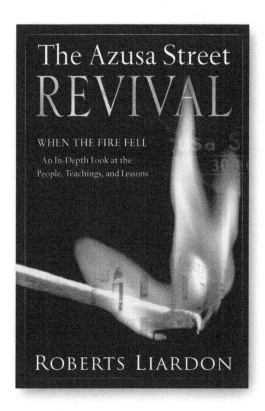

THE AZUSA STREET REVIVAL
When the Fire Fell

The Azusa Street Revival was as monumental as when Martin Luther nailed his Theses to the Whittenberg door. The fire that fell on Azusa Street spread worldwide and continues to fuel the flames of the Church today.

Who were the men and women dedicated to this new and exciting spiritual experience? What sparked their rise-and ofttimes-demise? How did this "mysterious" movement spread into denominational churches and become a major force in Christianity?

Roberts Liardon answers in vivid detail the bold beginnings and subsequent growth of the Pentecostal movement ignited by the Azusa fire in 1906. Read passionate testimonies from those who witnessed first-hand the revival's birth and its unquenchable Light.

Additional copies of this book and other
book titles from DESTINY IMAGE are
available at your local bookstore.

Call toll-free: 1-800-722-6774.

Send a request for a catalog to:

Destiny Image® Publishers, Inc.
P.O. Box 310
Shippensburg, PA 17257-0310

*"Speaking to the Purposes of God for This
Generation and for the Generations to Come"*

For a complete list of our titles,
visit us at www.destinyimage.com

Made in the USA
Coppell, TX
13 February 2021

50253121R00104